Mervyn Smith worked in the motorcycle industry for 30 years, travelling extensively in the UK and abroad in the pursuit of business. He has long been fascinated by travel stories and what motivates people to do out-of-the-ordinary things for others. A lifelong motorcyclist, he divides his time between long rides to anywhere, a garden that is just too big to be manageable, public speaking, writing and spending time with family and friends. He lives with his wife, Liz, in rural Shropshire and this is his first book.

For my grandchildren, Evie and Hugo.

Dedicated to the enduring memories of my dearly loved Aunt Madge, who always believed the best in me. To my much-missed friend, Paul Nelson, who was an avid supporter of the work of Open Doors and never gave up in spite of his illness. To Jean Banks, a lady who provided me with so much encouragement in my Christian walk.

All royalties from the sale of this book will go to support the work of Open Doors.

*https://www.opendoorsuk.org/*

Mervyn Smith

# ABOVE THE CIRCLE

AUSTIN MACAULEY PUBLISHERS™

LONDON * CAMBRIDGE * NEW YORK * SHARJAH

A CIP catalogue record for this title is available from the British Library.

ISBN 9781398430242 (Paperback)
ISBN 9781398430259 (ePub e-book)

www.austinmacauley.com

First Published 2023
Austin Macauley Publishers Ltd®
1 Canada Square
Canary Wharf
London
E14 5AA

20230606

My grateful thanks go to the following people:

My corporate sponsors. I was so proud to have been supported by you.

Kevin Bryan – Bryans BMW Rider Training, Stoke on Trent

Alex and the crew – Bec's Coffee, Bridgnorth

John and Norma King – The Bull's Head, Chelmarsh

Tom Neath – The Eagle and Serpent, Kinlet

Nigel Littlewood – Feridax UK, Halesowen

Eddie Floyd – Fireblade Ministries, Northern Ireland

Steve Ludlam – French, Ludlam & Co, Kingswinford

Steve Kelsey – Highley Garage

Steve Phillips – The Key Collection/Fowlers, Bristol

Peter Yeow – Motohaus Powersports Ltd, UK

Steve Moles and ALL the staff at The Motorcycle Mart, Kidderminster

Toby Dixon – Nevis Marketing UK

Barry Urand – Pirelli Tyres UK

Maggie Rogers – The Travel Wallet, Bridgnorth

Nigel Harris – Woolley and Harris Ltd, Kingswinford

Adam Kelley – Yamaha UK, Woking

To my major personal sponsors.

Pastor Will and Diane O'Leary and all at Jubilee International Church, Kidderminster

John and Jennie Home – Willowdene Farm, Chorley

Rev Mike Harris and all at St Mary's Church, Highley

To the staff of Open Doors and especially Fiona who believed in me and encouraged me every step of the way.

To Dr Paul Thompson for his professionalism in quickly recognising my heart condition.

To Mr Heyman Lukraz my heart surgeon and the wonderful team at the Cardiothoracic Unit at New Cross, Hospital. I cannot thank you all enough.

To my dear friend Ian Baxter for casting his expert eye over the text.

To Martin Rowe for my profile picture.

To Tim Down for the superb bike stickers.

To my sons, James and Gareth, who were always positive about what I was trying to achieve.

To each and every person who sponsored the challenge and indeed who bought this book. You know who you are – thank you.

Last, and by no means least, a huge thank you to my lovely wife, Liz, who was ever supportive of my craziness in undertaking such a challenge and had to endure my frustration when things weren't going too well.

Unless otherwise stated all quotations used are by the kind permission of Open Doors UK. If my account has stirred you to learn more about the plight of persecuted Christians then please have a look on the Open Doors websites. For the UK, the web address is *www.opendoorsuk/org.*

One Dream, One Challenge, One
Summer, One Ride, One Purpose

**Isaiah 40:22**

'He sits enthroned above the circle of the earth and its people
are like grasshoppers.'

# Introduction

*'20 years from now you will be more disappointed by the things you didn't do than the ones you did do. So throw off the bow lines. Sail away from the safe harbour. Catch the trade winds in your sails. Explore. Dream. Discover.'*

**– Mark Twain**

*'If your vision doesn't scare you, then your vision is too small.'*

**– Brother Andrew**

I had a bit of a silly dream. When I shared it, some people would laugh and say, 'What on earth would you want to do that for?' Such questions came from people who were settled, sound, steady, and non-risk takers and they made me feel as if my time for pursuing silly dreams had come and gone. But there's the problem. I was not ready to conform to such thinking in my so-called golden years, and I am still not. I welcome new challenges and hope I always will, because becoming old begins in the mind. I did not want to join the ranks of those for whom getting old is something to be fatalistic about instead of something to be resisted. It's a mindset that robs us of our potential, and age should not become a limiting factor in our ability to still be able to achieve and contribute.

My dream was this. I wanted to ride a motorcycle to, and, if possible, beyond the Arctic Circle. The thought of it consumed me at times, but even so I recognised something holding me back and that something was fear. It was almost as if my subconscious had been invaded by the negativity of others and I almost started to believe I could not do it. People who have dreams are not always popular because they challenge the mindset of the status-quo; some people prefer things to stay as they are. This book is about what happened to me to break free of such thinking and how events caused me to embrace a challenge that some thought was just plain daft.

We are forged by our experiences of life, both good and bad; some of us thankfully break free of the negativity imposed upon us by others and what we go through, but many of us still carry scars. Therefore, for reasons far too complex to go into here, I grew up learning to be comfortable with my own company and by my mid-teenage years, I had developed quite an independent, if not stubborn streak. Often, I did not fit in with the crowd, nor did I want to, not a loner exactly, but someone who was more of an individualist than a team player.

Perhaps these are the primary reasons why I have always enjoyed riding motorcycles and why, from the age of 16, I have rarely been without one in one form or another. They represent for me an escape, a way of travelling that brings a kind of individualistic freedom that is matched by no other form of transport. People who ride motorcycles are by nature different, not part of the herd mentality, and, as this journal may indicate, some can be justly regarded as being a bit odd.

Riding a motorcycle is a sensual experience because you are never divorced from the outside elements. You note changes in the weather much more acutely and often you can sense a storm before it arrives and you suffer it intimately when it does. You can smell the world outside and sometimes almost taste it. On a motorcycle you literally feel the road beneath you and become more sensitive to the subtleties of handling, braking and power than ever you would in a car. This means a motorcycle has to be ridden with finesse and control, for a lack of it can have you on your ear in seconds. There is a dynamism of poise, balance and power that very few other vehicles can match, but with that comes vulnerability and a need for far greater perception of traffic and road conditions. To ride a powerful machine well and safely is not something everyone can do, or perhaps would even want to. But it can be dangerous and statistically you are one of the most vulnerable road users. I have always known this. After 30 years of working in the motorcycle industry I do not have rose-tinted spectacles when it comes to understanding and recognising the dangers of riding one. I found this quote about it.

*Motorcycling is not of itself inherently dangerous. It is, however, extremely unforgiving of inattention, ignorance, incompetence or stupidity* (Anon). Hmmm, that actually makes it quite dangerous then doesn't it?

A long motorcycle ride would usually give me two very distinct mindsets. The anticipation of the adventure, and the fear of it (oddly the latter usually dissipated within minutes of setting off.) Before I embarked on my epic ride I read this somewhere – *why do we put ourselves through the act of going away?* I immediately recognised the condition. A fortnight's holiday away with my family also used to invoke this tension within me and I could be difficult to be around for the first 24 hours until I relaxed. Once the decision was made to do this particular trip, I found those old feelings resurfacing again.

But sometimes in life events push you beyond the confines of your comfort zone, even if the borders of it are quite expansive. That is when you have a choice to go with the challenges presented or to ignore them and settle for something less risky.

That is what happened to me with this challenge, and I chose to 'go'. People questioned why on earth at 68 years old would I want to risk covering thousands of miles on a motorcycle, riding alone through 8 unknown countries? Very simply for the remarkable people who stand firm in their faith under the most intense and sometimes deadly persecution.

My ride was for a Christian organisation called Open Doors. It was founded by a remarkable Dutchman called Andrew van der Bijl, better known as Brother Andrew. In his commitment to Christ when it was an extremely dangerous thing to do, he became best known for his exploits in smuggling Bibles into communist countries at the height of the Cold War.

This ministry grew and became known as Open Doors. Brother Andrew's story is told in the bestselling book 'God's Smuggler.' Christian or not, if you ever want to read an inspirational book, one that will challenge your perceptions and perhaps even your beliefs, I dare you to get and read a copy. It is a wonderful and challenging story, all the more so because it is absolutely true!

Open Door now works in over 60 countries, supplying Bibles, training church leaders, providing practical support and emergency relief and supporting Christians who suffer for their faith. In the UK and Ireland, Open Doors works to raise awareness of global persecution, mobilising prayer, support and action among Christians.

Christians living in these countries need the support of their family, the body of Christ, to help them stand firm in their faith. Today, perhaps more than any time in history, millions of persecuted Christians need fellow believers to stand with them to walk that journey of faith.

And this book is about a journey of faith too and in the 'going' I found a God who is faithful to the calling, as He always is, if we are brave enough to follow it. It was a journey within me as much as one without, and throughout it all I know I was being upheld by a supernatural and overwhelming sense of purpose gaining a trust that was never misplaced even when it didn't go quite as expected.

In a unique and odd way it was our joint journey of faith together, me in God and God in me and all for them. My hope, however, was that this trip would become a story for other people and not just a self-reflective journal of me and mine.

Unlike Brother Andrew my ride did not involve travelling in countries where to be known as a Christian could put your life at risk, but much of the inspiration for it came from him and those who do risk everything daily to follow Jesus.

How I arrived at that decision to support 'those who have no voice' with this challenge is part of the story. Many of you reading this account, I know, will not be Christians and I have long given up thinking I could directly argue anyone into becoming one. But writing this without making references to my faith and to the faithfulness of God would be impossible.

If I tried it would become a false representation of my motives regarding the challenge. I also hope it might help the reader to question their own response to these issues of faith and why, in the face of most intense persecution, even death, people still choose to follow Christ.

I suspect some who read my story, knowing of my faith, may find themselves being a little shocked at what I share (those who know me well will not be). I might come over as being a bit edgy, tetchy, hard, or egotistical perhaps and it might be obvious that I do not react well to bullies or suffer fools gladly. That apart, I am a fairly rounded person…mostly.

Perhaps it's a throwback to those teenage years, or the inherent northerner in me (I was born and grew up in north Derbyshire), or I am not yet grown in grace enough to be more like Jesus as I would one day hope to be. Like all of us, I am a work in progress. I once heard a pastor say *'the Holy Spirit will use you differently from anyone else in the universe.'* It is a statement that has never left me and has given me much encouragement over the years. It came from a sermon I heard preached on the Isle of Man whilst working for Honda at the TT races in 1990 when, as a new Christian, I had snuck away from my colleagues on a Sunday morning secretly to go to church – much like many Christians across the world who Open Doors support.

The difference was the cost of discovery would have been some mild personal embarrassment and not my very life. We are all unique and we are all different. If God can use an awkward so-and-so like me I guess He can use anyone, if they are willing of course. Some could say 'well that wasn't very Christian' at some of my actions and comments and they would be right for I am imperfect and human.

I have written my journey as I experienced and felt it 'warts and all.' Nevertheless, I am a follower of Jesus and I am committed to His cause and His people; I simply would not have done this challenge had it been otherwise.

To be frank it would have been far easier to ignore the calling and spend that simmering July of 2018 fishing or gardening and justifying my inaction, which is something I have done so many times before. Nothing of value though is ever achieved by laziness, vacillation and excuses.

I am not naïve either. I am very aware that riding from the UK to the tip of Norway is something any skilled motorcyclist can do – if they have a mind to. When compared to the real adventurer riders who think nothing of circumnavigating the globe and who seem to have an ability to disregard, or at least play down, the privations and dangers, my road trip, by comparison, was relatively insignificant.

In the countries, I travelled through the roads were good (the appalling condition of the pot-holed B4555 from my home village of Highley to Bridgnorth was never replicated anywhere abroad on the trip), accommodation was easily (mostly) found, and English was spoken almost everywhere.

There were no shortages of petrol filling stations, even in the extreme north of Norway, and food was available at most of them. No, what perhaps made this trip unique were the circumstances that brought it about and the fact that unbeknown, I was going to ride it during one of the hottest European summers ever recorded.

Additionally, what I wanted to do was record something for my family. With a new grandson (Hugo, our first) being born in March of 2018 and living in Australia, and our beautiful granddaughter Evie, a little closer by, I hope that one day when they are old enough, this book is a story to remember me by.

This record is primarily a legacy to them, and is not intended as a book that could make me famous, for I do not really class myself as much of a writer and have never been one for serious self-promotion.

Nevertheless, I wanted to tell the story that led me to fulfil a 'silly' dream ultimately motivated by a true cause, riding my motorcycle alone through that sweltering summer of 2018 to the very tip of Norway and back, and of the small adventures I had on the way. And to give testimony of a God who protected me and provided for me every mile/kilometre of it.

# Chapter 1
# Concept and Confusion

*'They killed my father because he was a believer.'* – **Bachu, an Ethiopian woman who, in spite of the persecution, has hopes to be trained as a preacher.**

The ancient Chinese philosopher Lao Tzu was credited with the proverb, 'a journey of a thousand miles begins with a single step.' Of course, physically he was quite correct, but there is another process that precedes any journey.

The journey of 1,000 miles, or in my case nearer 6,000 miles, begins first with a concept. No point in taking off to anywhere on a long journey unless there is some purpose behind it.

That dream, to ride a motorcycle one day from my home in Shropshire to the Arctic Circle, would simply not go away. It was not meant to. On dark rainy winter evenings I had even got so far as to look up possible routes in the AA Big Road Atlas of Europe.

The only reason I even had this book was not because I was a veteran European traveller (yes, I had driven some in France and Italy and had ridden a little in Spain, Holland and Portugal) but because our youngest son Gareth once lived and worked in Milan and it was he who would adventure in Europe and elsewhere. His elsewhere currently is Australia and he had left the atlas behind for me.

I find it amusing to thumb through its pages now to see I had even highlighted routes to Norway and back, but if I am honest the reality is the 'one day' would have probably been put aside and something would inevitably get in the way. Sometimes in life we need people who will spur us on and initially they were in a minority. As I have said many did not share my enthusiasm and they got to me because I began to think that the dream was too big. I was not yet at the point of saying 'I don't care what you think, or what the circumstances are – I'm doing this.' Liz used to listen to my plans to ride there one day with the inevitable comment, 'Well why not?' My wife was one of the few people who believed that I could do it, if I set my mind to it.

My dream was certainly attractive, but looking at the countries and distances involved psychologically it was all very daunting. I was allowing negativity to creep in where there should have been bold enthusiasm and I am not so certain, without some prompt or a very bold decision on my part, that my dream wouldn't have been consigned to the 'wish I had done it list'.

Remembering what Mark Twain wrote that,

*'20 years from now you will be more disappointed by the things that you didn't do than the ones you did do'* I began to wonder if that was me and concluded it could be. Two things were to radically change my perspective.

The first was in March 2016. I went to my trusted GP, Dr Thompson, with growing shortness of breath; it proved to be a very timely appointment. I really try not to do it, but when you get to a certain age you can be tempted to talk with your peers about your growing decrepitude and a good friend, Bob Brown, about my age, then 66, told me he had been recently diagnosed with something called late-onset asthma and the symptoms he described quite mirrored mine.

So when I announced to my doctor I thought I had this condition, he smiled and very wisely ignored my self-diagnosis. He sent me outside to walk up and down the corridors for a minute or two and then on return to the consulting room he listened to my heart.

After examination he sat back and just quietly said to me, 'Were you aware you had a heart murmur?' This statement came as a huge shock. Of course I wasn't. I was in other respects quite well, and it never occurred to me that my symptoms could in fact be related to issues with my heart.

The upshot of that visit meant I was very quickly undergoing cardiac clinical tests and being diagnosed with severe aortic stenosis. Basically, my aortic valve was 70% blocked and leaking. The aorta itself close to the heart was 50% blocked and dilated. In short, this was a very serious condition.

It wasn't many weeks after the diagnosis I started to experience some angina pain. Quite clearly this was not going to get better on its own or with prescribed pills.

I had been a walking health time bomb and didn't know it. Without that visit to my GP a few weeks later Liz and I would have got on long haul flights to visit Gareth and Charlene his fiancée (now wife) in Perth, Australia.

The whole trip was booked and paid for and I would have travelled with this unknown condition giving rise to the possibility that I could have taken ill or even died enroute. I underwent major open-heart surgery for a replacement aortic valve and a section of the aorta in October of 2016.

It transpired that my heart valve had a congenital abnormality from birth. The stress of my job, particularly in my final years with Honda, coupled with a less than healthy lifestyle had undoubtedly exacerbated the problem.

I confess I can also be predisposed to depression sometimes. I have learned over the years to hide it well, but sometimes dark thoughts can pervade. So facing very serious open-heart surgery I should have been terrified and worried to the point of becoming almost incapable of normal day to day functioning. I have been there before when I thought I was seriously ill, but this time I really was.

But something within me had changed; I was no longer the hypochondriac with a morbid fear of death. Yes, I was concerned, who wouldn't be at the prospect of such a big operation, but overall my demeanour was positive.

My consultant friend Paul Rylance who worked at the very hospital where the procedure was to take place, helped me see that for those on the cardiothoracic surgical team there the operation was just routine. His encouragement certainly helped but I couldn't help joking; 'Well it's only routine if it's not happening to you Paul!'

Throughout it all, I was sustained by a belief that this was not my time to die and the scripture Isaiah 26-3, upheld me throughout.

*'You will keep in perfect peace him whose mind is steadfast because he trusts in you.'*

This scripture was given to me by so many people before my operation that it could not be coincidental and I took it to my heart (perhaps literally). It gave me a peace I know was supernatural, even on the day of my surgery itself.

Following surgery, I made quite a remarkable recovery, surprising all by being in hospital just 4 days. The clinical care I received through the NHS at New Cross Hospital in Wolverhampton was second to none, but I am not sure if I could have survived another day of the appalling food!

The warnings about unpleasant and painful procedures, like the removal of the drainage tubes, I took in my stride and I know my faith and the prayers of many certainly helped me through the trauma of that recovery time. My wonderful surgeon, Mr Luckraz, beamingly informed me on his rounds that he was very pleased with me.

'I had three valves to choose from for you and I was able to insert the biggest of the three. At 25mm it is 2mm bigger than the one they gave to Arnold Schwarzenegger!' Any other physical similarities between us end there.

But later, when at home the experience made me seriously question what I was going to do with the extension of my life now so graciously given? The next months were focussed on regaining my fitness levels, but that nagging question remained with me throughout and to some degree still does.

12 months later, in October of 2017, the second life-shaping event took place. Liz and I attended the Open Doors 'Standing Strong' conference in Birmingham. There we heard first-hand accounts of the plight of persecuted Christians living in countries where to worship freely is impossible, places where dying for one's faith could be a daily reality.

Of course, being regular supporters of Open Doors, we already knew about this, but to hear testimonies directly from those who were affected had a huge impact on us. One testimony stood out for me above all others. It was from a Nigerian Pastor, a large man dressed in traditional African clothing who was an overseer of many churches in the north of his country.

I was already aware of what some of these churches had had to endure at the hands of the Islamist militants Boko Haram in the region, where there had been many killings. He told how his own church had been burned to the ground and as he shared his distress this godly man was literally bowed by the weight of responsibility on his shoulders for his churches and his people.

We were all led in prayers for him and his nation, and immediately following them, I felt a prompting. I prayed something like 'what can I do Lord to make a difference?' Sometimes when God answers prayer like that it is not in an audible voice; it can often be a 'penny dropping' moment when an idea, a nudge to do something suddenly has a spiritual illumination on it that it never had before.

Of course, we often ignore or don't recognise such moments and even when we do, we still have a choice to go with them or not. In the interval I went out into the foyer to talk to the Open Doors challenge team.

They were rather busy but eventually I spoke with a lady, Fiona, who was, it turns out, actually their challenge coordinator. I explained as I was recovering from heart surgery I did not think currently I was suitable material to climb Kilimanjaro or to ride a bicycle across the Jordanian desert.

'But,' I asked her, 'has anybody ever suggested riding a motorcycle to the Arctic Circle for Open Doors?' Her eyes widened. 'No, no, never,' she said in surprise, but seemed excited by the thought and wanted my contact details. 'We must talk again, very soon after the conference' she said. So I returned to my seat and I knew at that moment I had been given the very purpose of pursuing that motorcycling dream.

I was calm about it as I explained it to Liz, who was ever supportive and encouraging. 'Well,' she said, 'it is something you have always wanted to do.' But much later, as the realisation sank in, my calmness began to give way to some trepidation.

Suddenly, this became much more than some adventure before dementia or a tick off some silly 'bucket list'. This was way more than tracing routes with my finger on an old road atlas; it meant I was actually committing myself to this challenge and to riding those routes.

But I found a steely resolve growing within me and I knew there would be no turning back; I would have the tenacity to carry me through. I was going to be riding for the persecuted church, raising awareness of the plight of my fellow Christians and of course to raise funds for them through Open Doors in the process.

Back at home, I looked again at the map of Norway in the atlas. I had already noted that the nearest town to the Arctic Circle was a place called Mo I Rana, but now I looked beyond it to see exactly where the northernmost town was and what it was called and found it was Hammerfest.

Highley to Hammerfest – that had a really nice ring to it I thought. Excitedly I e-mailed this concept to Fiona to find she had already cross e-mailed me with her enthusiasm too for the potential challenge and within hours the Highley to Hammerfest Challenge was born.

Highley, my home in South East Shropshire, is a large village of some 3,600 folks and sits on a ridge above the Severn Valley. Apart from an infamous heiress kidnapping in the '70s, (a very sad story), the Severn Valley Railway, a coal mining heritage, and potholes on the access roads deep enough to create new mine entrances, it is notable for very little.

Nevertheless, it a village of friendly people and a fine place to live. Hammerfest is described by Bill Bryson in his book 'Neither Here Nor There' as *an agreeable enough town in a thank-you-God-for-not-making-me-live here sort of way,* which, given that Bryson originally hails from Des Moines, Iowa, a city once described as America's dullest, is a little harsh I think.

Highley and Hammerfest are both understated kinds of places but the inhabitants are justly proud of where they live. This made the two locations even more appropriate I thought. Using Google maps, I made a rough initial outline route between the 2 locations and it looked as if it was going to be at least a 5,000-mile round trip. Their mileage calculation proved somewhat optimistic.

I also had an idea to share about the persecuted church and my challenge en route. Noble ambitions indeed, but the reality proved to be very different. As time went on in the planning this became a distraction and in fact, my primary hope to speak in Denmark or Norway was scuppered by both proving to be 'closed shops' when it came to opportunities to share about the challenge. This was mainly due to the timing of my ride; I found many Scandinavian churches closed over the summer.

The other factor in the equation was fundraising and here I was a complete novice. I had some ideas of course and as some of the official Open Doors challenges seemed to centre on the figure of £10,000 I felt it right to set my challenge target at that figure too. Only later did I come to understand their organised challenges are set with a year or so of planning, promoting and fundraising behind them, whereas I had just months.

Reasoning that sponsorship money would be tight around the Christmas period I further delayed launching my challenge until way into the New Year which was a mistake. I was not focussing sufficiently and at this stage of planning I was allowing myself to become overwhelmed with the enormity of the undertaking and not thinking things through as logically as I would normally do.

Fiona at Open Doors was ever patient with me as I bumbled along. She was helpful and encouraging every step of the way and if she got frustrated with me (I would not have blamed her) she never once showed it.

By now I was beginning to share with others about the trip. Those that thought me seriously deranged at best, or weird at worst, (and there were some, I learned) kept their thoughts largely to themselves, which was probably wise. From my family and close friends, I had nothing but encouragement.

I asked them directly, 'Do you really think I can do this?' Not one person said no. I learned later there was some disquiet, but overall their belief in me outweighed any fears they had. But outside that group there were others who were vocally less than positive about it.

One person told me, 'Don't you think you're a little too old to be doing this sort of thing?' I retorted with, 'If I thought like that, then I would be!' So many times I was to hear the incredulous 'you're doing it alone?' that it started to get to me a little. People kept telling me I was brave. Brave means facing things with an absence of fear. Naturally, there were elements of this venture I was apprehensive about, but it was more the trip logistics and the challenge fundraising as much as the actual riding. I used to counter with 'I am not brave, those I am riding for are' and it became another opportunity to share about the persecuted church.

My financial advisor Nigel, a good all round chap and also a motorcyclist, made it obvious that he wanted to do part of the ride with me. He got a polite but very firm no. Undaunted by this, he went into the Yamaha dealership, where my eldest son James works, and told him he thought I shouldn't be doing it alone (I can just imagine also the unspoken – 'at his age'). He got short shrift from James too.

There were a number of other riders I knew who hinted they would like to join me on the ride and my response to all of them was the same. All this interest I sensed was nothing but misplaced enthusiasm, running on the back of a dream that was not theirs but in which they wanted a part. And that was precisely the core reason I did not want to share this trip with others because it was my dream, my challenge and my ride. I wanted to stop when I wanted to stop, to ride hard when I wanted to ride hard, to rest or sleep when I wanted to rest or sleep. The thought of my daily riding decisions and routine being influenced in any way by another rider, or indeed my safety being compromised by one, was an anathema to me.

The way things evolved as the ride unfolded it would have been impossible for another rider to share it because it became individualistic and personal in ways I had not anticipated. I will let the reader be the judge if I was being selfish or not.

And those other things that were given me cause for apprehension made me feel a bit like the rabbit in the headlights some days. It wasn't just the unknown concept of fundraising; it was the practicalities of the trip and the route and such things as how many miles/kilometres were sensible to ride in a day?

Did I forward book all my accommodation or go wild and take camping gear? How many days for the trip should I allow? With more and more people becoming aware of the challenge, I was also now in the spotlight and the expectations were high, adding to the pressure. I read some advice given by one experienced long-distance traveller.

He said, *'Don't over plan, just get on your bike and go.'* I know now the wisdom of that, but of course I read it after I had returned. Naturally, many riders had opinions about the ride too, but none I spoke to had actually done this particular trip.

One motorcyclist confidently said, 'Oh, if you are going to Norway, well then you must also go up to Nordkapp,' and wanting more information I asked him if he had actually ridden there. Looking down at his feet he shuffled and muttered, 'No.'

Nordkapp is marketed as the northernmost point of Europe, a day's ride from Hammerfest, and I was resolved to ride to it as part of my trip. (Actually, it isn't the northernmost point. That honour goes to Knivskjellodden which, as my Rough Guide pointed out, is *'a slender peninsula that pips Nordkapp by about 1,500m.'*)

You can hike to it but there is no road; in fact, I thought of doing that very thing, but as I was not taking extra walking shoes and as it would have meant losing a day's riding, it was impractical and therefore not included in my itinerary. I do regret that now.

Researching Nordkapp on the internet proved to be a real distraction too and reading some of the horror stories of riding a motorcycle there was not for those of nervous disposition. Part of the ride is along an exposed elevated coast road and thick sea fogs, horizontal rain, or snow, driven by near hurricane-force winds with the potential for huge waves breaking over you were not unusual.

One rider recorded it had been the most terrifying thing he had ever done on a motorcycle, (clearly, this man had never ridden the M25 at the start of a bank holiday weekend!). I could have been put off going there by these stories, but they are always someone else's story; the only way to know and experience it is to do it yourself.

My other major consideration, of course, was the cost. I was resolved from the outset not to use any donated money to fund the trip. Any money given was for the persecuted church, (unless a specific request had been made by the donor for it to be used by me for trip expenses.)

My recently deceased and dearly loved Aunt Madge had left me a small legacy. Funding for me was not an issue; however, I was still going to save pennies on the trip wherever I could because it was going to be an expensive one and I have never been one for wasting money unnecessarily.

Because of the fundraising requirement and shrinking timescale I just had to button it down. So, after weeks of unnecessary procrastination and unwise research, decision time came. Having read of one group of motorcyclists who experienced heavy snow in Norway in June the previous year on a mountain pass, I decided to go a little later.

The ride then would be in mid-July and the dates 7 to 22 July were chosen, with the flexibility to extend if there were problems. That decision taken meant I could now market the trip officially and get on with the practical planning and not least begin fundraising in earnest.

# Chapter 2
# Planning and Practicalities

*'We have made up our mind to die for Jesus and no matter what may be we will serve the Lord. Nothing will stop us.'* – **Aminu, a Christian from Northern Nigeria an area heavily targeted by Boko Haram.**

In the New Year of 2018 I was still spending too many hours online researching my ride, reading about those who had ridden through Europe to Norway and looking at the organised tours that were on offer there and at their routes as some suggestion of the ones I might take.

I consumed any article to do with long-distance touring on a motorcycle abroad looking for practical advice, much of it common sense and most confirming what I already knew anyway. I read one article from a so-called experienced touring rider in America that had a list of dos and don'ts and things to take or not that (I kid you not) ran to 6 pages.

It did not help in the slightest, especially when, almost hidden in the script, I read he had lost two sets of keys for his bike whilst on the journey. It can often be the smallest thing that could cause you to fail (mine was a function button, more on that later) and he had overlooked the blindingly obvious one. Without seriously protecting the whereabouts of your bike keys, every time you stop, you can have a 'to do' list longer than your arm but you aren't going anywhere if they have disappeared.

A friend bought me the AA map of Scandinavia and I wore it out, no really, I did. I opened it so many times to look at the routes that it started to fall apart. Initially, I thought I might cheat slightly, well actually more than slightly, and looked at the possibility of taking a ferry from the UK to Norway, or perhaps returning home from Norway by ferry. I found though there were none.

There was a ferry service once from Newcastle on Tyne but it had long been abandoned. The nearest any UK ferry operator could offer was to Holland, which would cut down my time riding through part of Europe but, as it was to turn out, not really by that much. I am not sure why I was even pursuing this line of thought.

Perhaps it was some sort of mental comfort zone wanting me to avoid riding through unknown mainland Europe. It was fluffy thinking.

Then, in my research, I came across an article by a journalist writing for The Daily Telegraph who claimed that riding a 'motorbike' (not a term normally used by those of us who work in the industry, it is either a bike or a motorcycle) to the Arctic Circle had been on his bucket list from a child.

He flew to Trondheim, hired a BMW (I mean, what else?) and all his riding kit and did the fairly short hop from there up to Mo I Rana and beyond to the polar visitor centre and back. Yes, technically he had ridden a motorcycle to the Arctic Circle, but he did not ride there and back from the UK.

Suddenly, it illuminated for me that there were to be no half measures. Doing it that way was too easy, required no real thought, effort or planning and he even got paid for doing it! Any thought of short-circuiting my trip went out of the window after I read that article. My challenge, after all, was Highley to Hammerfest and that is exactly what it had to be.

Riding through mainland Europe there and back was now a given. Reading back my early notes post-trip though, there were pages relating to potential routes and it is clear, now, that I was making the whole thing unnecessarily complicated. When I eventually decided an outward route I found it would unavoidably involve a ferry crossing. But there was a justified reason for taking it.

My ambition was to ride the whole length of Norway but practically, if frustratingly, I found I could only really do this by taking a ferry from the tip of Denmark to Southern Norway. From that route also it would much easier to explore Western Norway and the fjords.

Coming home was different. It would be the longer but faster route through Finland and Sweden with no ferries, or so I thought. I also decided that major cities, Copenhagen, Oslo, Stockholm, etc, were going to be avoided. I don't much like riding in city traffic anyway and I really needed to remain firmly focused on the primary motivation of the challenge itself.

The trip was not about city sightseeing. This made the ride the key objective and even though I did ensure my route took in some of the best Norway had to offer, it was at best passing and secondary. I was certainly no tourist, a traveller perhaps, but I felt I was a kind of journeyman, a skilled rider pursuing a set purpose.

The one essential item for the trip, of course, was the motorcycle. What was I going to ride? I had hoped that a manufacturer might loan me a bike but I did not approach Honda. Having worked for another manufacturer (BMW) since leaving them, it did not feel right somehow and anyway my chief contacts there had mostly retired or moved on.

I approached BMW GB, but they were unable or unwilling to help me, which came as some disappointment as I had been instrumental in restoring their police motorcycle business in the UK. I approached BMW in Germany where my business contribution was clearly better appreciated.

The answer was yes, if I could collect the bike from Munich. As I carefully considered this generous offer, I found it presented more difficulties than it solved. The security of my own bike left in Munich whilst on the trip and the specification of the loan bike; would it, for example, have fitted luggage and a Sat Nav which were essentials for the trip?

I was hardly in a position to dictate what bike to borrow much less the specification of it. Also, a detour out and back via Munich was a long way off my intended route, and there would be all the messing about swapping stuff from one bike to another. Practicalities overruled my hope to ride the challenge on someone else's bike and the more I thought about it, the less attractive it became.

I thanked my former colleague and friend Torsten in the BMW Authorities Department at Munich and declined his kind offer. I decided I was going to do the ride on my own bike, which had been at the back of my mind all along.

The bike in question is a Yamaha XT1200Z Super Tenere which, before I bought it, was a Yamaha UK demonstrator. As I still had some profile in the motorcycle industry, Yamaha kindly looked after me and, as a bonus, it came with full luggage (side cases, sometimes referred to as panniers, and a top case), and a raft of factory-approved accessories.

The Yamaha replaced an immaculate and low mileage BMW R1200GS which I had bought almost new directly from BMW when I retired. I loved riding the BMW, it was a wonderful motorcycle and, in many respects, I thought it would be the perfect bike for me in my retirement, but it proved a disastrous marriage, as I don't think the bike liked me very much.

There were too many recalls and expensive services (even at 'mate's rates'). It had to have two serious mechanical repairs due to bearing failures, one which resulted in a replacement gearbox the cost of which was only partially covered as it was outside of the warranty period, (BMW were very fair to me however because they could have said no to it all). It also gained the dubious distinction of being the only motorcycle (and in over 30 years working in the industry there have been countless) that I've ever had road-recovered. This, after an electrical component failed on the fuel system and stranded me in remotest Wales. It was to my embarrassment that my bike, perched ignominiously on a recovery trailer, did not slip into the village unnoticed and I came in for some gentle ribbing at the pub the following weekend. It had to go.

Like the BMW it replaced the Super Tenere is also an 'Adventure Sports' motorcycle, essentially a big trail bike that is primarily road focused in design but could, if one was so inclined, be ridden to a limited degree off-road. It has now been eclipsed by a raft of similar styled newer models by other manufacturers, but is still highly regarded by many motorcycling journalists, one even describing it as the thinking man's Adventure Sports bike. Where precisely I fit into that description is open to conjecture. It has a sensible upright and comfortable riding position, relatively good weather protection and the performance of a 1200cc parallel twin engine with enough power to propel one quickly through the autoroutes of Europe.

After all, it was a Super Tenere that Nick Sanders, a serious motorcycle adventurer, rode from Alaska to Argentina and back covering 51,000 miles in 46 days (I don't think Nick ever lost his bike keys) with no mechanical problems. Compared to his madness (I do respect what he did, but still think it was crazy to link such a journey to a time record) my challenge was small scale.

I wanted to use the trip as a platform to highlight the plight of the persecuted church, which was, and remained, my primary motivation. I knew all along that the bike was easily up to the challenge of this huge road trip and I had absolutely no qualms about going on it. The rider – well that was another thing.

I seemed to have made a good recovery from my heart surgery, and tried not to think about it too much. But from time to time a chest twinge would just make me think for a moment about what I had recovered from. But I could not, nor would not, dwell on it and at no time did my heart operation ever become a reason for me holding back from going.

For years, however, I have suffered from back problems. Being an ex-off-road competitor (trials), it came with the territory. Leading up to the trip my back was not in good order. An excellent chiropractor in Wolverhampton, Henryk, was recommended to me and I underwent some weeks of treatment which more or less sorted it.

I never had any major problems on the trip, even after having to pick the fully laden bike up off its side on a grassy hillside in Norway (more on that particular incident later) and, as I was to discover post-trip, Henryk also had some interesting links to Norway.

So physically, I was going in reasonably good shape, as was the bike being fully serviced with all new Metzeler tyres (courtesy of Pirelli UK) and crash bars fitted. On removal of the hardly worn existing tyres on the bike for fitment of the new ones (the idea was for the original tyres to be refitted after the trip) my son James rang me.

'Just as well we are changing your tyres dad, the rear tyre one is totally shot' he said. I was shocked as he went onto explain there was a nail right the way into the sidewall of the tyre rendering it useless. I have no idea where I picked that nail up and, being a tubeless tyre, it had stayed inflated.

I once asked a respected motorcycle journalist what he thought the major advance had been in motorcycle safety and he said without hesitation 'tubeless tyres.' Long after cars had progressed to tubeless tyres motorcycle design lagged behind this innovation.

Naturally, any foreign object puncturing an inner tube means a tyre deflation completely and often rapidly. A tubeless tyre puncture usually gives warning and, in this case, had even stayed inflated. That said, of course it was still possible for a rapid deflation and the thought of that happening on one of my faster rides out did not bear thinking about. That unknown nail in the sidewall of the tyre had negative potential. At times like these you know that you are being looked after.

There is also another advantage to a tubeless tyre; you can mend some punctures at the roadside. Part of my armoury for Norway was a tyre repair kit which would allow me to insert a sealing plug into the offending hole, provided it was not in the sidewall or too big for the range of plugs provided that is.

Such a repair is only meant as a temporary measure but at least it can get you to your nearest motorcycle dealer for a replacement. Trying to repair a tubed tyre puncture at the roadside on a large road bike would be a procedure I would never want to contemplate and at the very least would involve removing a wheel and the tyre. No thanks.

On James' recommendation I bought an air seat which proved to be a very wise investment. The standard seat on the Super Tenere lets it down; it is a very uncomfortable thing for long-distance riding and I wonder why some manufacturers do not pay more attention to this rather essential item. After all, to ride a bike you actually need to sit on it and often for long periods.

The next consideration was what riding clothing I was going to wear and take. It seemed I was going to have to cater for 2 possible climate extremes, summer in mid-Europe and potentially, very much colder and wetter weather in northern Norway. I was, after all, going to be way inside the Arctic Circle as far north as one can actually ride in Europe.

I did have 2 very good BMW riding suits at my disposal, one which was far too cold-weather oriented but the other allowed the jacket to be fully-vented to the outside in warm weather. However, promoting BMW-branded clothing whilst riding a Yamaha didn't seem appropriate (although as events were to prove, it was a decision I was going to regret.)

I was given a suit by a certain clothing manufacturer for me to evaluate for them during the trip, but the quality was so bad with seams splitting, and I returned it to them with a full report after just 2 rides.

After research, and with James' help, I bought a top of the range Gore-Tex riding suit from the excellent Richa Company which fitted perfectly and had all the features expected of a quality product. The jacket even boasted a pair of small front air vents which could be zipped opened if it got really hot, not a feature I gave much thought to at the time.

I was, after all, heading as far north in Europe as possible, extremes of heat were not really to be expected and therefore I was confident the suit choice would cater for the worst that northern Europe was going to throw at me – or so I thought.

I never ride in heavyweight gloves even in winter, hating the loss of feel to the bike controls. Fortunately, my bike has heated handlebar grips so my hands never get that cold when they are switched on. The 2 pairs of gloves taken therefore were lightweight, with 1 pair fully waterproof.

My boots were fully waterproof too and I bought a new lightweight Shoei crash helmet. My riding kit was the very best quality I could afford. Most motorcyclists use a layering method to supplement their outer clothing.

I reasoned that I would have to take both winter and summer under-garments; these were to take up a lot of space in the side cases.

I also bought a pair of Kevlar jeans which proved to be surplus to my requirements. So the bike, I, and my riding clothing would be ready.

Now, I turned my attention to the sensitive issues of fundraising. Let me say from the outset I did not find it easy to ask people to part with their hard-earned cash, but my vision for the needs of the persecuted church overrode much of my reluctance. This mission, if you want to call it that, was important to me, but more so to them and remained my driving force throughout.

Marketing wise, one of the first things needed was a publicity photograph, so a bitterly cold early Spring day had me riding around the local lanes looking for fir trees (suggestive of Norway I reasoned) which I could use as a backdrop for a photograph. I found some on a very quiet lane and set up my Nikon on a tripod to take suitable pictures.

If you had been witnessing this performance you would very likely have laughed. Focus camera, set the time delay, rush into the shot, forgetting your crash helmet of course, repeat with crash helmet until, more by luck than judgement, you got an acceptable shot. The picture chosen, I think, was actually not bad. Reminiscent of Norway? Not really, but I tried. It was a start.

I began to get promotional material made. My nicely designed T-shirts came up almost two sizes too big and were like tents to wear. When I complained to the local manufacturer he blamed me for ordering the wrong size.

I countered that he should have informed me at point of order that his XL size was actually equivalent to a normal XXL. He refused to accept a mistake had been made and change them and given time was now getting short I had to accept the situation, but it was an expensive lesson.

I had posters and postcards made by a printing business in the town and I found a great rapport with Tim Down, who ran a small sticker company in Dudley, and he made the challenge stickers for my bike. The learning curve was growing ever steeper for me but the mistakes were made which will stand me in good stead if or when I do my next challenge.

I attended outdoor events with the bike using the promotional material but very little by way of donations came from these. But I got opportunities to speak at many churches about my challenge and without exception, bless them, the responses were always encouraging. But as time went on the target of £10,000 was looking a very long way off.

I rang Fiona at Open Doors at one low point and suggested we reduce the target figure. There is an expression, 'O ye of little faith' and within 20 minutes of that conversation I took a call and was pledged £3,000 from one church! Humbled and a little shaken, I rang Fiona back immediately to tell her the target remained as originally set.

With advice from Fiona (it was needed as I am not really that good with IT), I managed to surprise myself by setting up a 'Just Giving' page on social media for fundraising, Facebook in my case. Once launched personal donations started to roll in very quickly and, again, my thanks to every single person who gave by this means. Time and time again the generosity of people was to overwhelm me. The challenge really captivated people's imagination and they believed in my cause and in my ability to deliver and, of course, I believe in all of this it was also a testimony of God's faithfulness.

Another one of my core ideas was to try to obtain trade and corporate sponsorship for the ride and to advertise them on the bike. I was still well connected within the motorcycle industry and knew some local businesses and I was genuinely moved by the response of people.

Maggie, the owner of my local travel agent, was so excited when I told her about the challenge that she promptly donated and wanted pictures of me outside the shop with her sitting on the back of the bike. This level of support and encouragement from the secular businesses was priceless.

All my motorcycle trade contacts gave towards the challenge either directly or by providing goods or services. I even contacted Yamaha and asked for some practical support for roadside assistance and recovery for the bike in the unlikely event of a breakdown and they did not hesitate to provide it. I cannot adequately express my gratitude to them all.

I once remember commenting to Liz, 'The motorcycle industry has a big heart,' and it still does. Bonded by a common love of motorcycling, some of the finest and kindest people I have ever met and worked with came from my time in the trade and I have retained many of those friendships. Yes, of course there was the odd rogue, they are found in all walks of life, but they were very much in a minority. So even years later when they knew one of their own was doing something a bit out of the ordinary the response from them was very positive.

Buoyed up by this level of support I confidently approached some Christian businesses and suddenly hit an unexpected wall of negativity; not one of them was interested in sponsoring the bike. One even told me, 'It doesn't exactly fit with our business profile' which, given the level of support from elsewhere, I found rather a hurtful response. The irony of this situation did not escape me. I had secular businesses genuinely proud to sponsor the challenge and Christian businesses who were embarrassed to, but their responses put me firmly in my place. Of course it was their prerogative not to support it and I accept that entirely, but the worst of it was the lack of encouragement from them. This was primarily because I felt it was about being strengthened and motivated by fellow believers to 'go for it,' because I really was stepping out of my comfort zone to do something a bit out of the ordinary for fellow Christians who were suffering. I felt this warranted some understanding and exhortation from them, if nothing else.

In fairness, all of them did make a personal contribution to the challenge and I was most grateful for it, but their business endorsement on the bike and their encouragement would have meant so much more. I questioned whether I should have even have mentioned it here, but this storyline is also part of my journey and therefore I felt it had to be included.


Back to other practicalities. One of my growing concerns was the Garmin Satellite Navigation system. I had paid Garmin for lifetime maps but found that I had to put the European maps needed on a separate SD card. This was a bit of a worry because the process to format the card did not make sense to me, even after 2 emails to Garmin for advice.

I knew that a Sat Nav was going to be vital so it was a bit of a stress point. Fortunately, James once again came to my rescue and he got the card formatted with all the right maps downloaded – I hoped. It was at this stage untested.

Then, for my birthday, the family had bought me a helmet-mounted intercom system that could connect to the Sat Nav via Blue Tooth, so I could hear the navigational instructions in my helmet. To my shame, I have to say I was somewhat sceptical of the usefulness of this gift, but James knows his stuff. He fitted it and set it up just prior to my departure. I was still not completely convinced though.

My idea was to just follow the Sat Nav 'on-screen' directions, as I normally did, when on the bike. How was I going to hear Emily, or whatever her Garmin name was, with earplugs in and above the road noise in my helmet?

My first ride to Bridgnorth, to try the system out, was a total revelation. I could not believe it. Despite the deeply planted earplugs, I could hear every blooming word she said (something my long-suffering wife Liz rarely manages to achieve) and this feature when riding through Europe was to prove invaluable.

My earplugs, I should say, were the expensive reusable type which had a road noise reduction filter but allowed other noise frequencies to be heard. Undoubtedly, these helped.

I began to turn my attention now to the detailed planning of the trip. My route was to include riding through 9 countries, England, France, Belgium, Holland, Germany, Denmark and Norway on the outward leg, plus Finland and Sweden on the return leg. Currency for each of these also had to be thought about.

Yes, of course, I would use my credit card but I would still take some cash for small items such as drinks, snacks, local tips or the unexpected incidentals, wherever they were. What I did not know, until I checked, was not all of these countries were in the so-called Eurozone.

I knew Norway had the Krone, but I was surprised to discover Denmark and Sweden also had separate currencies. My trip was going to involve taking no less than 5 of them (including sterling). A small detail perhaps but nevertheless I felt an important one. In my limited experience it is not a good idea to try tipping your server with the wrong currency.

My first actual travel decision (and booking) was how I was going to cross the channel and I decided it was to be via the Channel Tunnel and there was a slight ulterior motive to choosing this crossing route. Our old friends, Tim and Catherine Wilson, lived in Great Chart, Kent.

Tim was once our Curate at Highley and was now the Rector of 2 churches there. And Great Chart is, practically, very close to the Channel Tunnel terminal. 'Could I come and stay and speak to your churches prior to leaving for my trip' I asked? And naturally, the answer was yes.

I had my first 2 nights' accommodation sorted. I also planned to meet up with ex-Honda Netherlands colleagues in Ermelo for 2 nights and booked further hotels and Airbnbs to cover my first week of travelling. However, I had long since discounted the notion of camping.

I did not need the distraction of finding a suitable location or the frustration of setting up some un-erectable tent at the end of a long day's riding in bad weather. The extra space and weight to carry all the additional camping gear did not appeal either.

Eventually, something rather more than an outline plan began to emerge and I felt the trip and challenge was, at last, starting to come together. I still gave myself some needless sleepless nights trying to wrack my brains of things I thought I may have missed. In the end, there weren't so very many.

As I said earlier Norway seemed closed to me at times, and almost everything beyond that first week became difficult to arrange, hotels chosen were full or had closed, and churches, where I had hoped to speak, were all on summer recess during July.

One particular frustration was having been promised by e-mail accommodation near Trondheim for one night. This was arranged through a good friend of ours, whose nephew is a well-known TV fishing personality and just happens to co-own a fishing lodge on one of the best-known salmon rivers in Norway, the Gaula River, famous for its very large salmon.

I was really excited by this prospect and wondered if I might even manage an evening's fly fishing on the river. As another close friend of mine often says, 'Be disappointed but never surprised.' It didn't quite work out as expected, the offer was not withdrawn exactly but in spite of a couple of e-mails was not confirmed either and I did not want to just arrive there speculatively.

In fairness to them, I found out later that they were dealing with an extraordinary set of business problems. The Norwegian fishing authorities had closed the river (and all others in Western Norway) that July to salmon fishing. I learned also that those who did arrive at the lodge to fish for salmon were being taken instead to nearby lakes to fish for other species which would have been a difficult situation for the business as the fees charged would have had to have been slashed.

I started to book some accommodation but, following days of frustration, I got fed up with dead ends and resolved just to find my further ongoing accommodation as I travelled. Yes, without a doubt I could always find top-end accommodation but prices in Norway are not cheap, and I was trying to be sensible with my budget and stay within a limit of £100/110 per night and not stay in city locations.

Sounds easy to do, but actually it wasn't because often the cheapest prices were in the city locations. I tried using Airbnb. Never again! I was to cancel both my accommodation bookings through them because, as will become evident, there were pitfalls.

As I over-planned and contemplated the trip I was becoming more and more fidgety. I was about to launch myself into the unknown. Yes, I know that is possibly an overworked cliché, but it was true. My secure world of home and friends, of church and riding along well-known routes, of locals and warm pints, was about to be exchanged very soon for a life on the road, on the wrong side of the road at that.

I'd even had 'keep right' stickers made up which were liberally placed anywhere within eyeshot in front of me on the bike. Increasingly, I started to feel as if I did not belong here because it was not where I was going. Suddenly, I felt I needed a break from it, but with a practical purpose, I needed to go and ride a motorcycle.

# Chapter 3
# Discouragements and Disappointments

*'The Bible warns us that things like this will happen, but that does not reduce the agony when they do.'* – **Mary, from Tanzania, whose husband was killed whilst guarding their church.**

I decided to do some shake-down trips on the fully loaded bike. Having appointments with Open Doors HQ in Witney to discuss the challenge in more detail, I decided to ride down the day before and stay overnight with my good friend Ian at his cottage in Binsey, which is a small village on the Thames near Oxford.

So, early in the 1st week in March 2018, I went on a simple run down to Oxford. I decided not to do the usual and easy M40/A34 route but go over the Cotswolds from Tewkesbury instead. I should perhaps mention at this point the UK was not yet out of the winter by any means and by our standards it had been a hard one.

It had snowed heavily the week before and as I rode over the Cotswolds there were still shoulder high cut-through snowdrifts and even slush on the road in places. Then it started raining and my goodness did it rain! This was my first wet ride on the new Metzeler Road-Tec tyres which had been fitted a few weeks earlier and they inspired much confidence, with never the hint of a slide despite all the slime and mud on the road. It did not stop raining until the wee small hours.

But on the A40 Witney by-pass I had a real scare. In the nearside lane, I was closing quickly on a car ahead that, like me, was almost shrouded in a blanket of heavy spray. I remember I had become distracted by some setting or other on the bike (I cannot remember exactly what) and only did a cursory check in my mirrors. As I started to pull out to overtake, an Audi being driven at extremely high speed with an unexpected 'whoosh' almost brushed me as it came past. It was pretty close and it scared the living daylights out of me. In fact, had I pulled out hard…well, possibly best not to dwell on that.

The speed of that Audi could only be guessed at (and I wasn't exactly hanging about) but I think it would have been above 120 mph. In my defence, the rain was so appalling with incredibly heavy surface spray which limited my ability to see him coming up in my mirrors, but to be truthful I just wasn't being as vigilant as I should have been.

I was riding quickly enough and was blasé enough in thinking that another vehicle couldn't possibly be going so very much faster in those conditions. Wrong! His closing speed on me would have been extremely high. Even so, there is no doubt it was inattention on my part for not being more careful in those conditions. It was also a wake-up call for what I might have to deal with on the autobahns in a few months' time.

Bad, inattentive riding on my part, no question, and no excuses, but then he probably did not see me either in all that dreadful spray till the very last moment, so it possibly shook him up too. I pulled out and accelerated hard for a second or two with a ridiculous notion of catching him to register some disapproval.

Thankfully, common sense quickly prevailed and I slowed down to my previous cruising speed. I confess though, the incident gave me a big shock, it had shaken me and I am usually quite cool and don't frighten easily when riding or driving.

Being a little too early to call on Ian, I squelched into the Oxford Waitrose café for a calming coffee leaving a trail of pretty little puddles in my wake. I was feeling a bit cold but as I sipped my drink, I sat thinking about my close call today and of a time when, on that very same by-pass some years earlier myself, then Honda UK's Police Sales Manager, my former boss at Honda, Bob McMillan, and Grant Goodings from Thames Valley Police (one of the most respected police motorcycle instructors in the UK) were road testing marked Honda Police ST1300A-P's.

Riding also in torrential rain and at speeds which would have matched that Audi, (as official testers of police product on the day and riding with police instructors we were given speeding dispensation to do this) I recall I was relieved to end that day safely after riding at a pace and in conditions which had pushed me beyond my comfort zone at times.

It did not prove, incidentally, to be of any value in establishing why we were having such big problems with high-speed stability on some of those police bikes. Like the incident this day, I was so very thankful that in both cases I was being watched over.

Overnight at Ian's, I started to feel ill with a high temperature and a very sore throat. Next day meetings at Open Doors went really well. The people I met were so encouraging about the challenge and gave me lots of practical advice, but I was hiding the fact that I was feeling quite unwell.

By the time I mounted the bike to ride home I was shivering uncontrollably and absolutely freezing and I tried to ignore the thought of how wonderful it would have been to have climbed into a nice warm car. Somehow, I rode back home in the now cold, dry and sunny weather as quickly as I could.

Upon return, I immediately washed the bike down (necessary as there was still salt on the roads from the previous week's snow, corrosive salt and motorcycle cycle parts are not a good mix) then crashed out. I am not one for 'taking to my bed' but nevertheless I was out of action indoors with 'man-flu' for over a week, which was very frustrating.

What did I learn from this trip? Check your mirrors carefully before you go for that overtake? Of course. But clearly, I was rusty in other areas too and I noted the need to get myself better organised with the bike for the real event.

Scrabbling around for a flat stone to put under the side stand on Ian's gravel drive showed a complete lack of forethought and my packing skills certainly needed honing. Tugging to extract an overfilled inner side case bag in heavy rain was not an auspicious moment either. Oh…and ideally after riding through cold and very wet weather, to find a place to warm up properly when stopping, which was certainly not the café at Oxford Waitrose, but then perhaps, I was a bit traumatised.

My second shakedown trip was a long weekend in Northern Ireland. Why there exactly? Firstly, it was a good long ride and it would provide me with the basis of a working routine with the bike. Secondly, having worked in the province for many years, I had a lot of contacts there. I reasoned that with a very high interest in things motorcycling generally there I would get good support.

It didn't quite work out as anticipated, for my high expectations for the challenge were not met with the levels of enthusiasm or indeed, the support I expected, and sadly it almost mirrored my experience with the Christian businessmen earlier. However, undaunted, I had real friends there who gave me lots of encouragement and that counted for much.

The last weekend in May 2018 was chosen, a bank holiday weekend. I booked a trip to take the ferry from Holyhead to Dublin riding north up the A1 into Northern Ireland. I was staying with old friends, the Holdens, who lived in the orchard county of Armagh, and I had arranged with Eddie Floyd, of Fireblade Ministries, to speak about the challenge in a church in Belfast on the Saturday evening.

Fireblade Ministries is a story in itself and it may seem to be a slight diversion from the tale of the challenge, but it bears repeating for those who do not know it.

In 1996, I was an Area Sales Manager for Honda UK Motorcycles and my area included Northern Ireland. I was attending a motorcycle show at the King's Hall in Belfast and at the end of the day as we were preparing to close the stand a man came to talk to me. His opening words to me were, 'I'm a Christian, right.'

Now, those of us who have regularly worked major bike shows know there is a phenomenon that often occurs at the very end of show days when we have all manner of often strange people suddenly coming up to talk to us. It is almost that they are too shy to approach us at any other time and from experience I knew that some of these folk could be really very odd indeed.

The man in question that evening was Eddie Floyd and I confess initially I was not really in receptive mode and possibly even rolled my eyes to my colleagues who were already sniggering. He told me he was starting 'Fireblade Ministries' using a motorcycle as a Christian outreach and went onto explain about the blade being the word of God and fire representing the Holy Spirit.

It should be noted, had he approached any of my other Honda colleagues in attendance that day, this would have been as far as the conversation would have got, but God goes before. What he shared did spark some interest, and I told him I was possibly the one person on the stand who actually understood what he was talking about.

He showed me a letter signed by a known manager at Honda UK HQ who had given him written permission to use the name Fireblade for his ministry. That really got my attention for the Fireblade was, and remains, one of Honda's iconic and top-selling sports motorcycles and in my experience, Honda never gave permission for their model brand name to be used by outside sources for other purposes. But there it was, in black and white.

I asked Eddie how I could help. He explained that he did not have a Fireblade motorcycle, nor did he currently have the money to buy one but he wondered if we could help. I told him I couldn't promise anything (there was no way I could get him a free bike) but I would see what I could do and to be honest, I was being a little bit condescending for it had been a very long day, and I had no vision or expectation to be able to offer anything.

Nevertheless, and being true to my word, early the following week, I rang the office to ask if we had any Fireblades on the demonstration fleet that were due for disposal and remarkably, because the dealers usually snap them up, there were 4 bikes, so I asked for a trade price on one.

I gave Eddie the price, £6,000 I believe, and he asked if we could hold the bike for him, which we did. A week or so later he rang me back. After putting out an appeal to his contacts somehow he had raised the amount needed to buy the bike to the penny which just amazed me because I had not really been expecting a positive outcome.

So, more than a little humbled, I arranged shipment of the bike to one of our Honda dealers, R. F. Linton and Sons in Ballymena, explaining the situation to them and who the bike was for. They knew Eddie and were supportive of his ministry and agreed to process and invoice the bike to him for just an administration fee.

Later, I asked Eddie if he was going to change the original registration number and re-register it on a Northern Ireland plate. He asked me if I had noted anything significant about the bike's number N188 GLY. I told him that I hadn't. GLY, he said, stands for 'God Loves You. And look up Numbers 18 v 8 in your Bible'. I did and this is the scripture,

*'Then the Lord said to Aaron, 'I myself have put you in charge of the offerings; all the holy offerings the Israelites give me I give to you and your sons as your portion and regular share.'*

I was stunned that this motorcycle could have such a significant registration number and even a reference to the offering received and given and knew that it was more than mere coincidence and could have only been from God. I was, and still am, amazed how all this came about.

Eddie still uses the bike to support his ministry, often speaks at churches in Northern Ireland and attends all the Road Race meetings there and at the Isle of

Man TT, where he witnesses and offers Christian support and Bibles to anyone interested or in need. I am ashamed of my attitude towards him when we first met; he is a great guy, does a great job and, graciously, he has forgiven me.

**Day 1 – Friday** 25th May 2018. Highley to Portadown, Northern Ireland. Leaving time – 06:45: temperature range 7°C to 23°C; distance ridden 227miles.

I set off through the familiar Shropshire countryside and lost the rain within 5 miles. I joined the A5 at Shrewsbury riding the length of it to catch the fast ferry which left Holyhead at 11:30. It was a pleasant enough morning riding up through Wales, although following the overnight rain the roads were wet in places and thunderstorms had also been forecast for later in the day.

This was the first time I was using the helmet intercom system in anger. I put my destinations in the Sat Nav and Emily and I went away for our long weekend together.

I was riding in a BMW Rallye 11 suit which proved the right choice for the weekend and could have been the pointer for clothing choice for the main challenge. I felt a bit rusty as I had not done a long distant ride since Oxford in March.

I had a trouble-free ride along the surprisingly quiet A5, where beyond Betws-y-Coed I was really able to enjoy the 'twisties' due to the light traffic. Crossing the bridge over the Menai Straits onto Anglesey it was dual carriageway from there, all the way to Holyhead.

About 10 miles south of Holyhead something brushed against my right arm and flew away. At first I thought I might have hit a small bird but found it strange I had not seen it. As I queued for my ferry I noticed the windshield was at a slightly odd angle and checking further I found the height adjusting knob and the associated bracket were missing.

When cleaning the bike days earlier and had obviously forgotten to re-tension it. Another lesson before the challenge – check everything is 100% secure.

On the ferry I spent some time talking to 2 Dutch riders both in their 70s who were off to tour Ireland on their Hondas. One of them, a retired pharmacist, told me he had never enjoyed his life so much since he had stopped working and it was clear motorcycling was a large part of that for him now.

Somehow I felt I had never quite managed to achieve that level of contentment in my own retirement, but I was happy for him. He kept sniffing

44

and the oddest thing happened, as he suddenly became really quite offended by the smell of a perfume being worn by a lady sitting close by and moved away to sit somewhere else.

His action threw me a little. He was quite unnecessarily demonstrative in the way he changed seats and I was suddenly glad I had not been wearing after-shave. Who knows what triggered that reaction? I felt there was a little more to it than it not being his favourite scent. His friend shrugged his shoulders, as if this was nothing new, and stayed chatting to me.

It was a very calm crossing, taking just over 2 hours, and the road network out of the dock area was excellent. I had remembered to bring some Euro coins and, predictably, there was soon a toll booth. Now one of the things not so easy to do on a motorcycle is to pay tolls. I expected them, but no matter how you plan it, it is always a pain.

Normally, it will involve you removing your gloves, finding the pocket the money is in, trying to count it out, paying it, then reversing the procedure, or similarly extracting your credit card from some deep inside pocket. If you have intolerant drivers behind you, not good; if you drop a coin or your card, even worse.

What I did was dive into my right jacket pocket and offer up a load of Euro coins on my right palm for the toll booth operator to sift for the right ones. He must see motorcyclists everyday fishing around in pockets trying to find means of payment and I know that many of them behind me that day would not even have thought about it prior to leaving the ferry as I had.

He was actually quite amused by my solution to the toll predicament and we had a good laugh about it and he wished me a good onward journey with a smile. I just love the Irish. I repeated the same exercise again an hour later at the toll booth on the A1 with much the same result and kindness.

As I rode north the day grew progressively hotter and I was able to zip open the very generous air vents this particular riding suit had. This design feature might have been more carefully considered by me when making my final clothing selection for Norway had I known what I was in for. But it had disadvantages because the suit only became waterproof when inner Gore-Tex liners were zipped in and, as can be imagined, this is not something which can be done quickly.

I had them with me on this ride, but with it being so warm and dry they were in the side case. So, the dilemma with this suit would be trying to work out if you were going to get a wet period during your ride and whether to insert them at the beginning of the day or not. Okay to take a chance on a weekend away in Ireland, but weeks on the road in Europe? I discarded the idea as being impractical and knew I would not have enough luggage space to take 2 riding suits.

Unlike the early days when I used to work in Northern Ireland when there were army or police road-blocks everywhere, especially at the border, the crossing now is seamless with just a simple road sign to say you have moved from the republic to the province.

As I rode across the border I thought about blocks, particularly what a stumbling block this border was then, and remained, in the UK's Brexit negotiations which, at the time of writing this, were unresolved.

I thought of the hard-won Good Friday agreement and the astonishing friendship that arose between former enemies Ian Paisley and Martin McGuinness which helped bring an end to the 'troubles.' I also thought how lightly our current crop of politicians were handling the ever complex and sensitive situation in Ulster in those Brexit negotiations. The thought of the good people of Northern Ireland being tossed as some game chip on the gambling table of opportunist career politicians did not rest comfortably with me as I rode.

At Newry I left the A1 to enjoy the eminently ridable minor roads in Armagh, losing my way a little on the back roads where Bill and Claire Holden live (even the Sat Nav got confused), but I was soon relaxing with this lovely family in their new home. I may not have seen them for a few years but as ever with true friends it seemed as if it was just yesterday.

In the evening we all went out for a very non-Irish meal…a curry. Bill, a recently retired traffic officer from the Police Service of Northern Ireland, I knew both as a friend and professionally. With Honda, and latterly BMW, I had supported the superb PSNI road safety initiatives for motorcyclists that Bill and his colleague Steven Nugent ran. I might add, as an ex-traffic motorcycle policeman, he also is a seriously good motorcyclist, one of the best to ride out with.

**Day 2 – Saturday** 26th May 2018. In and around Northen Ireland. Leaving time – 08:30; temperature range 14°C upwards and sunny; distance ridden 240 miles.

The following day, Saturday, was a busy day for me. I was up early and on a mission. I explained to my hosts I was unsure what time I would be returning that evening. I rode first to Hurst Motorcycles, in my time a Honda dealer but now the sole Yamaha dealer in Belfast.

David White, the manager there, remembered me and as I explained about the Norway challenge, one of the salesmen interrupted. A customer with a problem motorcycle had arrived. David sighed and gave me a long-suffering look, 'Sorry Merv, I have to go and road test this bike' he said.

I knew exactly what he was dealing with; the fact the complaint had even escalated to his level meant it was serious. Such is life at a motorcycle dealership, in my experience, often the problem being more with the customer than the machine. There is simply no pleasing some people and problem customers became well known both by the dealers and the manufacturers.

I'd had to deal with my fair share of them over the years. David was very happy for me to pin my promotional poster on his notice board and knowing what he was about to get involved in, I did not outstay my welcome.

I rode onto to Ballymena and to another one of my ex-Honda dealers, R.F. Linton's, the same people who had looked after Eddie Floyd's Fireblade, I had such fond memories of my calls there. The owners, Ronnie, Raymond and Adeline were always a delight to do business with and looked after their customers similarly.

They were not expecting me and I was greeted like a long-lost friend. I was very sad to learn that their long serving mechanic Davy, a gentle and friendly man, had recently passed away from cancer, an evocative reminder of the march of time. One thing that had not changed over the years though was one of their daily traditions, the provision of excellent cakes with the tea.

I had a flashback from 20 years ago, sitting in their small back office, trying to be deadly serious about some burning business issue they had caused for Honda (usually a complaint from another dealer about grey-imports, or excess discounting, but frankly none of the dealers in Northern Ireland were whiter than white in this regard) and having the wind taken out of my sails by their friendliness, kindness and hospitality.

Underneath my hard exterior, I am a big softie really. Suddenly also, I recalled the appalling machine-dispensed drinks, made with powdered milk that I used to be offered by some of my other dealers there. They were undrinkable and were so bad that sometimes I secretly poured them away. I suspect many an Ulster office potted plant quietly met its demise at my hands.

My poster was left with them and I was sorry to have to leave. My next call was also a poignant one for me; I was going to Joey's bar in Ballymoney.

Joey Dunlop was a motorcycle racing legend and a Honda rider for most of his career and he hailed from Ballymoney. He still holds the record number of Isle of Man TT wins at 26 and was revered in Northern Ireland. Toward the end of his racing career he bought a bar in his home town which rapidly became a Mecca for motorcyclists.

I have many a tale to tell of Joey (he was a very special man) and my times in Northern Ireland working for Honda, when shots of Bushmills whiskey came over the bar for us in waves, but these stories are for another book. Not having been there for a number of years, I noted immediately that most of the places where you could once park your bike had been dramatically reduced by the unwelcome introduction of double yellow lines.

Being the awkward type, I upheld historical tradition and parked right outside the pub. I had never been here other than in the racing season and it was very quiet. I tried to imagine where on earth all the motorcyclists would now be parking during the major race meetings, especially the North West 200, when this bar would be full to overflowing with bikers worshipping at the shrine of Dunlop.

Inside, I recognised the barmaid, Joey's daughter Donna, and after a nice catch-up conversation with her over my cola, I left my challenge poster on their notice board.

Road racing takes place on closed public road courses and is very popular in Northern Ireland. There is no way it can ever be made 'safe racing' (there is actually no such thing even on a closed purpose-built race circuit) but here the risk is far higher as competitors race between hedges, fences, kerbs and stone walls.

Joey was one of the fastest and safest riders and he rarely crashed, but, even so, sadly he was killed at a road racing meeting in Estonia in 2000 after riding suddenly into unknown wet weather on the far side of an otherwise dry road circuit and lost control of his Honda RS125 motorcycle.

It was estimated that over 50,000 people attended his funeral in Ballymoney. As the Honda motorcycle representative for Northern Ireland I was privileged to be asked to be one his many pallbearers that day as we carried his coffin in relay the mile or so from his home to his final resting place at Carryduff Church.

2018, in fact, was to be one of the worst years on record for the number of riders killed road racing including, tragically, Joey's own nephew William Dunlop. I both love and loathe road racing in equal measure. Love the atmosphere and the close racing when it is free of crashes, but hate the injuries and deaths when it isn't.

By choice I do not attend these events anymore. Fireblade Ministries attend them all; Eddie and his team are there to provide spiritual support, if needed, for those attending those racing meetings.

By now it was mid-afternoon and I was free to ride at leisure until my meeting in Belfast in the evening. I headed east from Ballymoney to arguably one of the most beautiful roads to ride in the UK – the Antrim coast. By now it was a very hot day (for reasons lost to me, I was not really recording the day time temperatures on this trip) without a cloud in the sky and as I turned south onto the A2 I was shocked by how many vehicles were about.

Yes, it was a bank holiday weekend but even so this did not seem normal at all. The North West 200, one of the top sporting events in the Northern Irish calendar, would not create this much traffic along the coast road. There were masses of hire cars, most of them identical grey Renaults with Republic of Ireland number plates, which given the somewhat erratic nature of the driving were probably being driven by overseas visitors. I was suddenly very much on my mettle.

I rode down the narrow and steep winding access road into pretty Port Ballintrae, one of my favourite places, but today it was just a mob of people and vehicles and had I been in a car there would have been nowhere at all to park. I nudged my bike in between cars close to the harbour slipway and leaned against it allowing myself to take in the rugged grey stonework of the walls and the beauty of surrounding coast.

For a minute or two it brought back some happy memories of a family holiday and our visit to this normally peaceful haven. But not today, for my reverie was soon interrupted by a young foreign man, possibly Spanish, who was having a complete meltdown at his family and that situation quickly became public viewing.

Wearing a wet suit, shouting and waving his arms at them, it was not a happy scene as he walked off in a sulky huff. I walked in the opposite direction to the small café where I had hoped to buy food but found the queue was out of the door. I overheard someone talking about it being exceptionally busy with all the 'Game of Thrones' tours around that weekend.

Amidst this gathering of awe-struck adherents I felt ill at ease seemingly being one of the few people in the northern hemisphere who has never seen one episode of this particular TV drama and having no idea until I learned, listening to conversations, that much of it had been filmed in the area.

Suddenly, it explained all the parked coaches, vehicles and the mass of people. For goodness' sake, I thought, haven't people got something a bit more interesting in their lives than to visit an area just because it had been in some big budget soap! It was becoming uncomfortable and much as I loved this beautiful little harbour, I could not tarry there.

As I rode back up the access road many more grey Renaults with determined looking drivers were coming down and even for me on the bike it was tight getting past them. I anticipated that it would not be too long before the route, in and out, would become completely impassable, no doubt with more angry shouting and arm waving foreign visitors.

Back up on the A2 I stopped in a lay-by overlooking White Park Bay, another stunning vista where the beach below was relatively quiet but up top it certainly wasn't. I followed a promising sign to a café slightly inland from the coast road and I was quickly reminded that parking a motorcycle on a gravel surfaced car park should come with a public health warning.

It too was very busy and I seem to recall I had been here once before. The gravel covering proved to be very thick and the side stand on my bike was immediately sinking in too far and not finding solid ground underneath. If I had tried to park it there and walked away it would have eventually sunken in to the point of no return and fallen over.

Now, here at least, I had taken on board my 'flat stone' experience at Ian's in Oxford because I had actually brought a plate to put under the side stand to cater for this very situation i.e. to widen the stand footprint enough to prevent it from sinking in. It was in the top case. To get to it, of course, I would have to park the bike to access it. Doh! Lesson No 2; make sure your side stand plate is easily accessible whilst you are sitting on the bike. I didn't get any food there either.

I rode on with hope to the small and normally pleasant hamlet of Cushendall and found it totally gridlocked. Well, for the cars it was. On the bike, I squeezed myself through the stationary traffic where tempers were beginning to get frayed in the heat.

I cannot say I had a nice ride to the next small town, Carnlough, either. It should have been given the beautiful scenery, but the traffic was so heavy that day it was impossible to get an open run for any distance and the constant overtaking of hire cars being driven very slowly by arm pointing drivers was spoiling it. There were lots of oncoming motorcyclists too and they had to be noted carefully as some of their overtaking towards me became a slight concern.

I did stop at Carnlough for a break and finally got an indifferent meal in an unremarkable café there. Later, licking an ice cream, I sat on the harbour wall, as I have many times in the past, but the constant coming and goings of so many people and vehicles became tiring. As I have indicated, I am by nature always more at ease being alone in the quieter places.

The run from there into Larne was a little easier but now I made for Belfast. I knew I was too early to access the church for the evening meeting, so I rode to Hollywood on the other side of Belfast Lough and parked the bike by the sea on a small service road I knew.

Here there was to be no respite or quiet sojourn either as my spot was suddenly overlooked by a group of noisy men who appeared on a balcony opposite and were clearly intent on getting drunk, perhaps in the interval of a sporting event they had been watching on TV inside.

The day was proving a real disappointment. I had so much looked forward to riding in Northern Ireland and especially the Antrim coast road again but on a hot bank holiday weekend it did not match my expectations. In spite of my disappointment and the noise of a semi-drunken reverie, I did actually manage to grab a little snooze, leaning against a huge rock by the seashore.

Later, as I rode into Belfast, the city roads were oddly empty and early evening found me sitting on the bike outside Covenant Love Church on the Albertbridge Road. Eddie arrived, unusually in a car, and he seemed a bit flustered. He was not, I thought, quite as enthusiastic as I expected, but I reasoned this was because he had a lot of things to organise.

He told me my church meeting had been well publicised as 'An evening with Fireblade Ministries, Mervyn Smith, and Amy Roberts.' Amy was a singer so I expected some worship before I spoke. We manhandled my bike into the church foyer; I changed out of my riding gear and retrieved my notes from the top case. I was ready and expectant.

Eddie and his co-workers with Fireblade Ministries were carrying tray after tray of food into the back hall, having ordered enough food to feed a small army. Blimey, I thought, they really must be expecting a lot of people. But my Northern Ireland shakedown was again being shaken because, as the time approached for us to start, I realised there was hardly a soul there.

My spirits lifted when I heard some very loud Harley Davidsons pull up outside the church, sounding as if there were 20 (just 6 in fact), but so loud had I been in Larne, or indeed Dublin, I would still have heard them. A number of bikers came in dressed in their 'colours' with that 'hard' Harley biker look about them, but in fact were part of the Christian Motorcycle Association.

Amy got up and sang quite beautifully, her hubby providing pre-recorded backing tracks from one of those 'boxes', but it worked. She had a great voice and her songs were personal testimonies, quite thought provoking in their way, very Irish I felt but not the type of worship I was expecting and although she was really quite brilliant, her time slot overran.

Once she had finished singing the Harley riders just got up and decamped en masse, having only called in on route to something else and left just as I was getting up to share. 'Was it something I said?' I quipped as they walked out, but actually, at this point, I had said nothing. This wasn't going well.

So, to my much reduced audience I shared with those who remained about how Eddie and I had met, about my time working in Northern Ireland for Honda and BMW, about the persecuted church, about my Norway challenge and I know that those who were there were touched and encouraged by it. I am so grateful to those faithful folk who did come and who supported my challenge that evening generously.

My primary focus though was not to talk about my past life or indeed to encourage people to sponsor my challenge, but to highlight the plight of the persecuted church and I was disappointed that more people did not come to hear their stories of courageous faith.

Only later did I realise that our relatively insignificant event was competing with major rugby and football matches, a big concert elsewhere in the city (something I was to fall foul of again, during in my challenge proper) and, being a lovely bank holiday weekend, lots of people were away. I confess I was quite crestfallen. All this planning and hardly anyone came.

Not Eddie's fault. He had done his best. More my fault for not realising this weekend was not a good time for an evening meeting in an empty city centre.

We waded into the excess of food as best we could, but out of respect to my hosts I had to depart earlier than I wanted. I left with that hollow feeling of failure; it was a very fast ride back to the Holdens in the dark. Bill had graciously waited up for me.

**Day 3 – Sunday** 27th May 2018. Mainly a rest day, just 64 miles ridden locally today.

I cannot think of many better ways to start a day than with a famous 'Ulster fry breakfast,' not at all healthy (I think the cardio-rehabilitation team at Kidderminster would have had a fit) but a very tasty treat. Later, following Bill on his Honda VFR1200, he took me on a sight-seeing trip on quiet roads skirting the huge Lough Neagh and then to the Ulster Grand Prix course at Dundrod.

I had never been to the Grand Prix as it is held in late August and that was always family holiday time. Being a public road (as I said the public roads are closed for the racing) I got a taste for the circuit as we rode briskly around it but at speeds much less than those the racers would be doing, all the while marvelling how they would cope with it where, on some sections, they would be approaching 200 mph.

At one place where the road fell in a series of dips I mused that just there at race speeds it would be like dropping off the edge of the world. When you do watch a pure road race the bravery of the riders is breath-taking.

On our way back a pony and trap driver deliberately waited till the last minute before trotting out in front of us. We were not riding fast so it was easily covered and then, as we carefully overtook, he was gesticulating angrily as if it was our fault. Bill was not impressed and had I not been with him I think he would have turned his bike around and gone back and had a few words officially.

The evening had become hot and sultry as we gathered for a family barbeque. Inevitable at some point in the evening, the subject of Brexit came up. One of Bill and Claire's guests, we'll call him Darren, who was also a retired policeman and had served for a long time in 'security', issued these chilling words to us.

'If they don't get it right, if Northern Ireland is forced by a bad agreement into a hard border with the Republic because of Brexit, then there could be more bloodshed here.'

The rest of the party nodded in silent agreement. Even though I understand the situation there slightly better than most outsiders, there are times in Northern

Ireland when it is unwise to offer an opinion and this was one of them. We all became very quiet until, thankfully, someone changed the subject.

Brexit, without doubt, has heightened tensions in Northern Ireland; they always quietly simmer away under the surface anyway, but it has certainly not helped. The day to day outworking of this is rarely reported outside of the region these days which is a deliberate policy in my view.

It is only when an extreme act of violence, such as dissident Republicans shooting a young journalist in Londonderry recently, that it gets reported. Without wishing to become political here, we in the rest of the UK are blissfully unaware that things in Northern Ireland are not always as calm they appear. Whatever peaceful balance there is could still easily be tilted by ignorant and unthinking politicians.

**Day 4 – Monday** 28th May 2018. Portadown to Highley. Leaving time - 08:30; temperature range 8°C to 25°C; distance ridden 229 miles.

My time with Bill, Claire and family had been delightful and it was good to catch up with them and Eddie again. But riding away next morning I found myself filled with mixed feelings, as was often the case when I left Northern Ireland after conducting business there. I love the people but hate the politics and as one of Northern Ireland's greatest comedians, Frank Carson, once said, *'the problem with Ireland is too much religion and not enough Christianity.'*

I had also been shocked and saddened by Darren's comment last night, reflecting as I rode that history could prove him right and that thought depressed me. This, coupled with my challenge promotions having proved disastrous and the disappointment of my Antrim coast road ride, made me just want to get home. My shakedown seemed to have achieved very little in fact but at least I had formed a relatively good routine with the bike.

But my sombre reverie was interrupted by the daily realities of riding for within half an hour of leaving my guest's home, on a local A road, I had to cope with a broken-down truck on a blind corner and then with two bullocks wandering aimlessly about in the road. It jolted me back into a need to be thinking more objectively about my journey home.

Once on the A1/M1 it was an uneventful but hot ride south to Dublin ferry port. Whilst there sitting in the blistering dockside heat (or so it seemed then) waiting to be called to board, I heard the unmistakable rumble of a Harley Davidson.

The Irish rider came over to talk to me and, seeming unable to construct a sentence without copious use of the 'F' word, he told me he worked in London and it had been the first time he had been back home for 10 years. I sensed there was perhaps a little more behind that statement than met the eye.

He was loud and a bit 'in your face' and he made me feel uncomfortable. Whilst boarding in the bowels of the car deck he almost knocked me off, catching my right-hand-side case with his massive leather pannier bag as he brushed past me. It was clear he hadn't a clue about ferry boarding etiquette, much less how to secure his bike, so I obliged by strapping it down as tightly as I could for him.

As I felt uneasy around him, I tarried pretending to attend to things on my own bike as he went up to the lounge area. Unobtrusively, I slipped in a bit later, avoiding him. The thought of being talked at with profanities for 2 hours did not really appeal. My reserved character came to the fore and as I write this, I wonder how much I missed of his story by ducking the opportunity to listen I am not proud of it but, I confess, I can be very guarded at times.

Briefly, he wobbled away in front of me off the ferry in Holyhead; he was not a very confident rider either and I wondered why he had chosen to ride what for him would be an ungainly Harley. I was past him before the A5 and did not see him again.

Back in Wales and being a bank holiday Monday the A5 from the ferry was very busy. I know how keen North Wales Police are for setting up speed traps on such weekends. My former boss Bob McMillan and his riding pals were all pulled over for speeding on a bank holiday on the road from Trawsfyndd to Bala. Bob rightly claimed they weren't speeding (possibly, in his case, one of the few times ever!) and took the police to task. Due to his sheer tenacity not to accept their version of how they had allegedly filmed him speeding from a parked helicopter up in a quarry, he eventually got his case dropped. I was taking no chances either and stuck more or less to the limit.

But some drivers certainly weren't, especially one guy in a blue Volvo 4x4 who forced a late overtake on me right at the end of the dual carriageway section. Within a mile, it was with a certain amount of satisfaction that I filtered past him, stuck in a huge traffic jam approaching the Menai Bridge.

The traffic on the other side seemed lighter than expected and things like loose sheep running about in the road and a car suddenly turning across in front of you to enter a car park on your side of the road are what make you sharp when riding a motorcycle. Betws-y-Coed was surprisingly quiet too.

The following few miles on the A5 can be a biker's delight if you are not baulked by slow drivers as today. But the section of road beyond was fast with lots of straights where you could make good progress, and thinking of the possible activities of the police this day and the dreaded speed camera vans, which can record your speed up to a mile away, I was not getting carried away.

I was overtaking groups of slow cars, but once past I was sticking to the 60mph limit. In one of these groups a young man driving a silver Fiesta seemed to take exception that I'd overtaken him and passed me at high speed as I cruised along on a quieter section of road at the legal limit. But he was soon snarled up behind slower vehicles and being on a bike, I was not.

Passing this group and in front of him again I had him marked as being erratic and potentially dangerous, for I noted his aggressive driving in my mirrors. He was now cutting up other road users in his effort to catch me again to prove his point (whatever it was). I allowed him to overtake me a second time but by now, I was getting a bit put out by this 'cat and mouse' silliness.

Inevitably, I caught up with him when again he was stuck in the middle of another pack of slower moving vehicles. However, before he could do anything about it and using the bike's far superior acceleration, I just overtook the lot.

This time, however, I took the risk of not slowing afterwards, blow the speed cameras I thought, and nailed it for good measure quickly taking the next 2 small strings of cars before he had even caught them. As we came down into Llangollen there was a long traffic queue and I gently rode down the road centre past all the slow-moving cars. I had now placed a hundred plus vehicles between us and I was thankful.

I should point out here to the non-motorcyclists among you that being seated higher up on a bike you have a much better view of the road and incredible acceleration on tap to pass anything quickly. Also, without cutting anybody up, you can legitimately pull in between vehicles in a way no car ever can.

But, believe it or not, I am courteous and I do plan my overtakes with care, always looking for an acceptable gap between cars so as not to cause any motorist to have to brake unnecessarily.

After Llangollen the driver of a black BMW Coupe respectfully let me complete my overtakes before pulling out behind me. This guy was in a fast car and he could drive it. I could see in my mirrors that his overtakes were clean and clinical but, unlike the Fiesta driver, he was content to let me make progress and he stayed behind me and did not push me. But inevitably, he's in a car and I was on a bike and a familiar traffic scenario was repeated, and I lost him well before Oswestry.

As I rode the quieter sections from Shrewsbury to home I was once again in reflective mode. Had this trip been worth the effort and expense? Had I actually achieved anything of value that would prepare me for Europe and Norway? I arrived home safely but pretty tired and it was still very hot. Liz told me there had been terrific thunderstorms for 2 days; I did not see a drop of rain all weekend.

This is the post I made on Facebook immediately on my return.

*'The N. Ireland run has been a good shake down for the Norway trip. It is strange how quickly one forgets how to get properly organised for a trip of days away on the bike, rather than the usual quick day's blast into Wales. Things that should be obvious have become awkward.*

*Examples. Checking all that can be adjusted has been. My windscreen adjusting nut and bracket disappeared somewhere along the A5. Working out what pocket (only one is waterproof in this suit) to put your essentials. Becoming aware that your additional side stand footplate is locked in your rear case as your bike slowly starts to sink into the gravel covered car park of a road side café.*

*All these things I actually know, all these things had been forgotten because the bike and I had not been sharing a touring role for some time. Lots of other small things to change before the big trip, but they all add up to making life on a long bike trip as uncomplicated as possible.*

*If you have to think about it, it's a problem, I want to concentrate on the primary thing, the riding.'*

But the reality was, I returned home quite downhearted. Things really did not go that well in Ireland, although I was thankful for the good things it brought, renewed friendships, a shake down on the bike, safe riding and the kindness of people I barely knew.

My chief disappointment was the lack of promotional support from an expected quarter. My time there could have been so much more productive. Frankly, I was questioning if I should even continue with the challenge. I actually felt like calling the whole thing off.

# Chapter 4
# Departure

*'This is how we work: we always try to know what the needs of the families are, and provide for them according to their needs.'* – **Pastor Boutros from Syria.**

Ireland taught me something I already knew but was failing to apply. No matter how much you are skewed by people, circumstances and your own mistakes, you have to keep faith with the vision and the calling.

It boiled down to one key question. Was I given a dream to ride to the Arctic Circle for the persecuted church or not? The answer was of course yes. If nothing else I am resilient, and the encouragement I received from Fiona at Open Doors and many others made me dig in again.

The month of June was spent in more fundraising and promotional activities but the nearer my departure date came the more fidgety I was becoming. Word was getting around generally about my challenge. Our local MP, Philip Dunne, had kindly endorsed the trip and publicised it on his website. That, in turn, was picked up by some of the media in Shropshire and I was interviewed by BBC Radio Shropshire which entailed a super and very quick early Sunday morning ride to Shrewsbury.

The interview went really well but did not result in much feed-back, let alone donations. I was asked if I could come back to speak after the ride and of course, the answer was yes. On my return from Norway, I was never contacted by them. I suppose I really should have pushed it but didn't.

The weather was hot and becoming hotter. I occasionally checked the temperatures in Norway and noticed they were also quite warm but I reasoned going so much further north this would not last. I was still planning for and expecting colder weather in North Norway so my choice of riding suit was the

Richa Gore-Tex suit, not ideal for hot temperatures I knew, but perfect for the expected rain and cooler climes of Scandinavia.

And I still believe I was right to be so prepared, having watched a few videos taken by summer riders in Norway in teeming rain riding along snow edged roads, much like my March ride over the Cotswolds. And, as I alluded to earlier, in June 2017 a group of motorcyclists riding in an area I knew I too would be passing through recorded this in a 'Bike' magazine article.

*'Then we're climbing again, and rain morphs into a full-frontal blizzard, clarting us with a comical arctic layer. The final climb is abandoned in the white-out.'* As I was intending to ride above the Arctic Circle and on some of these routes it was not unreasonable to suppose it was going to get cold and wet even in July and all the evidence I found backed up the theory. In fact, I could not have been more mistaken.

In the period just before leaving I spent time going through everything again and again, especially relating to the bike. I had 'fun' applying my challenge graphics but obviously, unlike a car, display space was limited so I had to be quite inventive in where to place them for maximum impact.

Overall, I think they did give the on-bike publicity of the challenge I wanted, but after application decided were not quite as 'eye catching' as I hoped. The time had arrived also for me to make the final decisions on how to pack the bike, and what clothing to take.

My Sat Nav was still a nagging worry. James had formatted an SD card and we downloaded pretty much all of Europe on it from the Garmin website. I tested some of the hotel addresses and it seemed to accept them but I would not really know how well it was operating until I crossed the channel and started to use it in earnest.

I had bought zip-up compression sacks to squeeze in as much as I could and tried to have the smaller and mid-sized ones for things like phone and other chargers (an absolute pain but vital these days), another for medication and toiletries and yet another for books and writing material, a small sketch pad and box of coloured pencils (why?).

But no matter how much I pared this down I still had too much stuff. I had 2 side cases with inner bags (these allowed me to leave the side cases attached to the bike at all times), 1 top case (also permanently fixed) and I was going to take a large tank bag.

But the Northern Ireland run had not really given me all the indicators I had hoped with very different packing needs for 3 or 4 weeks than a simple weekend. My main clothing filled one inner bag and I soon found it was easier to slide a neatly packed pile into the inner bag directly rather than use a large compression sack.

I placed the smaller compression sacks containing my toiletries and medication on top of my clothing and that was side case (pannier) 1 filled. Side case 2 had the riding suit liners and other riding clothing I expected to need when the weather went cooler and I managed to get these condensed into two large compression sacks and they lived (unmolested) inside the bottom of the second inner bag and even then they took up too much blooming space.

Smaller compression sacks of books (e.g, my diary and a read) and other slightly less essential items were placed on top of these. This inner bag was always the more difficult to refit into the side case each morning. The top case contained some basic tools, a tyre repair kit, fishing tackle, a crash helmet sanitising and visor cleaning kit, disc lock, spare tie downs, drinking container, a lightweight fleece and hand cleaner.

Since I am commenting about packing space I should perhaps explain the fishing tackle. My hope was to catch a fish in Norway (silly really, I rarely catch anything when I try fishing abroad – or anywhere else for that matter) so I took a 6-section travel fly rod which was strapped unobtrusively under the rear carrier above the right-side case.

And, being a fly fishing set up the only other items needed were a light reel, a small fly box containing artificial flies and nylon leaders. They took up hardly any space and weighed next to nothing and proved completely superfluous.

My tank bag held my essential bike documents, passport (in a weatherproof wallet), spare gloves and earplugs, my camera, the side stand plate (I did learn something from Oxford and Northern Ireland), a backup phone and that already well-worn map of Scandinavia.

Being magnetic, I knew the tank bag would gather road dust beneath it and scratch the paintwork on the bike's tank when used for such a long period. Some riders use a cloth underneath the tank bag to stop this happening.

I considered this but decided that as the bag needed to be removed to refuel and with an expected 2 or 3 fuel stops a day, a cloth flapping about in wet and windy conditions was an additional concern I did not need.

So I boldly masked the tank in the affected area with some wide black gaffer tape, not pretty, but pretty effective as it turned out. The tape adhesive residue was a bit of a job to clean off after the trip though.

And the bike keys? After a few anxious pocket-slapping moments in Northern Ireland, I bought a small carabiner and attached it to the lanyard for the earplug case which was worn around my neck.

Riding the bike on the weeks leading up to Norway I made it a habit at every stop to simply slip the bike key onto that clip; it was going nowhere and the system worked perfectly. That said, I still did not entirely trust myself so I took off one of the side panels of the bike and secreted the spare key in a hidden location – just in case.

It sounds like I was prepared and largely I was, in fact as it proved, a bit over prepared but that was part of the story and part of the adventure.

**Day 1 – Saturday** 7th July 2018. Highley, Shropshire to Great Chart, Kent. Leaving time – 13:20; temperature range – 28.7°C to 33°C; distance ridden – 216 miles. My opening mileage was recorded at 6,315 miles.

I had not slept well for days and the night before departure was no exception. The enormity of the ride was weighing heavily on me. I never doubted the capability of the Super Tenere, but I was in uncharted waters regarding my physical and mental capability to ride solo for so far and so long.

Naturally, I had thought much about the unknowns of riding on the continent and the realisation that all the research possibly counted for very little. Basically, I was now about to be 'out there' and whatever I had to face I had to face. My riding ability did not so much concern me but the one thing that persistently nagged my mind was rider fatigue and I was right to be mindful of it.

I read what the Royal Society for the Prevention of Accidents (ROSPA) has to say about fatigue and wish I hadn't. It is sobering reading.

*'Driver fatigue causes thousands of road accidents each year. Research shows that driver fatigue may be a contributory factor in up to 20% of road accidents, and up to one quarter of fatal and serious accidents.*

*Sleepiness reduces reaction time (a critical element of safe driving). It also reduces vigilance, alertness and concentration so that the ability to perform attention-based activities (such as driving) is impaired. The speed at which information is processed is also reduced by sleepiness. The quality of decision-making may also be affected.'*

What I didn't know yet was exactly how far I could stretch myself in terms of riding distances and time in the saddle. This ride would not be anything like a 200-mile riding day in mid-Wales or a blast up to Belfast from Dublin, and there was the uncertainty of the weather (the Arctic is supposed to be cold right?). These were the unknowns that were still robbing me of my sleep.

On the day of departure initially I was calm, but as the morning progressed, I felt I was being pressurised. Everybody seemed to be hanging around to see me off. I should have been flattered but actually it made me even more nervous. I couldn't think straight and my final packing was proving an issue and I made a mistake by leaving an important item on the bedside table.

James, bless him, went home to get a large bag to fix on the rear seat. I did not have the heart to tell him I did not want it. I had the less than generous air vents in the riding jacket fully open and I decided to ride to my first stop in Kent wearing my new Kevlar jeans which I reasoned might be a little cooler than the Gore-Tex suit trousers. It was a decision that determined at least one item of clothing that I would not later be taking across the Channel.

So, at 13:20, being waved off by close friends and family and being videoed by James, I left the safe confines of the barns complex courtyard and was quickly winding through familiar country lanes and local towns to the M42/M40.

It must have been a pretty uneventful ride to Oxford services because I cannot really recall any of it. In retrospect, I think it was just the enjoyment of riding again knowing that the trip was at last a reality and not a concept. I was taking my metaphorical single step of 1,000 miles and, as I rode along, I did become aware of the tension suddenly easing. This was it, no turning back, I was on the way and it felt good – very good.

I have never liked the Oxford M40 services. Any motorway services that serve both sides of the carriageway these days are almost always congested to the point of unpleasantness and today was no exception, but it was just the appropriate time to take a break.

The heat intensified as I rode slowly to find a suitable place to park the bike and I was sweltering by the time I was walking into the services. I could not believe how hot the day had become and it was uncomfortable. I re-hydrated myself with a drink and did not linger there.

Back on the bike later, I noted the M25 was much quieter than anticipated (the England football World Cup quarter-final match with Sweden was in full flow at that time) and the outside temperature was hitting 33°C.

But as I rode I sensed I was getting somewhat fatigued. On the M20 I turned off at Junction 9 for Ashford and headed towards my final destination for a few days, Great Chart. My decision making was becoming a little impaired by tiredness and I missed my turning for the village and had to turn around.

As I rode up the main street I passed the Swan and Dog pub and with it being so hot the garden was full of drinkers. Many were smoking and nobody looked particularly happy or celebratory, so I assumed England had lost their quarter-final match. (They hadn't).

For the next two nights I was staying with old friends Tim and Catherine Wilson but I had only been here briefly once before and I could not remember exactly where the rectory was; I was not thinking too straight. Assuming it must be very close to the church, I stopped outside the nearest house to it and asked a skinny looking middle-aged man who was tinkering with his car in the garden if he knew where it was.

Displaying a lack of interest that would have done a moronic teenager justice, he looked at me blankly clearly bored with my question, shrugged his shoulders and said, 'Dunno mate' and sank his head back under the car bonnet which, just at that moment, I felt like dropping on it. A younger man joined him and smiled but I was feeling fazed and did not want to embarrass myself further by repeating the question.

I rang Tim. 'I'm right by the church, I must be close' I told him. Tim wandered out into the road and immediately caught sight of me and waved. The Rectory proved to be just 50 yards up the road from where I had stopped. As I dismounted, I told Tim his neighbours didn't seem to know where the Rectory was which he found odd. First impressions of Great Chart were proving to be not so very favourable.

Tim, the Rector of Great Chart and Singleton, and Catherine his wife were set for a very busy weekend. Catherine was about to lead her last service in the area marking the completion of her Curacy in the Church of England. Tim also had extra activities that particular weekend. If I was an intrusion on their busy schedules (which I must have been) I was never made to feel like it.

The Rectory they lived in was a huge and rambling edifice that I suspected would be difficult to heat in the winter. They were living in happy clutter preparing for a move to Bedford where Catherine was to embark on her own ministry and calling as an Anglican priest.

They seemed completely unfazed by the logistical uncertainties that any house move brings in a way I probably wouldn't be. These are people who just seem to take everything in their stride and they had a calming effect on me. I had asked to stay with them for 3 good reasons.

1. They were old friends and, although we did not see them often, it was great to catch up. Tim had been a wonderful mentor to our son, Gareth, when they had been in Highley.
2. I had asked and kindly been given permission to speak at their services about the persecuted church situation and my challenge,
3. Great Chart is conveniently close to the Channel Tunnel terminal.

Before socialising I headed for a much-needed shower. The shower itself proved to be a bit like Awkright's till out of the old BBC series 'Open all Hours', ready to trap the unwary and as I closed the shower doors hefty bits of trim fell on me and clattered noisily to the shower tray.

It was obviously a regular occurrence and I think it caused much amusement below. Afterwards, I spent some time pruning down my equipment before crossing onto the Continent. The Kevlar jeans had proved to be just too hot to wear in the 30°C heat. These, James's extra seat bag and some other things were discarded and left with my hosts for collection upon my return. I should have pared my luggage down even more, I now realise.

But I could not find 2 important items I know I would need, my reading glasses and my leather slip-on mules. I rang Liz and she confirmed I hadn't packed them! All the self-created stress and pressure in that 'official leaving' had me forgetting to pack two essential items. I was not best pleased with myself for such an obvious oversight and hoped there wouldn't be others.

Fortunately, I had the foresight to bring a pair of spare reading glasses, which were cheap drug store backups given to me by American friends and not the varifocals I was used to. My feet would just have to suffer.

It was a very busy weekend for Tim and Catherine. I was just so thankful for their hospitality and kindness. Catherine was preparing her last sermon and Tim was musing how he might be able to make the garden acceptable for a summer event in a fortnight.

Looking at the long dry grass and the complete lack of anything remotely green or colourful growing, I didn't doubt he had a task on his hands. Tim though, never seemed to get rattled by anything and I smiled knowing somehow he would make it work. Special people, they had opened their home to me at a time when it was not really convenient and made me feel like one of the family.

### Day 2 – Sunday 8th July 2018. A non-riding day.

I spoke at the main church service at Great Chart and as we took the path to the church the ever-friendly Tim said hello to the young man next door from yesterday who he obviously knew quite well, 'I hear you didn't know where the rectory was?' he quipped to him cheerfully.

Now, I am guessing that yesterday, his morose mate had informed him of my question. 'My mate was visiting yesterday' he said, 'he didn't know' and I felt slightly better about him as a result and a bit embarrassed I had not repeated my question.

I found myself at a traditional 9:30 'Morning Service' and I was quite nervous before I got up to speak. They were not the stuffy middle-class Anglican congregation that I had feared, but enthusiastic and friendly down-to-earth folk. My talk about the persecuted church and my challenge seemed to go down well and I had a lot of positive feedback.

Then later, a few miles away at Singleton, I spoke at a more informal service at 11:00 which was held in a school. Again, what I shared was well-received. Before I left, Steve, one of the leadership team, gave me a scripture Isaiah 41:10,

*'So do not fear, for I am with you, do not be dismayed, for I am your God. I will strengthen you and help you; I will uphold you with my righteous right hand.'*

This was an incredibly timely word for me and how true it was to prove in the coming days ahead. Tim, being tied up with a retirement lunch for another local priest, arranged for me to have lunch with members of their congregation, Alan and Leigh, who were such a hospitable and kind couple and I could sense it was going to be a wrench for Tim, and indeed Catherine, to leave these wonderful people.

The lovely folk of Great Chart and Singleton were to collect in excess of £230.00 to support me in the challenge. I am forever in their debt.

**Day 3 – Monday** 9th July 2018. Great Chart, Kent to Ermelo, Netherlands. Leaving time – 07:20; temperature range 26ºC to 33ºC; distance ridden 17 miles (to the Channel Tunnel) then 434 Kilometres.

And so this was it, the day the challenge really began. Being awake early I permitted myself some thoughts on what lay ahead. Once through the Channel Tunnel I had no real idea what I was facing in riding through 8 different countries, or the traffic conditions and weather ahead.

If I started to question the relevance of it, or indeed the sense of it, I would not be riding into mainland Europe today at all but turning around and heading home. Each day though, my thoughts and prayers were helped by the Open Doors prayer diary for July, and when you began to read and pray about lives of Christians facing the most appalling circumstances to follow Jesus, then the core reason for doing this once again came into sharper focus.

If it was just about me and my desire to go to the Arctic Circle on a motorcycle trip, it would not have had the same impetus behind it. It would be a shallow self-indulgent thing, a tick off some bucket list with a 'been there done that' tee shirt. I had to keep in mind this was not a trip per se, but was a challenge, and something I had committed to in prayer, as one of the stickers on my bike was to proclaim I was 'riding for those who have no voice.'

As I packed my bike ready to leave, Tim was tinkering with an old Hayter lawn mower. He was still scratching his head over the church event there in a fortnight and how he might cut the grass into a maze. It had not rained for weeks and looking again at the browned grass I wondered, even if he could get the mower started, if this was actually possible.

But now once again I was feeling quite nervous and did not contribute much by way of encouragement. I was both sorry to leave but equally keen to go and say my goodbyes and as I rode out of their driveway suddenly it all felt a bit lonely.

Riding back through Great Chart I was soon reminded that this was a Monday rush hour and very much commuter land. I followed behind a blue VW estate car driving so close to the back of the local bus he could not see around it.

However I could, but because of continual oncoming traffic I could not take advantage and frustratingly we were stuck there for a while until the bus pulled over into a lay-by for passengers.

As we joined the A28 dual carriageway the driver of the VW, now on the inside lane, absolutely floored the accelerator and began to pull across in front of me in an attempt to out-accelerate me into the outside lane before the upcoming traffic lights. It was probably something he did every commuting day and was quite deliberate but his car was no match for the bike and before he could complete his intended manoeuvre I was already gone.

However, it brought home to me just how competitive and aggressive commuting can be, especially in the wider London area with these daily little 'wins and losses.' It had been a long time since I had been in this fray, and then mainly in a car, and exposed to the silly tension which is something all too easy to get caught up with.

I wonder sometimes if the 'me-first' attitude set one up for the competitive working day. I really should not be so judgemental. In times gone by, with a then very much 'A' type personality and a driven mindset, I have been that driver, and very possibly much worse, with a not-to-be-out-done selfishness and the tension that stupidly builds by being beaten by another driver into that gap or to those lights.

On a bike it is just so much easier to deal with and, in spite of the mild risk, I was calm about it. The lights were on red and he was directly behind me now but I did not react to him in any way. As they changed once again using the bike's far superior acceleration, he rapidly becames a speck in my mirrors and a memory. Shortly afterwards, I pulled into the local Sainsbury's for my first fill up, the first of very many.

A brief ride down the M20 and following the signs for Eurotunnel I was soon exiting for 'Le Shuttle.' My train was scheduled for 09:20 but I had arrived in enough time to be squeezed onto an earlier train. I found the ticket processing, immigration and boarding procedure very well organised, and the staff were friendly and helpful. I was impressed.

Bikes were last on behind the already boarded cars. I parked my bike diagonally across the carriage and next to another bike, a Triumph, and as the doors closed the train sped away towards France.

I was a bit surprised that the train was a bit of a rattler, not quite as smooth as I expected and at times my bike swayed alarmingly on its side stand. As we lost the daylight for 20 minutes or so I tried not to think too much about the fact that we were under the English Channel.

I recalibrated my Sat Nav and the bike computer to kilometres and changed the time zone. I chatted to the middle-aged couple riding the Triumph; I noticed they were very tactile with each other in a way most couples of a certain age are usually not. They asked me where I was going and I told them of my Scandinavian challenge and gave out the first of my promotional post cards.

They told me they had married in Finland last year and clearly marital bliss was still fresh. She was very chatty and outgoing; he was quieter. They were heading for southern France and were politely encouraging about my trip but I sensed they thought me a little strange, not so very far from the truth. I chatted to some of the car drivers, everyone was in good humour and it was a pleasant crossing.

Exiting into bright sunshine at Calais, now 40 minutes earlier than expected, I was expecting a French border control customs check and in anticipation of this had not fitted my earplugs or even fastened my helmet strap; my passport was accessible and at the ready and I breathed a sigh of relief as my Sat Nav was alive, well and functioning.

Emily, or should it now be Emilie, was telling me the way to go and, far sooner than anticipated, I found myself on a dual carriageway and only then did the penny drop. The border controls and checks for France had already been completed on the other side in Kent! I felt a little stupid as I pulled over onto the hard shoulder, secured my passport, inserted my earplugs and fastened my helmet whilst watching the better prepared couple on the Triumph disappearing away at speed.

Only now could I set off properly on my continental adventure, initially riding the A16 North through France into Belgium to my destination Ermelo in Holland where I was staying and meeting up with my old friends and ex-colleagues from Honda Netherlands.

As I rode the busy autoroutes through this part of Europe I began to realise just what a neophyte I am when it comes to riding there. I had anticipated 3 lane roads but these were dual carriageways. I had expected obvious border crossing signs, but there were none and as I passed from France into Belgium, (and indeed later into The Netherlands), it was seamless and not very obvious that I had slipped from one country into another.

If there was a border sign, I certainly did not see it and wanted to. Not because of the potential nationalism it might represent but because it would have been nice to know I had ridden through France and was actually entering another country.

Near Ghent, I make a navigational error. Misreading the not-quite-so-clear signs I thought I was exiting for a service area but instead I found myself off the autoroute and suddenly into a busy town. This was challenging so soon into the trip. My bike was festooned with small but specially made bright orange arrowed 'keep right' stickers on the screen, on the handlebars, on my tank bag and possibly elsewhere, and I became suddenly very mindful of the need to obey them.

I had to turn around to regain the autoroute and Emilie was becoming fractious in her attempts to get me back there. But first, I pulled into a local petrol station and decided to fill up there. Here, my obvious lack of experience especially at the vagaries of the 'pay at the pump' instructions came into play.

I was rescued by a kindly Belgium van driver who, of course, spoke perfect English. When he showed me what to do, it was actually pretty obvious. I felt a bit, well, stupid. Fully fuelled up, I was soon back on my intended route.

Nearing lunch time, I got it right next time and exited correctly for the services. I now needed a refuel, not the bike, and as I parked up I was amazed at how hot it was again at 33°C and just how tired I had already become. This was just day one in Europe and I was beginning to feel as if I was in the middle of some Bear Grylls challenge.

I entered the rest area and dropped my tank bag and helmet down on a table by a window seat and popped to the loo. I was halfway through my deliberations when I broke into a cold sweat. What was I thinking of leaving my tank bag and helmet there unattended?

I think it was the quickest wee I have ever taken and again my lack of forethought had me castigating myself for the next hour or so. Fortunately, all was okay but it was a sign perhaps of just how quickly heat and tiredness could affect judgement. I bought a coffee and small cake and could not help but watch a woman, a few rows down, eating the longest panini I have ever seen. She needed longer arms! It was not an endearing sight.

For the next few hours, I made my way inexorably towards Holland but around Antwerp the traffic was very bad and I found myself filtering between stationary traffic following a rider on a KTM motorcycle who, sensibly, was doing it with his hazard flashers on.

When I eventually located the never-before-used hazard flash button on the Yamaha, I emulated him and felt almost like a continental rider for the first time blinking my way between rows of stationary vehicles. On the A27, I stopped at Kalix Berna services. I liked the name and remembered it for some odd reason.

By now I was pretty exhausted, and parked the bike on baked hard ground under some trees. I was aware I had become dehydrated, headachy and really quite fatigued, conditions which would become familiar over the next few weeks.

Fare in these continental services seemed to major on sausages of some sort. I bought one in a roll and a coffee but they were both pretty horrible. I texted my old friend Eddy Tromp to inform him I was less than an hour away but I received no response.

Kalix Berna services is not a huge site and it was very busy with limited parking spaces. It was smelly too. The enormous rubbish bins were full to overflowing and in 30°C heat, well you don't need too much imagination. I sat at the furthest bench away and rehydrated myself from the special gel water bottle Liz had bought for me for the trip, and watched the occasional bad parking effort opposite.

In the shade opposite, under the trees my bike was well out of their way. Even so I was keeping a close eye on it. By now, it was late afternoon and I was reflecting on my day so far, of riding though 3 countries already, thinking of how easy it had become to travel across borders these days.

I was wearing one of my 'Open Doors Highley to Hammerfest Challenge' T shirts, you know the ones that were almost 2 sizes too large. A lady noticed and approached me saying her family were supporters of Open Doors, (the founder Brother Andrew was a Dutchman), and asked me about my challenge.

Her name was Daphne and she told me that she, her baby daughter and her mother, were heading north for a holiday. She told me it had taken ages to get through the traffic around Antwerp, which did not surprise me.

I gave her one of my challenge postcards and told her I had hoped to share about the trip whilst riding through Norway but had drawn a blank. She suggested I contact her Christian friend there, Jonathon Bott, who she informed me was very well-connected and asked me for my e-mail address to forward his details to me.

I left the services well-encouraged but again and immediately finding heavy queuing traffic and having to filter again. Thankfully, before too long I was exiting for Ermelo. I stopped soon afterwards to check for any texts but worryingly I had heard nothing from Eddy. The Sat Nav, however, took me right to his doorstep in a very nice part of the township. I saw him and his wife, Ineka, look out their kitchen window in surprise at my arrival. He told me he had received no text from me.

After coffee with the family, I followed Eddy who was riding an old BSA M21 and managed to get us a bit lost on our way to B&B 'Joy'. Dick, the proprietor, was a very friendly man with a hint of sadness about him as he showed me up to a really nice room. Eddy left me to refresh and relax for a few hours and collected me at 19:00 in an old but perfectly serviceable HRV, one of those bullet-proof Honda cars of the late '80s.

After saying grace, it was nice to relax over dinner with them in their lovely home and they quizzed me about my challenge and Open Doors. I think they were quite taken by what I shared. Afterwards, Eddy took me to visit a friend of his, Nico, who had the most amazing collection of off-road bikes, mainly European Motocross machines, some of them very rare, all of them immaculate.

He was also into other classic bikes and owned some makes I had never even heard of. Nico was a real enthusiast and I was a bit overwhelmed by the sheer number of bikes he had. I wondered how it is that many enthusiast collectors of motorcycles I knew always seemed to have an inexhaustible amount of funds to buy them, the technical skills to restore them and the space to display them.

Nico had been in business and, I was not surprised to learn, had been a very good off-road rider in his day. A thoroughly nice man, it was a pleasure to meet and share his enthusiasm in enjoying his bike collection. I returned to B&B 'Joy' in a similar frame of mind, but quite exhausted.

**Day 4 Tuesday** – 10<sup>th</sup> July 2018. A non-riding day

As I woke up and checked my communications, there was one from Google, suggesting my email account may have been compromised by a sign-in attempt at a location more or less where I was. It was me of course and I ignored it. I just didn't want to go through the rigmarole of changing my password…again.

We're not so good at IT, are we? I mean those of us of a certain age. The kids tackle the complexities of iPhones, tablets and social media with such breath-taking confidence whereas I find it all a little intimidating. I secretly watch them when I am out and about.

They can email or text using their 2 thumbs quicker than I can think and they don't ever walk into things while they are doing it! My IT skills are okay (ish)

but basic and I confess I would have liked to have had a broader knowledge of things especially for media posting.

I wish now I had made more time to learn those things before the trip. But I was writing and posting a daily 'blog' with pictures on Facebook. What a difference the odd video recording would have made though.

Eddy picked me up early and we enjoyed a family breakfast together. Today I needed some stitches, well not me personally; the seam of my air seat cover was coming undone. Thankfully, Ineka had a friend who was a seamstress, so our first stop was to her small shop close by. The lady had it sorted in minutes and refused to accept any payment from me. It left me thinking about the kindness found in small communities and how shops like hers were becoming a rarity in Britain.

Eddy took a little time to show me around Ermelo and especially the wonderful windmill which he told me had fallen into serious disrepair before the town realised it was an asset that needed to be saved. Now, they are justly proud of it and it is indeed a splendid icon for the town.

Ferry, another friend of Eddy's, does not have a car. He rides an old Yamaha XS1100 with a sidecar fitted and he rides it all year round, even, he proudly told us, in snow. He was wiry, very clever, a superb mechanic and engineer and clearly passionate about his interest.

He too has a wonderful collection of motorcycles and we happily talked bikes for an hour or so. Bikes are an obsession with us all, but a harmless one.

Back at Eddy's for coffee, we were joined by Franklin Coppen, another ex-Honda colleague and friend. Eddy, Franklin and I joined forces to try to sort out the ill-fated ST1300A-P police bike issues. Much time, resources and money were expended by Honda Netherlands and Honda UK in trying to cure a high-speed stability issue on this model.

The problem was exacerbated by the fact that not all the bikes manufactured were affected. In the face of a coming Yamaha model contending for the same market segment it is my opinion that the bike was signed off into production before full development had been completed on it, an indication perhaps of the type of company Honda had become at that time.

It made the mid 2000s a very stressful time for us all, and me in particular because of what happened in the UK with our police riders, but we were bonded by the adversity of those experiences. But they paled into insignificance when I was faced this day with the reality of wartime occupation.

Eddy took us to a forest outside Ermelo where he wanted to show us a particular war time site and I was made to face for the first time the reality of what Holland had to endure at the hands of the Nazis in the last war.

Onderduikershol Drie was a self-contained underground complex dug out of the soft sandy loam and was used between February 1943 and July 1944 as a hiding place and staging post for shot-down English pilots and fugitive compatriots.

In July 1944, the location was betrayed and one night the Germans raided it but, such was the clever twisting design of the 75-metre escape tunnel, they found it impossible to get their guns accurately trained on the escaping men.

The 13 men living there took flight wearing night attire only but they all escaped safely into the dark forest. Local farmers hid them and helped re-clothe them and they all survived.

We drove a few kilometres to the lovely Dutch town of Putten. Eddy's idea was for us just to catch a bit of lunch there but we had to walk past a plaque, the details of which made for sobering reading.

In early October 1944, in retaliation for the death of a German officer by local resistance fighters, 661 men were rounded up from the town and deported to the concentration camps (some did escape en-route) but, of the 589 that did arrive at the camps, just 49 returned to Putten after liberation.

As I digested these stories of German occupation, it occurred to me quite powerfully that this was just one very small locality. Multiply this kind of oppression by the enemy across the rest of Holland (all the while remembering Anne Frank's story and the deportation of so many Jews) and indeed throughout invaded Europe, it conjured up a very sombre picture. I was deeply affected by what I had learnt.

We crossed the town square to a bar with outside seating. The day, once again, was warm and we passed an hour reminiscing over our beers and balls, the latter I should add being a local savoury and very tasty they were too. It was here I discovered I had lost my B&B room key.

We retraced our steps carefully and checked every nook and cranny in the car; it was nowhere to be found and there was nothing that could be done. After taking a tour of the local vicinity, and where Eddy proudly showed off the local Motocross track (he is quite involved in the organisation, off-road motorcycle racing is still very popular in Holland), we went back to the guest house to get a spare key.

I have stayed in countless hotels and guest houses over the years and this was the only time I had ever lost a room key. Dick, the owner, was not best pleased with me, and I could hardly blame him.

Of course, I immediately told him I would cover the cost of a replacement which defused the tension a little. I later learned very sadly that his father was dying which I think was the main reason behind his stern reaction towards me.

We took an early dinner at the Napoleon Bonaparte restaurant in town. An odd name for a Dutch restaurant I thought, but it was bustling and quite excellent. However, I was struggling. I found myself tense and very down and, although I put on a brave face, I could not quite shake it off. We put the world to rights, especially the Honda world.

We were all casualties of a time when 'lunatics had taken over the asylum' in all the Honda Genpo's (Japanese business HQ's) throughout Europe and the new brooms, mainly young know-it-all and ambitious Japanese who had no regard for the historical culture of the Company and were not sympathetic to the old way of doing things.

Of course within any company, large or small, this scenario is played out countless times. The truth is both old and new ought to have a place in any business. The old because experience and wisdom really does count and give a voice that can help stave off business pitfalls, and the new because things are ever evolving and should be embraced.

With the dropping of key popular selling models and their uninspiring replacements, business throughout Europe for Honda motorcycles was to suffer for well over a decade as a result of the actions made by them at that time.

And of course we talked about the ST1300 police motorcycle and as we did, I found myself becoming quite depressed. Some say it is cathartic to go over past events but I was finding it a struggle mentally to relive that old and, for me, painful Honda history, for tragically in the UK, we had 2 police riders who had accidents and died whilst riding that bike. In neither case could it be proved the motorcycle was to blame and the fact both riders were on advanced police riding training courses when they died was significant in my opinion. However the tragic circumstances surrounding the accidents affected me deeply and to some degree still do. Those thoughts, the lost B&B keys and the war sites today did not help. I did not let it show to my friends (at least I hope I didn't) but it was by a supreme effort of will.

Eddy was Honda Netherlands motorcycles technical guru, a top technician and engineer, the man you would call on when you couldn't solve a Honda technical problem. He was hugely respected throughout Europe but he took early retirement.

Franklin had been in sales like me, but was even more outspoken than I was over the way he saw the future Honda business going and paid the price for it. And me? Coinciding with a head count reduction at Honda UK and suffering from the effects of 2 plus years of severe stress due to the insurmountable issues on the police bike, I took voluntary redundancy.

Well, you see, I had no ST1300A-P police bike to sell anymore as it was, on my recommendation, withdrawn from the police market and unjustly my 23-year career with Honda went with it. There is another background story to be told one day about this situation, but it is not for this book, but one day it will be told.

Back at Eddy's, it was his turn to show off his own bike collection which was also excellent. As can be expected, Eddy's bike restorations were superb and his latest project was a very rare early N800 Honda car.

I admit to being quite envious of his skills and of his motorcycles hoard. Franklin, being diabetic, had left his insulin pack at the restaurant and left us early to go and retrieve it.

I spent a little more time with Eddy, Ineka and Stephen their son and departed early for my B&B. I was sad to leave them but wanted to start my adventure properly now and was keen to be back on the road.

# Chapter 5
## Alone with the Challenge –
## Germany and Denmark

*'If believing in God is a sin, I'd rather die! Just kill me! It's my mission to live according to God's will!'* – **A North Korean Christian's response to his torturers.**

**Day 5 – Wednesday** 11th July 2018. Ermelo, Netherlands to Neumunster, Germany. Leaving time – 08:30; temperature range – 13ºC to 23ºC; distance ridden – 496 kilometres.

Next morning I awoke to fear, which had come back like some unwelcome overnight guest and I was still feeling a little low after yesterday's dinner discussions. Shrugging it off because I had to, I found I was the only guest for breakfast. Dick told me that he would be travelling 200 kilometres that day to see his father for the last time.

The thought of that had me also quite emotional, especially when Dick kindly gave me a special candle as a memento of my stay; I still have it as a reminder of some very kindly people. The breakfast was superb and I settled my account, including extra for the replacement keys.

Outside, I noted it had rained a little overnight and how the vegetation all around was wilting indicating just how much it was needed. My first decision of the day was getting my bike out of the car park because, on arrival, I had struggled to park it and Eddy had helped me push it backwards into an out-of-the-way spot.

The reason for the difficulty was the small B&B car park was covered in the hated deep gravel and my bike was parked on the side stand plate so the logistics of extracting it on my own had to be thought out. I decided the best plan was to get the bike out first onto the hard surface service road before loading my luggage because the extra weight would impede the process.

It proved a good plan as I found that, indeed, the gravel was much deeper than I had thought and without Eddy's helping hand, I had to waddle it out of the car park in first gear digging a bit of a trench in the process.

Hoping Dick was preoccupied with the washing up and had not noticed, I returned to carefully kick all the gravel back into shape. Did I tell you I hated gravel car parks? Well, I do and with good reason; they are not motorcycle friendly in any way.

At 13°C, the day started as one of the cooler riding days of the trip. Soon, I was threading through the outskirts away from lovely Ermelo and quickly on the autoroutes north. The ride initially was fairly unremarkable and this was not bad news, meaning I was adapting and becoming more relaxed in my continental riding.

As I slipped from Holland into Germany I thought how the whole region was so aptly named the low-lands. From France into Germany, it must have been 750 kilometres at least before I noticed anything remotely resembling a hill. Germany also made much more of a fanfare of the fact you have entered it with their road signage.

I still found it very odd that you could exit and enter another country without even really knowing it. I mean, where I live in Shropshire, it is only 35 miles to the Welsh border and you are left in no doubt when you are crossing it with unmissable signs announcing 'Croeso i Gymru / Welcome to Wales'.

I just happen to think it is a nice thing to know you have passed from one country into another as an indicator of your travel progress if nothing else.

I was now on the famous German Autobahn Road system. The E37 becomes the E22 and I was disappointed. I had expected 3 if not 4 lane super highways, for these were 'Autobahns' after all and had a reputation. But they too were 2 lane and more akin to our dual carriageways leaving a slight dent in my imagination.

Also, I had expected them all to be unrestricted speed-wise and for the most part they were not. When the limit did end and I had a few bursts to the higher speed range and this day hit 170 kph (105mph) a few times, even then it wasn't too long before a car of a certain make was bearing down on me.

You will not be surprised to learn that Audis, BMWs and Mercedes figured prominently in these but I noted also the standard of driving generally was very good. No lane hogging and no one tailgating you if you were stuck waiting for a slower moving vehicle ahead to move over.

I was impressed. Staying with these faster drivers was a possibility I did not really explore. Whilst the XT1200Z is not the fastest motorcycle out there it is no slouch either, 200 kph being easily within its capability. Tempting though it was the extra mental effort needed to ride at those speeds for long periods was not something particularly attractive nor was it good for fuel consumption.

I resolved to pace myself so my normal cruising speed gravitated to around 130/140 kph, i.e. 80/90 mph, with the occasional boredom-breaking acceleration burst to remind myself, and the odd BMW driver, that the bike and I can do high speed when the occasion calls for it.

I make a few stops because I sensed tiredness creeping in; this was to become my standard operating procedure. If I felt tired, I would stop at the next available service and rest, a pattern for the rest of the trip began in Germany. Although tired, my body was holding up well, I was not tense on the bike and I had no back issues either.

At one nondescript services a man tried to converse with me in German. 'Nein Deutsch,' I tell him, and remembering all those old POW war films I point to myself and say, 'Englander'. He laughs heartily, and says 'Honda cruiser', points to himself and adds 'vroom, vroom!' We both laughed; he needed to say no more – a fellow motorcyclist.

I was now heading west around Hamburg on the A28, had noted the dark storm clouds ahead and soon it started to rain…heavily. Riding the next 30 kilometres or so were to be some of the most challenging of the outward leg of the trip.

The A28 was just a mass of road works and contraflows and the lane widths had been reduced with no hard shoulder and the traffic was just horrendous. I was aware I needed to stop to fit the waterproof cover over the tank bag but there was absolutely nowhere possible I could do this.

After my test ride in March to Oxford in the rain I knew my new suit was 100% watertight and I thought briefly of how wet I would have been had I been riding in that BMW riding suit with the waterproof liners removed.

I filtered between the rows of vehicles where I could but often they were so tightly squeezed up that at times I could not get safely by and then I became stuck too. Even when I could make progress it was not comfortable and very slow because of the narrowness of the traffic lanes which made it hard work.

I saw some German bikers ahead (all riding BMWs of course) who made no attempts to filter so, with my hazard warning flashes winking merrily, I slowly overtook them and left them to their car park. I wondered why they didn't follow me, and only later was I told it was technically illegal to filter in Germany.

I say technically, because apparently you can filter on a motorcycle if the traffic is stationary. Well, how are you going to cater for that with any degree of certainty? You can be filtering and the traffic ahead and alongside starts to move and then suddenly that makes what you are doing illegal? Go figure! In my ignorance I did filter past a slow-moving police car, but he gave no visible signs of annoyance and showed no inclination to pursue me. Perhaps my UK number plate made him think it not worth the effort or, practically, how could he even pull me over in the melee of so much traffic? I was in unknown territory here, abroad and still on a steep learning curve about European road and traffic situations.

The thunderstorm began to ease off but ahead was one ridiculous heave of now non-moving traffic. I was gently filtering, inching past vehicles one by one, focusing on my very narrow pathway and I saw the reason why it had completely stopped.

A driver of a red Hyundai had tried to change lanes from the slowly moving outside lane into the non-moving inside lane (as I recall we were nowhere near any sort of exit junction) and instead of waiting for that lane to begin moving before manoeuvring, he was now diagonally stuck, a car wedge between the two lanes and he had completely gridlocked all the traffic behind him as a result.

Of course, as I arrived in-between the lanes, he was now directly ahead completely blocking my path also and there was no way around him. I stopped with a resigned sigh. I was not happy and none of the drivers near him were either and many horns were being blown.

I did start to feel a little bit sorry for him, he had made a mistake and it must have been embarrassing for him to endure the wrath of the drivers around him. After what seemed like a lifetime the inside lane slowly began to move and he was able to complete his manoeuvre and I was able to inch past. I confess to my shame; I also give him a toot of displeasure as I went past. I am not proud of that reaction.

Now tense and a little irritable, as much with myself as anything else, I was allowing the circumstances to get to me. This was not helped when, shortly afterwards, I had a misunderstanding with the driver of a white van who, because his lane had almost stopped, tried to intimidate me by deliberately starting to move over towards me to change lanes, forcing me towards the horrible Armco barrier.

He had seen me, for I could see he was leaning over slightly and looking intently into his door mirror to assess my reaction. The misunderstanding came about because he failed to realise I was not braking (in itself dangerous given the closeness of the vehicle behind) or going to be intimidated to let him force his way in.

There was actually enough of a gap ahead of him for me to accelerate into and it was he who had to wait. I really don't like these traffic games and I tried to assess the situation afterwards. If he had been a reasonable distance, even just half a car length ahead of me and had actually indicated a desire to change lanes, I would have simply let him in. But to try to force me to give way, quite dangerously as I was alongside him, simply because I was on a bike, a soft target if you like, annoyed me.

It would not to be the first time during the trip I would experience something similar, and as an experienced rider I ought to be used to it, but when you are deliberately put in danger this can provoke a reaction from me…sometimes.

Eventually, the rain stopped, and I was back on dry roads, not that I saw much of them for mile, sorry, kilometre after tedious kilometre, we this 'happy' band of road travellers slogging along through the endless road construction. This being early afternoon, I wondered what it would be like in rush hour and I made a mental note to try to avoid Hamburg on the return leg.

Eventually, the road works became less and slightly better onward progress was being made until, on a lovely piece of all new open autobahn, I was beset by another hazard, a wide-load! I could just about make it out in the distance, a huge earth-mover, an excavator, being transported on a long slow moving low loader with an attendant vehicle behind and lots of flashing amber LED lights.

This, after the chaos around Hamburg, did little to improve my mood. Filtering again through the inevitable queue that had built up behind it I was of course eventually at the head of it. Well, not quite, because I was now presented with the problem of the last two cars side by side at the head of the queue who seemed to be deliberately trying to baulk my onward progress by positioning themselves awkwardly.

One vehicle kept dropping back and was occasionally crossing the centre lane line then moving close up to the other car. I hung back trying to work out if they were officially escorting vehicles because their road positioning was certainly odd or, more likely, having seen me filtering up through the jam behind, if they were just ganging up on me to stop me going through.

Their mobile chicane was not really a challenge. I just waited until there was safe space to easily pass them both but they held me up a little while.

Now, in front of me, I had a more difficult decision to make. I was pretty certain that to pass a wide-load under (in this case civilian) escort was illegal. This was quickly confirmed as I approached the escort 'rear guard' van which had an illuminated 'no overtaking' sign on the roof (I got that even though it was in German). It was very much straddling the centre line behind the load to make the point. 'Blow this' I thought and, giving him no time to react, I was quickly past and coming up behind the wide-load itself.

If I thought the baulking cars and van were taking up too much road space, this leviathan was altogether another proposition. It was massive and no car could have ever squeezed by this thing anyway. But I was not in a car and one thing I knew for certain as he was so big and long was that he could not move off his driving line quickly. I rapidly assessed I could get through width wise without too much of a problem.

I did not slow after overtaking the escort van and in a flowing movement the decision was made. I accelerated hard between him and the central reservation to ensure I was alongside the thing for as little time as possible, but even so I sensed he had moved over a little on me. It was clinically done.

I did not dwell on it and soon the flashing amber lights were a speck in my mirrors and I had a blissfully clear road ahead of me, but I did wonder if I had been reported. I now know that no German biker would ever have overtaken that vehicle. Bob McMillan, my former boss at Honda, himself an ex-police motorcyclist, has a lot to answer for with regard to being bold in making my riding decisions.

Half an hour further on, and under threatening skies, I reasoned there was no point in trying to stop just to weatherproof the tank bag and hoped the water ingress from the storm hadn't been too bad.

If I had been moving at a reasonable speed through the rain I doubt if much would have got in as the bike's fairing would have deflected it away, but being in that traffic, often stationary or at very slow speeds in what was a torrential downpour, had me fearing the worst. I would know soon enough. Soon Emilie had me taking the exit for Neumunster and the hotel.

Hotel Kuhl was a budget hotel and I had pre-booked it weeks in advance, for Neumunster seemed to be a good stopping point between Ermelo and Hirtshals in Denmark, and so it proved to be. I was welcomed by a lady in her fifties I guessed, who was very smartly dressed and had a commanding way about her that led me to believe she was one of the owners.

Of course, her English was perfect and, with typical Germanic efficiency, in a thrice I had my room key, was told exactly where it was located, had my evening meal slot booked, and given instructions to park my motorcycle safely in their storage garage. She also reminded me that England was playing Croatia in the World Cup Semi-Finals.

I confess I was a bit cocky about that and even suggested our winning score. She was gracious about my confidence. 'We shall see' is all she would commit to. I have stayed in many hundreds of hotels in my 30 years travelling the length and breadth of the UK, and elsewhere, for work and the attention to detail here at this budget hotel was excellent and I was impressed.

I unloaded the bike and as I checked the tank bag indeed there had been some water ingress but it was just a case of drying out a few affected items. It could have been much worse. My room was basic but spotless. After freshening up I went down to the restaurant for an early dinner as I wanted to catch the match.

I was served by a chubbly-bubbly waitress, and naturally her English too was flawless. She tried to wind me up by suggesting a Croatian win, and I told her what the final score would be, in our favour of course.

I ordered a Weissbier, a salad starter and, because I was in Germany and slightly by way of celebration of that fact, a curry-wurst. The last time I had a curry-wurst was on a special and private visit to the BMW motorcycle factory in Berlin sitting with Herman Borer, who was then the factory boss, in his private dining room. I had fond memories of that day.

'Do you want the yellow or the red curry sauce' she asked me. 'What's the best?' I inquired. 'Try the yellow; it is the best in my opinion.' And so it was. The meal was excellent but the second Weissbier was probably not such a good idea and I left the restaurant with a mild headache, no doubt exacerbated by some dehydration.

Back in my room, I scrolled through a myriad of satellite channels on the TV before eventually finding one broadcasting the match with commentary in English. Outside, in the courtyard, sitting on plastic chairs were a group of worker guests watching it all unfold on a TV which oddly was inside a ground floor room.

Why didn't they just go inside to watch it? England scored first and I cheered loudly. From behind my screening curtain I could see they were looking up unimpressed. German they might be, but clearly they were not on our side in this. Croatia equalised, the courtyard erupted, and I stayed mousily quiet.

And when Croatia did win, they were doing little jigs around the car park and I felt, well, a trifle intimidated. A little later, when they had all retired to the bar, I sneaked downstairs and checked my bike over. All was well, I was yawning, very tired and I slept well that night.

**Day 6 – Thursday** 12th July 2018. Neumunster, Germany to Hirtshals, Denmark. Leaving time – 07:40; temperature range – 20°C to 32°C; distance ridden – 480 kilometres.

With England now out of the World Cup and being the only 'Englander' in the hotel, I sneaked into the breakfast room trying to keep as low a profile as possible, although I was wearing my riding trousers and boots which ordinarily might have prompted a conversation.

I noted yesterday that this hotel catered primarily for what we used to call 'blue-collar' workers, of which, as this trip was to prove, Europe seems full, because they still 'do' stuff whereas in the UK we seem to have lost much of this. To be a tradesman is a virtue, well certainly in Germany it is, the genre is respected and they are clearly well paid.

There are gangs of them, all wearing their smart but different corporate personal protection clothing. I noted from the badges that one crew had something to do with industrial structures. But, and perhaps they were all hung over, they were a pretty cheerless bunch.

They were barely talking to each other and breakfast was conducted over the odd grunt with very few smiles and I found it quite odd. I had never experienced anything like this from my German colleagues when at BMW, quite the reverse in fact.

I also recalled when working at major trade exhibitions with colleagues and competitors alike, even if some had bad heads from the excesses of the previous night, there was always good-natured banter going on. It set you up for the day. Not here though and I don't want to be unfair to these German workers, but this lot turned being taciturn into an art form.

Can I state here I do not care much for buffets and particularly not breakfast buffets. The restaurant was heaving with these large and determinedly hungry men and, though the hot food serving dishes were loaded generously, I found myself dancing around the more experienced buffeteers, who knew exactly where everything was located.

I eventually found the scrambled eggs and, after queuing 3 deep just to get to them, they ran out the moment I approached the serving dish. I watched the man in front of me leave with enough on his plate for 3 people.

Waiting for it to be replenished whilst the rest of my breakfast on my somewhat smaller plate was going cold, was not good planning.

Then naturally, I had forgotten to put my bread slices in the toaster (I couldn't find that for ages either) and had to stand around with a now loaded breakfast plate looking like a complete chump waiting for the toast to pop up whilst the rest of the guests were all tucking in.

I managed to get an out of the way table on my own and was served coffee by a quiet, emaciated, but friendly waitress. I was relieved in one way it was not her alter ego, the hearty girl who had served me dinner last night, as no doubt she would have made much of the England defeat.

As I sat eating my now barely warm food I decided this had proved a sombre and somewhat dispiriting eating experience, hopefully not to be repeated on this trip, but it perhaps illustrates my point about breakfast buffets.

I noted the workers who had finished their breakfast were now attacking the serving tables again stuffing bread, cold meats, cheese, and fruit, actually whatever seemed readily available, into large clear plastic bags. I assumed this extra food was for their lunches and I was a bit shocked by this behaviour if I'm honest.

But later, I was to witness this again on my trip and came to realise that hotels who cater for working crews do expect them to help themselves from the buffet for their lunches. It then made sense; the food wasn't being stolen! I learned from this not to make snap judgements when you are living around a different culture.

I went to check out; I had actually pre-paid so it was just a formality. Just as well really as the receptionist had absolutely no English but the sign language worked okay. I had already loaded my bike, so it was just back to the room to collect my jacket, helmet, and gloves.

I dropped the room key off and left at 07:40 noting the outside temperature was already 22$^\circ$C, there was no wind and not a cloud in the sky. I was leaving with just a third of a tank of fuel and had hoped to find a service station before I hit the autobahn, but according to the Sat Nav they were located inconveniently out of my way.

On the autobahn many kilometres later and now with the low fuel level indicator blinking, I breathed a sigh of relief as eventually the next services were reached. I resolved at this point in the trip never to let the fuel level fall below a third if I could.

A rider once described long distance travel on a motorcycle having moments of unremitting tedium. I can but agree. For me, these were the open motorway sections. Any motorway, autoroute or autobahn is always pretty boring for a bike rider until of course you had to ride through a gridlocked Antwerp or a Hamburg which does tend to focus your attention somewhat.

It is not our natural territory, simply a means to an end, a way to get from A to B in the shortest time and by the quickest route. The temperature climbed up into the 30s and because of the monotony of it a little tiredness was beginning to creep in, so I occasionally blasted the bike up to 200kph to break the humdrumness. But even then, with the odd Audi behind (oh and a lone Honda car too I recall) catching me, these cat and mouse games kept me more alert.

I was fully focussed though as I approached the Danish border. It was actually staffed, which immediately had me thinking of the logistics of finding my passport. There was no need to be concerned as the red bearded border guard just seemed to wave every vehicle through anyway, but it was a striking contrast to the other borders I had seamlessly crossed through Europe so far and, as they were all in the EU, I wondered why Denmark chose to be different.

Denmark was different in another way too. At last, the topography of the landscape was slowly changing. Not big hills but more rolling countryside, not exactly pretty either but then I was probably too tired and overheated to fully appreciate it.

I stopped at a rest stop and refilled my water bottle. But there was no rest here, for as soon as I sat down I was attacked by midge like insects which I might have called 'thunder bugs' in the UK. Tiny they may have been but they were merciless, biting and crawling onto every exposed part of my skin. And this service area stank worse than the one in Holland. I couldn't wait to get away from the place.

When you are riding it is hard to visualise the distances you are covering. Today, for example, I was to ride the whole length of Denmark but in those tired, hot and sweaty riding moments, all you can think of is the destination rather than the actual journey.

It is not exactly feeling that you are physically remote, for that would be potentially disastrous on a motorcycle. But, as I said earlier, riding long distances on motorways does not help a rider to feel fully connected with the landscape, or indeed the country.

For the car driver even less so. I played mind games to keep from falling into a road noise induced coma, mine by trying to pronounce the town and village names in a local accent, not that I had actually any idea what a Danish accent sounded like, but I improvised.

I particularly enjoyed Middelfart and Aarhus. Occasionally, shouting at myself in my helmet also helped to keep me alert, but over the years I have never had many sensible high decibel conversations with myself or indeed anyone else for that matter.

Just north of Aalborg, I pulled into a service for a now much-needed break. It was quite up-market and, compared to the last stop, very clean and not in the least smelly. I bought a nice coffee and snack and sat outside listening to the burbling of some German motorcyclists at the next table.

They were arguing mildly about something and I noted the lady bikers were holding their own; it made me smile and they nodded kindly and waved to me as they departed.

Soon, I arrived at Hirtshals, the tip of Denmark and Emilie guided me expertly to my accommodation, Motel Neordsean (North Sea). I also noted its location was right next door to a major visitor attraction, an aquarium.

At reception, I availed myself of the guest-discounted rate to visit the feature and, although I was very tired, after freshening up I strolled down there because this would be the only opportunity I had and, being late afternoon, I had just enough time. The unmasked sun created a glare from the white concrete pathways that was merciless on my tired eyes.

Since a small child, I have always been fascinated by aquatic life and wherever there is an aquarium I always take time to go and have a look around. From Sydney to Vancouver, I have seen those that are rated as the very best and I am surprised to say that this aquarium, here at the neck-end of nowhere, was alongside them all.

It was superb. Every tank was well-lit and you could sense the care, if not pride, in how they were set up and presented. The information boards had

English and the species identification was assisted by excellent photographs. There were good background features about marine Denmark and fishing industries, but what really took my breath was a massive tank (possibly the largest I have ever seen) containing every species to be found in the North Sea.

I sat there spell-bound and thought of the time when as that young kid my interest in under-water life was sparked by watching the spawning minnows in my local stream. It was awesome. The fish were going about their lives as if they were actually still living at sea; huge shoals of horse mackerel glided by, cod as big as star ships and species I would never have associated as cold-water marine were there.

I confess I sat there for ages and it was almost closing time when I came out to be blinded again by the blazing sunshine. There were not going to be many other opportunities in this ride to take time out for myself and I enjoyed the self-indulgence of it.

I decided not to eat at the motel but have a tour around, not least checking where the departure point was for tomorrow's ferry. I rode down to an adjacent beach and took a selfie with the North Sea as a backdrop and found Hirtshals to be a nice seaside town with a lovely harbour and, unlike many other ferry ports I have visited over the years, it was quite classy.

For that of course, also read potentially expensive. I sat down at an outside table of a little bistro and the lady owner came out to serve me, telling me they were all enjoying the beautiful weather for a change. I imagined from that comment that they could experience some pretty extreme weather up there.

I paid the equivalent of £18.00 for a glass of Coke, and what proved to be a very small bowl of local prawns accompanied by a minute piece of brown bread. Let me just say, I thought this was somewhat excessive for so little.

As I parked my bike back at the motel an older couple were getting out of an immaculate black BMW X3. Sometimes, you just sense things; he looked as if he was chewing a wasp and, despite my nodded smile and hello, or possibly because of it, was brusque and unfriendly.

Perhaps he didn't like my bike being parked near to his spotless car or more likely, they'd had a row, but it made me feel a little uneasy as it was almost a portend.

Back in my room I discovered a problem, a big problem. My brake disc lock, the one key security item brought to safeguard my bike when parked, had failed.

It would not lock, although I was grateful it failed at locking rather than unlocking because that would have been an even bigger problem.

No matter what I did it simply would not lock, so now overnight, the bike had no additional security at all other than the standard steering lock which a determined thief could easily overcome. This was a worry. I inserted the now unlockable disc lock through the front brake disc anyway as a visual deterrent, but an investigating felon would not have been easily fooled by it.

Lying on my over-firm motel bed and trying to put it out of my mind, and following the information forwarded by Daphne, I emailed Jonathon Bott about speaking possibilities whilst in Norway as my Dutch friends had suggested, but I was not that hopeful and, as it proved, it just didn't work out. At 10:30 I turned in exhausted – it was still bright light outside!

# Chapter 6
# Into Norway

*'Evin Prison became a church for us. We were able to speak to more people about Jesus there than in freedom.'* – **A young Iranian woman in prison for distributing Bibles.**

**Day 7 – Friday** 13th July 2018. Hirtshals, Denmark to Bykle, Norway. Sailing time – 08:30; temperature range – 20ºC to 34ºC; distance ridden – a mere 194 kilometres.

A week away already and, though I am not superstitious, I noted it was Friday the 13th. I make mention of it because today things could have gone horribly wrong but, as you will learn, didn't.

I was up, ready and loading the bike at 06:00 and being amazed because it was soaking wet! As I looked about, I noticed a sea mist just starting to burn off which must have been quite thick to generate so much moisture. I strolled down for an early breakfast but, as I walked into reception, I was not the first.

There were two families of determined looking Germans who were like horses at the starting gate. I decided to stroll around the car park until the restaurant opened and noted a UK registered Hyundai i30, similar to Liz's car, even to the colour.

The number plates showed it came from Gloucester, a long drive and some commitment, I thought. I looked across to the restaurant window and noted my fellow guests were in and already attacking the inevitable buffet. Fortunately, there weren't quite enough of them to completely deplete the service tables in one hit, but my goodness they did try!

These people are buffet experts, having the art of locating the food, always seeming to know where the jam, the sauces, the juices, the bread, and the toasters were located. I wondered if they had done pre-breakfast reconnaissance the night before.

The Germans are just so well organised, super-efficient in these matters whilst we are more laid back, usually, and then moan because we get out-manoeuvred. I should explain, having worked for BMW I have some wonderful German friends. I like the country and I like the people. But on this trip I noted a trait that seems to mark some Germans and where food was concerned it's definitely me first. Just an observation, not a generalisation.

That said, it's me first in the line for the ferry. This was unusual and, given my experience of boarding ferries, it usually meant very little. You might think you are at the head of the first boarding line, only to find row 5 is actually the line they will board first. Many times I tried to work out the logic of what and how they load these ferries and finally decided there wasn't any.

There was not a cloud in the sky and set to be another scorcher of a day and I hoped for a calm crossing. We were going to cross the infamous choppy stretch of water called the Skagerrak and, even before I had any notion of this challenge, I knew that it had a fearsome reputation for rough crossings and I was not the best of sailors.

I was joined in my line by some fellow shipmates, a retired Danish couple, former schoolteachers, who were cycling through Norway on electric bikes. They looked over my motorcycle with all its stickers and ignored me for a while before actually speaking.

At times, I wondered if some people were a bit embarrassed to approach me given the nature of the challenge and who I was riding for. Another motorcyclist pulled up behind me, a big guy dwarfing his Yamaha XT660 and he too was Danish.

His bike mirrored his physical shape, with huge panniers overloaded beyond capacity and other items such as his tent and camping stuff, tripods, spare fuel tanks crammed into every available nook and cranny. Seeing this mobile hardware shop, I was immediately thankful I had junked the idea of camping and I suspected the suspension on his bike was going to come in for some punishment.

We all passed the time away now chatting about our respective trips. He was from Copenhagen and going to the Lofoten Islands, a trip he told me he did regularly. Looking up at the sky he said, 'I have never been to the north of Norway without experiencing at least one full day of rain.'

We talked about Norway's less than generous speed limits – 'just ride at 80 (kph) and enjoy the trip' he said. I never caught his name but he told me he was the Danish classic motocross champion. I didn't question it, but it must have been some time ago because he really didn't look anywhere near fit enough to be able to compete now.

The brightly coloured Fjordline ferry from Kristiansand arrived and we watched as the ground crew efficiently dispatched the vehicles onto the Hirtshals roads. Actually, I was the first vehicle on and was loosely guided to the area where the motorcycles are expected to park for the crossing.

Here, things began to go a little wrong because Fjordline do not assist motorcyclists to secure their bikes in any way. Car driver? 'This way sir, that's right, line up just there, stop, yes okay sir that's perfect.' Motorcyclist? 'Over there mate, sort yourselves out'.

It may not have been actually spoken but practically that was precisely what we were subjected to. I noted a curt disclaimer sign; let me quote it to you.

*'It is your own duty and responsibility to make sure that your motorcycle is properly fastened during the crossing. Straps are provided on board. Please leave the straps behind when disembarking the ferry, other motorcyclists will need them on the next crossing. Have a nice trip!'*

Now…does anyone else see the flaws here? My duty and responsibility? Just imagine for a moment you happen to be the only motorcyclist travelling this particular day, and for argument's sake, this is your very first ferry crossing.

You have absolutely no idea how to secure your motorcycle and, since all the deck staff are pandering to the needs of the car customers, which they were, who could you even ask? So your bike falls over and is badly damaged because it is a rough crossing and this is entirely your fault?

By this sign, Fjordline seem to be absolving its duty of care to motorcyclists who are, after all, also fee-paying customers. In fact, I am certain it is their responsibility to ensure all vehicles of any sort are properly secured for the safety of the vessel.

An unsecured motorcycle in a big storm could be a potential fire risk. And, if the straps were really stolen on one crossing, what about customer needs on the return one? I can guarantee you that no such sign existed in the car deck area.

I emailed Fjordlines later complaining about this fiasco. You will not be surprised to learn I received no reply. Motorcyclists the world over are often treated as a lower species when compared to car drivers and, sorry, I don't think that is right.

And here is how it played out this particular morning. There were a number of us by now and the space to secure the bikes proved very limited indeed and the camaraderie normally enjoyed between fellow motorcyclists began to be stretched as we jostled our bikes into the ridiculously small area designated for us.

As first in, I took what I thought was the furthest spot away and parked leaving myself a little wiggle room. But, Hamlet my Danish friend (my new name for him by the way), now being pushed by other bikers behind him, had underestimated the room he needed to park his two-wheeled mobile home, and suddenly wanted me to move my bike even further over because he could not get his in.

It is not exactly easy to reposition 700lbs of motorcycle on a slippery slightly sloping deck floor when someone else's pannier bags are pushing at you from the side. I tried to be gracious, but I was not happy. But he was clearly an old hand at this and had his bike rapidly secured and, instead of offering assistance to the others, just cleared off, leaving the rest of us to fend for ourselves with his bike leaning uncomfortably close to mine now.

Then, cheekily, a young Scandinavian, riding a mid-sized Yamaha sporting large Norwegian and Danish flags, deftly squeezed in the other side of me. Quite how he managed this I don't know, but he did. However, once there, he looked bewildered and a bit lost as to what to do next.

Because he seemed a nice kid, I took pity and helped the late-comer secure his bike because, case in point, he hadn't much of a clue how to do it. But if I hadn't, then who else would have done it? If nobody and the bike did fall over, whose fault, Fjordlines? I think you know the answer.

Fjordline does indeed provide securing straps which were quite dreadful things, tangled, complicated to release, difficult to tension and absolutely filthy. It did not provide any foam rubber or cover to use underneath the straps to protect your bike either.

I was now fuming; this was appalling. Here was I kneeling down in £300 Gore-Tex trousers on a slightly oily floor, undertaking a job that deck staff are, or at least should be, paid to do.

Not being 100% satisfied my bike was secure, and concerned about the domino effect should it cut up rough at sea, I lingered on to make it extra safe. Based on, admittedly, a rather better experience on the Irish ferry in May, I had the foresight to bring my own securing straps on this trip to supplement those provided.

Using a combination of these and the dreadful straps provided, which, being twisted up, took ages to untangle and tighten down, I left the deck confident that my bike at least was going nowhere.

Of course by the time I got onto the passenger decks they were now busy. Hamlet had, naturally, managed to secure himself a prime spot. He waved but, just at that moment, I did not feel very kindly disposed towards him and hunkered myself down sulkily near the deck access door.

The crossing in the Sea Cat was quick, just 2 hours, mercifully smooth and trouble free and I even managed a little nap to prepare myself for Norway.

As we approached the port of Kristiansand I was up and out of my seat like a greyhound out of the trap and first in the queue for the car deck door to open and first to get to my bike too, but of course it meant very little.

The young man by the side of me, the one who I had helped secure his bike, was clearly in no hurry and I forgot that without him moving first, I was trapped. Without risking over-balancing my bike I could not go anywhere or even get to my straps to free it.

I had to stand and wait whilst he adjusted both his flags (for goodness sake!) and repositioned everything before he finally decided to release his bike which, given his unfamiliarity with the accursed straps, naturally he struggled to do. Hamlet chose 'not to be' and had gone, of course.

Eventually, the young man moved and now I was last man standing, but it was not easy pulling backwards a heavy fully loaded bike and turning it around on a camber. I feared a situation that would cause the weight of the bike to go away from me, giving way to that horrible over-balancing situation that most motorcyclists will have experienced at one time or another.

I did that once on an Isle of Man ferry, much to the amusement of my then Honda colleagues, not a nice scenario. I was almost last off the boat it seemed, but not entirely unhappy, I was, after all, in Norway at last.

By the time I got to exit the ferry area to take the E9 road north, (there were no border formalities), I noted with some alarm how swelteringly hot the day had become. My fellow motorcyclists had long gone.

Norway is described in Rough Guide as *'a wilderness outpost in a tamed and crowded continent.'* How that description appealed to me when I read it and indeed after the unremarkable scenery from Calais and the mind-numbing monotony of autoroutes and autobahns nothing really quite prepared me for Norway.

Sometimes, the only expression that really captures an astonishing new vista is simply – wow! I was instantly enthralled; it was immediately and dramatically different. Mountains, foaming rivers cutting through deeply shaded valleys, forests and roads with sinuous curves; even in those first few hours riding it was already shaping up to all I had hoped it would be.

However, I quickly became frustrated with the ungenerous 80kph speed limit and wondered how strictly it was enforced, for these were roads just begging to be ridden. Not far out of the little town of Kristiansand, I noted the tarmac was covered by scores of burn-out skids for mile after mile. Clearly the local car drivers like to smoke their wheels and I suspected the tyre businesses did a good trade here.

It was odd because I was to come across the phenomena elsewhere in Norway as I rode, and I meant to ask the locals about it but never did. One thing made me smile was the moose warning signs appearing. I was a little taken aback, knowing, of course, there were moose in Norway I had, for some reason, assumed they would be far north, in the remote arctic areas.

Given these signs were just within a few kilometres of Kristiansand it seemed their distribution was pretty much universal throughout the country. As a way of keeping myself alert, I made strange moose-like mooing sounds every time I saw a sign, silly I know, but it amused me. Actually, I have no idea if I sounded like a moose or not and am relieved to say nothing responded to my efforts.

But the warning signs are not just for show. As my American and Canadian friends told me, moose are to be taken deadly seriously when travelling, especially at night. They are apparently very difficult to see after dark and have a habit of standing smack in the road centre and, having absolutely no road sense, they do not move away when a vehicle approaches.

I was told, if you were unfortunate enough to hit one at speed…well let's just say it would not end well for either party, for they are very large animals indeed. One of my Canadian friends told me he simply refused to drive certain routes at night because of them.

Working my way along Highway 9 enjoying, even at 80kph, the beauty of the scenery I noticed billows of smoke and columns of fire rising from the side of a close mountain – a forest fire. I took a gently sloping gravel road down off the main road allowing me to get a little closer to take some pictures whilst back up on the main road cars were now stopping to do exactly the same.

I was fascinated and horrified in equal measure and watched as the helicopters fought it by dropping water bombs on it from large suspended slings.

When my morbid curiosity had been fulfilled, I continued down the gravel road but it did not, as it promised, take me back up to the highway further on. The road was quite narrow and being lazy in not wanting to do a 5 point turn I decided to put my off-road skills to the test and simply ride the XT up a grassy hill back up to the road.

Normally, this would not have presented any difficulties and all went really well until, three-quarters of the way up, the bike's traction control system (TCS) engaged just at the critical moment when I needed that grip finding/wheel spinning technique that all off-road riders would understand.

Losing momentum unexpectedly, and to avoid the potential of a bigger crash, I had no option but to shut off and gently lay the bike down to the left as a result. I was both shocked and annoyed. Of course, my dilemma now was picking up a fully laden bike from the side of a Norwegian hill and holding it there whilst deciding how best to extricate myself from this self-made fiasco.

I knew from my off-road riding experience that the ideal way was to position myself between the bike and the camber of the hill and slowly waggle the handlebars to drop the front wheel down until the bike was level with the hillside and then ride it back down. That would work perfectly with a light bike, but trying to do this with such a big heavy bike on a steep camber would, I knew, be way too dangerous.

Trying to remount such a tall bike on a hillside with the potential of the weight of the machine falling away from you had all the ingredients for a disaster. My options, I felt, were limited. The only way was up.

Infuriated at my stupid TCS error and with an adrenalin rush and slipping feet, I somehow managed to wrestle the bike upright. The bike being stalled and in gear was held at the rear wheel. But I had to start it which meant pulling the clutch in, so any braking effect there would immediately be lost. This made it a more precarious situation.

Transferring the braking carefully to the front brake, I pulled the clutch in and was relieved that weight and gravity did not cause the front wheel to skid backwards. I hit the start button, but it refused to fire up. It took multiple attempts and quite a few stupefied seconds before I realised that the bank-angle sensor had deployed.

This is a device that cuts the fuel off to avoid a potential fire situation when it senses the motorcycle has achieved some critical angle i.e. a crash. After switching the ignition off and on again (reaching over to do this had risks also when you consider I had to take one hand off the handlebars) mercifully the bike started.

The situation was still very fraught however, but with gear engaged and with careful and judicious use of throttle and clutch, I pushed the bike slowly back up the slope to the road edge. It was not so very far but it was really hard work, and the heat of the day and the stress of the predicament did not help.

I was drained by the time I got it back to level and safe ground. It was an embarrassing and undignified situation fortunately witnessed by only a few passing motorists and it ended better than it might have. But I was very annoyed with myself for a number of reasons.

1. Because I should have remembered to switch the TCS off before attempting to ride off-road.
2. Because if it had gone horribly wrong and the bike had pitched sideways down the hill, the resultant damage may have terminated my challenge. I might also have been injured (see below).
3. Because I could have put my back out so badly picking it up that I might have been unable to continue.
4. Because, frankly, I shouldn't have done it at all.

A footnote to this story was given to me later by a friend. He was talking to a guy at a motorcycle event who was recovering from a broken collar bone. He was injured by riding a large 'adventure sports' bike, a Honda in his case, off-road up a steep hill and he failed to make the top because he too forgot to disengage the TCS on his bike.

He, like me, was also an experienced off-road rider, but his outcome was far worse than mine. His bike fell over awkwardly throwing him off and he sustained that injury as a result.

Back on Highway 9, I rode on simmering from the heat and fury at my stupidity. It was 34°C which, considering I was now over 1,600 kilometres (1,000 miles) further north from my heat discomfort on the M25, just seemed ridiculous.

After my bike recovery efforts I was so unbelievably hot for the first and only time on the ride, that I strapped my riding jacket to the rear seat and rode on in shirt sleeves, but it made me feel quite vulnerable, so I stopped after about 20 minutes in a shaded lay-by to collect myself and try to cool and calm down.

I checked the bike over and, apart from some very minor scuffs, I was relieved to find no damage thanks to the excellent fitted crash bars. I said a prayer of thanks. I was being looked after, and it was only then on refection did I realise just by how much.

Something else suddenly and chillingly came to me. The summit of that hill proved to be almost at the road edge itself. I could not have known this without walking up there first. I knew I would have had to carry a reasonable amount of speed and momentum just to crest it, but here's the thing. If the TCS had not cut in when it did there was a real possibility I may not have been able to safely stop before the road itself.

The thought of that and me inadvertently riding into the path of an oncoming vehicle sent shivers down my spine. I just blindly and stupidly made a decision through laziness and bravado to ride up that hill without giving any thought at all as to how close the crest might have been to the road edge.

Some might say coincidence, but I firmly believe the TCS engagement was God's protection. You will be hardly surprised to learn I did not engage in any more off-road exploits for the rest of the trip.

I heard a motorcycle approaching and it was Hamlet, our Danish motocross champion, pipping his horn as he passed. Fully expecting to see 'convoi exceptionnel' signs plastered across his rear I cannot quite believe how wide and overloaded his bike was.

But I was glad he did not stop for I was not really in casual conversation mode, glad too he had not been passing 25 minutes earlier to witness my predicament. I wondered how he had ended up behind me because he was off the ferry ages before me and I had not seen him parked up anywhere on the way.

A few kilometres later, the sky darkened ominously and I thought my Danish friend might be right in his rain prophesy – until I smelt the smoke. I stopped to look. This forest fire was below me down in a river valley quite close to the road and the smoke was becoming thick and menacing.

The authorities were there in a big white van with orange flashing warning lights obviously assessing if it was sufficiently dangerous for them to close the road. Not wanting to be physically caught the wrong side of that decision I jumped back on the bike and got away from there as quickly as I could.

From what I could see it looked a big fire. As the road climbed steeply from this point, I looked in my mirrors and could see little but thick blue smoke behind me.

I have never experienced forest fires before and have to say, seeing one at close quarters, they are a bit terrifying. I did not want to imagine what could happen if one flared up in trees right next to the road and prayed it would not be part of my experience on the trip.

When in Western Australia in 2017 (yes, we did get there 6 months after my operation) we visited Dwellingup, a place that had experienced an appalling bush fire in 1961. Going into the local museum there and reading the reports of what happened and who perished in the region was not for the faint hearted.

These things kill people, lots of people. And 2018 proved to be a terrible year for wildfires world-wide, in Europe, Russia, USA (especially bad in California) and even in the UK. A very worrying trend, I think.

My Sat Nav had become a little confused. Perhaps Emilie did not take kindly to being dumped ignominiously on her side on a Norwegian hill. I stopped outside some shops in the village of Bykle and asked a couple of locals where the hotel was.

A guy about my age laughed, 'Are you blind?' he says and points to a posh building at the top of the hill. 'It's the smoke' I quipped and he laughed again.

I had pre-booked the hotel many weeks in advance without really checking that it created a shorter than ideal riding day. That said Hotel Bykle, my overnight stop, was a most welcome relief after the stress of fires and TCS foolishness.

Can I just say here the hoteliers on my trip were mostly very kind to me with reduced room rates given when I told them about my challenge. I was disappointed to find the manager here was on leave as I wanted to thank him here personally for his kindness; however, I did leave him a little note expressing my gratitude.

Arriving earlier than anticipated, after freshening up, I went for a walk up the hill behind the hotel and watched the helicopters swooping down to drop water bombs on the fire in the valley below. I was amazed at the bravery and skill of the pilots. I also stumbled across a little museum of traditional Norwegian log buildings which looked interesting enough for me to investigate the following morning.

Walking back down to the hotel, I noted that all the watercourses on the hill had dried up, with not even a trickle to dampen them. A kid passed me on a mountain bike doing a wheelie all the way down the hill, which is a tricky thing to do. He's good, he knows it and I was suitably impressed.

Back at the hotel, I witnessed a smartly dressed young woman putting her equally smartly dressed infant into the bespoke baby seat of a large black Tesla. I would not have taken much notice ordinarily but Tesla cars are not so common in the UK and this was a seriously posh one. These people clearly had money, in fact illustrating perfectly Norway as being a wealthy country.

I had observed that approximately every sixth car coming towards me today had been a Tesla. Based on my observation, I reasoned that Tesla's market share in Norway would be very high and I wondered about that. I was to learn later the reason why.

I enjoyed an excellent dinner at the hotel with a single beer. Alcohol is extremely expensive in Norway. Furthermore, the police rigorously enforce the zero-tolerance legislation when it comes to drinking and driving, so one would be quite enough today, thank you.

Being away over a week now, my hotel routine now was pretty much a replica of the set form I had now gained on the trip and beginning to become almost second nature. Each night I would ring Liz (I never failed to ring her every night when I was working away). Then, I would write up my daily journal and download my pictures from my phone to update my Facebook page which I was trying to do daily. My little report on the day, I was to learn later, achieved quite a following.

This night, I also cancelled my Airbnb booking at Trondheim for 2 reasons. It was bad planning on my part for on closer examination it was too close to Kristiansund, my stop the night before, and would have meant another unnecessarily short riding day following. Also, the host, a young oriental man called Boo, was badgering me by email to let him know at least 30 minutes in advance of my arrival time.

I don't know why but this also made me feel uneasy. Airbnb were starting to get a bad reputation, stories of teenage children letting out their parents' home while they were away on holiday were quite common. I was suspicious. Was it even his apartment he was renting out?

I had a premonition of the owners returning early to find me in their home and bed. I cancelled and got a full refund I am pleased to say.

By now, I was happily exhausted. One final job was to pretend to secure my bike with the disc lock and park it close enough to my bedroom window to hopefully hear if someone did mess with it.

# Chapter 7
# Mountains and Fjords

*'I praise God that some survived, many in truly miraculous ways. However we are deeply traumatised, broken, and in need of prayer.'* – **Federick Gitonga after Al-Shabaab militants attacked the university campus at Garissa, Kenya.**

**Day 8 – Saturday** 14th July 2018. Bykle to Rongen Farm, Bolstadoyri, Leaving time – 06:00; temperature range – 14°C to 22°C; distance ridden – 323 kilometres. At this stage of the trip I had ridden cumulatively 1,917 kilometres, or 1,405 miles (with the extra UK only miles added).

Actually, I would have heard nothing. I slept like the proverbial log and awoke refreshed at 05:00 and, although early, there was quite a noise just outside my bedroom window. I took a peek and it was a fire crew getting into a large Avis rental vehicle going, no doubt, to take on another forest fire.

I silently wished them well because their day was going to be a lot more unpleasant than mine. Once again I noted there was not a cloud in the sky. My back was aching quite badly, which given my history was a slight concern. The escapade of picking the bike up yesterday would have exacerbated it and I prayed it would settle down.

At some point on my ride today, I would be further north than the most northern point of the British Isles, Unst in the Shetland Islands. Over breakfast, I sat thinking about how far I had ridden to achieve this and how far I had still to go. Once again it brought the enormity of the ride into focus.

I tried not to dwell on it, just one day at a time moving ever closer to the goal. If I thought about it too much it would be a distraction that would rob me of the enjoyment of it. This, after all, was still an adventure, albeit with a serious purpose behind it.

Happily too by now, I seemed to have got my routine more or less together both personally and on the bike. In the torrid heat hygiene and cleanliness became vitally important and I became a bit obsessive about it.

I would turn my riding suit inside out to air every night and treat it with a fabric freshener and the inside of my crash helmet also. I am sure the question had entered your head. What about fresh underwear? I had a wash/wear routine and would hand wash some of my underpants, tee shirts and socks on alternative days.

I was to find they never completely dried overnight in spite of the warm conditions, but after a day roasting in the pannier found they were perfect to wear the day following. Rolling this system on every other day meant I did not start my day riding in anything other than clean underwear. There, now you know.

Whilst riding, my essential items, glasses, phone and wallet, were now designated their own jacket or trouser pocket. My glasses, needed only for reading, were in my right trouser pocket, my phone in the left and my wallet secured in an inner pocket of the jacket.

The only problem I had was remembering to zip close the trouser pockets; this failure caught me out a few times and had me frantically tapping my pockets when riding to make sure nothing had fallen out, then stopping urgently to ensure they were closed.

The pockets in my riding suit were generously deep enough for the items not to fall out, but having lost 2 pairs of prescription spectacles from unsecured pockets in another suit (you think I would have learned after the first time, wouldn't you?) it really should have become second nature. Eventually it did.

Before riding each day, I gave the bike a quick check over, especially the tyres. I made sure my helmet intercom was fully charged overnight and working so Emilie could nag me as I go along, or the unit 'ping' me to let me know of a speed camera site.

I ensured my helmet visor was clean at the start of each day's ride and, of course, that my entire luggage was secure and the pannier and top case lids were locked before I moved off. The bike has an external temperature gauge and I recorded the temperature at the start of the ride and checked it constantly whilst riding.

I was aware that in slow traffic or when stationary it would always record somewhat higher than the ambient temperatures due to engine heat build-up, but on the move it was pretty accurate I think, shockingly so some days.

I checked I had my full bottle of water and that my phone (also fully charged) and all my pockets were zipped up and secure. I stopped at the nearest service station for fuel when my fuel gauge was showing below 1/3 left in the tank, almost all my petrol purchases being 'pay at the pump' by credit card.

I even developed a routine of filling the tank by sitting on the bike whilst fuelling up and rocking it gently when near full to ensure trapped air was released and the tank filled to the absolute maximum.

At these stops, I would buy food, if needed, water, which was always needed, drink my now favourite chocolate milk drink and sometimes buy chewy fruit sweets. If I was feeling very tired I might take a wee snooze and, if necessary, clean my helmet visor once again before riding on.

With regard to packing my luggage, I had achieved a level of efficiency here also by now. By using those zipper compression bags and redistributing specific items to make them more accessible and packable the inner bags were less bulky and could be inserted into the side cases without being forced.

Equally importantly, they could be extracted without me standing over them and tugging at them like an Arthur trying to extract his Excalibur. I also knew now, from familiarity, where any item was located in the cases or the tank bag.

Closing and locking the lids was, however, a bit of a chore some days. This is because the single lock securing mechanism of the Yamaha cases is not particularly well designed (I note on the more recent model this has been addressed) and early on in the trip a few times they had not closed correctly with the lids no doubt flapping up and down like a hungry crocodile's mouth.

Thankfully, nothing was lost and no damage done but it became one of those double check items before riding off each day. These may only seem like small things but they served to make life on the road easier.

This particular morning I had to wipe my bike down as once again it was covered in condensation. I rode up the hill and wandered around the museum grounds but was unable to gain access internally to any of the buildings. I took pictures for my American friend Bob Kellum who, having his own log cabin in Canada, has more than a passing interest in their construction.

The functionality of these pretty buildings was quite evident but it made me wonder how hard it must have been for a family to live in one in a Nordic winter. Perhaps they were much snugger than they looked.

Back at the bike, I looked for the forest fire in the valley below. The smoke levels were like a faint mist compared to yesterday. The fire fighters clearly had done a good job.

I put Bergen into my Sat Nav reasoning that my overnight accommodation, a fisherman's lodge on the Vasso River, would be close enough for an easy commute back from the town but today my calculations proved a bit wrong.

It was not long out of Bykle that I was bearing left onto the E134 which runs alongside a topaz blue river for many kilometres. A vole-like animal ran out in front of me and I managed to avoid it. I am certain it was a lemming; it was certainly suicidal enough to be one.

The road began to climb steadily. For the first time in days, it became comfortably cooler, and suddenly I was into my first mountain pass which was easy riding when compared to the later ones. There are huge lichen covered 'Erratic' boulders (a boulder carried by glacial ice), beautiful glacial lakes, patches of still lying snow and truly wonderful vistas of distant peaks.

I thought of those motorcyclists who were driven off such a mountain road by blizzards in June last year. Hard to visualise on this day because there was no such issue for me. Cooler it may have been but there was still not a cloud in the sky.

However, for the first time, I did put on that extra warming fleece layer. It was wonderful and technical riding until I encountered my first Norwegian road tunnel at a place called Dyrskard and, although pre-warned about them, the experience still gave me a bit of a shock.

There are over 900 road tunnels in Norway; in a country so mountainous it is an obvious engineering solution to overcome that very problem. Varying in length from a few hundred metres to almost 25 kilometres, some have a dark (no pun intended) history.

Henryk, my chiropractor, told me of his father's wartime experiences in Norway. How, as a 15-year-old youth in Poland, the Germans took him, and other fit and able young men, from their homeland to Norway to be used as forced labourers building these road tunnels. Another small example of how normal people were affected by that dreadful war.

And as I entered this, my first tunnel at a relatively modest speed, I was disorientated by the immediate contrast from the extremely bright sunshine outside and the inky blackness inside which was barely relieved by the appalling roof lighting.

I was further shaken by the sudden appearance of a huge truck, lights full on, that just happened at that precise moment to be coming the other way. After the bright sunshine outside and even with my own headlight and auxiliary side lights on, my eyesight had not made the necessary adjustment quickly enough for me to see safely and make safe assessment of the width of the tunnel on my side of the road and the bright headlights of the oncoming truck made it worse.

There was more room than I had first thought, but I confess I slowed dramatically and pulled over to the right as far as I dared, and in the dimness I could see there was also quite a nasty drop off the tarmac road edge. In short, it was not a forgiving environment for even a minor riding error.

As you read my exploits on this trip, you may note I am not often fazed by much when riding, but, I confess, I was a little unnerved by this experience. It was especially annoying as I hadn't seen a truck all day up to that point. This particular tunnel, I was to learn, was one of the older ones, possibly even built by German slave labour force. But it brought home very forcibly the need to be prepared when riding from extremely bright sunshine into one of these.

I had read somewhere in my research that the trick was to close one eye before you enter the tunnel. I tried it from here onwards and it helped a little but it was still an unsettling experience and it was one of the reasons I never rode with sunglasses on whilst in Norway. A few kilometres further on, I was better prepared for the next longer tunnel which descended downwards quite dramatically too.

At a nice little town called Odda I bore to the west of Sorfjorden and followed its shore on the 550 till I came to a rather spectacular waterfall tumbling off a mountainside. The area was obviously on the main tourist route, with many camper vans and tour buses in abundance.

I stopped for a comfort break, a coffee, and a rather splendid waffle served from a kiosk by friendly staff. Somehow though I was a bit confused. I was anticipating the next town would be Voss and widening the map screen the Sat Nav somehow had me on the wrong side of the fjord.

I brought my trusty paper map out and, after taking some time to actually pinpoint my location, realised that Emilie was taking me south west of Bergen which would involve ferry crossings. After further examining the map, I decided the route was so tortuous that it was going to consume too large a part of the day and as it was now past midday it didn't make sense for me to be a late arrival at my next accommodation.

So, reluctantly, I retraced my steps and rode back to Odda. With Rongen Farm now entered as my final destination for the day, Emilie had me skirting Sorfjorden again, but now correctly on the east side on road 13.

Road 13 did not prove to be very pleasant riding being very busy with lots of camper vans (they will be referred to as RVs from this point and, for those who may not know it, this means Recreational Vehicle) and caravans. And it became narrow, suddenly, without warning. I observed many skid marks where 2 vehicles had met at one of these points.

To further focus my attention, like the earlier road tunnel, at the road edges on both sides there was a very vehicle-unfriendly, sharp drop off of about 6 inches from the tarmac bounded by either an Armco barrier, on the fjord side, or, on the single lane sections, a rock face on the other.

To stray off the road edge on a bike would prove very costly and, if you were unlucky enough to be forced there, I doubted you would escape without serious machine damage or indeed injury. At one point, the driver of an oncoming red Ford van tried to steal my road space a little too much, but I did not let him force me into an erroneous reaction and squeezed by him without undue drama. But it concentrated my thoughts about the unforgiving nature of this road.

It wasn't long before I was at the tail of a road train of 5 vehicles behind a very slowly driven car towing a caravan. Fortunately, there was an all-new stretch of road wider and absolutely clear so I just overtook the lot. As I approached the caravan, the towing car put on his left indicator and moved over a little to try to curtail me. I ignored him and was gone.

Technically, as this new stretch of road was in a 'road works' zone, my overtaking was illegal. I did not realise this until later, but even had I known to be honest I would have still done it. Why ride a motorcycle if you don't take advantage of its versatility?

In places the land at the edges of the fjord was very cultivated, with many orchards and lots of vendors selling fruit, and at the end of it I crossed over a beautiful bridge, but sadly there was nowhere safely for me to stop to take a picture.

Across and still on Road 13 approaching Voss, there were more tunnels, one being 7.5 kilometres long, modern with much better lighting, whilst yet another even had a traffic island in it. Turning onto the E16, the main route into Bergen, it was quite busy and so far in Norway I had not come across this much traffic, although compared to many congested roads in the UK it was nothing.

Thinking that it could have more speed detection (so far I hadn't seen any) and police I decided not to exceed the now rather frustrating 70 kph limit out of Voss. I noted a motorcycle slowly catching me and being the sometimes-competitive type the choice to keep him behind or let him pass was difficult.

I decided that lost pride was better than a speeding ticket and let him come by. It was Harley Davidson and as he passed I noted he had a pillion and that he didn't wave as motorcyclists normally do to each other. But then he was riding a Harley, which made him by association some aloof bad-biker type, who wouldn't stoop to acknowledge one of us lesser mortals riding an inferior machine.

If noise equated to horsepower, then Harleys would be the fastest bikes on the planet and they are not. Harley riders seem to like to use the noise of their bikes as some sort of weapon, certainly the noise of a big 'V twin' engine being blipped on open exhaust pipes by your car window can be intimidating, and it's meant to be, it's a 'don't mess with me I'm a bad ass' statement. It seems to me to also there are two types of Harley Davidson riders. The genuine 'outlaw style' biker gang riders (there are some Christian riding groups who fall into that category) and those who pretend to be. Since Harleys are quite an expensive bike to purchase, over the years I have seen many well-heeled middle-aged men growing stubble, donning their chaps and bandanas and strutting around their parked machines trying to look 'hard' and fooling absolutely no one. But actually that's okay for there is one thing I will say about Harley riders, they do use their bikes and they are fellow motorcyclists after all, even if they don't want to associate with the rest of us.

I sensed this rider was one of the latter group and, on the next twisty section of road, I decided to catch him up and stayed with him for a few kilometres just to prove I could. But my heart was not really into playing with some disaffected Hell's Angel, and eventually I let him burble away from me.

I stopped at a large parking area by a pretty lake and bought a large ice cream from the kiosk and sat to watch the world go by for a while. It would have been sensible if I had bought myself a meal, but I was not thinking about dinner at this point. I should have been!

Having decided that it was now too late to be riding into Bergen, I did not hurry from my lakeside sojourn. I looked at the map. I already knew from my internet research that to get to my overnight accommodation would involve a river crossing of some sort, but the map was not of sufficient detail to inform me how. As the river was very big, I was hoping it was not a ford of some sort.

Back on the bike with Emilie happily chirping away in my ear I was following the Vosso River on my right. After 26 kilometres, I knew this precisely as it formed the basis for a decision the following day, she indicated to turn off to my right. As I approached, I could not see the junction clearly as there was a wall and it was angled away obliquely with the small road dropping steeply to the river valley.

As, of course, I was riding on the right side of the road I deliberately rode past the turning so I could assess it more accurately (to avoid a situation where I might have to stop and dance the bike around to exit). Actually, I could have turned into it without too much issue but stopping to assess it was not really safe. Given that, and with the E16 being quite busy, I tried to be conscious that my indecision could confuse other road users and put myself at risk.

About a kilometre further on, I had enough room to turn the bike around safely and approaching it from the left meant I could see it clearly enough to just ride down it which I did. It was indeed quite steep and I could see a narrow bridge across the river which came as some relief. The track off it up to my destination was gravelled and deep in places and, once again, this caused difficulty in turning the bike around and parking it.

At Rongen Farm, I knocked on the door of the main house and was greeted by Astrid, a friendly Norwegian lady, in her 70s I would have thought. She gave me the keys to my overnight stay which was a fisherman's lodge.

She asked me if I had brought any food to cook, which of course I hadn't because I had completely forgotten that this was self-catering accommodation. I admitted this to her. 'Well,' she said, 'if you are desperately hungry, there are some rice cakes in the cupboard and a jar of strawberry jam in the fridge.' It would have to do.

The lodge was immaculate and laid out in typical Scandinavian style for which read 'lots of pine'. I had a huge bunk bed, washing and cooking facilities and a fabulous view over the Vosso River flanked by distant peaks. It was peaceful and it was beautiful. I decided to move my bike to firmer ground nearer the lodge itself where I was more confident about safely extracting my luggage from the side cases.

Did I tell you I hate parking on gravel? I think I may have! As I settled into my new surroundings, there was a knock at the door and an elderly man stood there with an outstretched hand. He told me his name was Torsten, Astrid's husband. A friendly man, we talked for quite a while. He told me he worked at the UN for many years as a representative for the trade unions of Norway.

As an angler, I knew the Vosso River was famous for its salmon fishing, and also that the fish that ran this river were often very big indeed so I asked him about it. Torsten told me the biggest fish caught last season was 45lbs in weight. I asked him about the fishing this season.

'It is a disaster, there is no fishing at all at present,' he said. 'The river is too low and the water temperature is too high,' and added, 'the authorities have shut it to all fishing for the moment and July is normally the height of our season. All the salmon are still in the fjord waiting for their time to run, it is just not right.' (Ah, and there was me hoping I might have hired a rod to fish for an hour or two).

He went on to tell me of the environmental concerns he had over this and the other Norwegian rivers, and of the many fish farms in the fjords overrun with sea lice, a natural parasite whose population explodes due to the intensive fish farming methods.

'They get into the gills and kill many of the outgoing smolts,' he said. A smolt is a juvenile salmon running to the sea for the very first time and naturally, if they are being killed in high numbers, this does not bode well for future generations of fish returning to the river to spawn. I know this is a fact because there are also massive concerns over the issue in Scotland.

'They found a high concentration of aluminium in the fjord, but nobody knows where it has come from or what has caused it,' he added, 'and there are big problems in the Atlantic for the salmon too,' but he did not specify what they were, and I suspected overfishing from netting.

The wild Atlantic salmon, the 'king of fishes,' is sadly under serious threat. It is not only the over-fishing at sea, but the siting of the fish farms, often in sea lochs, or as in Norway, fjords, directly on the migration route of outgoing and returning wild salmon.

The pro-fish farming lobby is strong and well organised, effective in its marketing of the benefits to local economies and jobs, playing down with some effectiveness the fears of the environmentalists. But over the years, I have read enough to convince me that fish farms are incredibly damaging to the environment.

Just consider this for a moment. The sea lice mentioned earlier are ineffectively controlled in the farms by the use of chemicals. I am no expert, but it seems to me that water borne pesticides, for in effect that is what they, are historically bad for marine and human life alike.

The genetic purity of the genuinely wild fish is also being compromised by inferior force-bred farmed salmon which have escaped to spawn with the wild fish weakening the strain. Farmed salmon is big business in Scotland and Norway and, as ever, it seems to me that money overrides the obvious environmental issues. I would rather not eat a farmed salmon, but a wild caught fish would be very expensive now.

As one who does care about such matters, I found it was quite a dispiriting conversation especially as I held Norway in high regard regarding its environmental policies. We discussed my trip and Torsten graciously took one of my cards and said he would support my challenge.

My evening feast was rice cakes and strawberry jam washed down with water and half a packet of Haribo sweets. As I could not go fishing, I walked the banks of this iconic Norwegian river for an hour or so and looked intently into the crystal-clear waters for any signs of fish; there were none.

At 21:30, I sat in the huge lodge window and watched the light slowly fade into a kind of twilight. As I have said, it does not go dark, as I was too far north for that at this time of year. But I found myself quite unsettled, not exactly homesick, but concerned about the vast riding distance to Hammerfest I had yet to cover. At times, I had not enjoyed today's riding so much as the roads were not very nice in places and quite busy.

I woke at 03:45 sweating profusely with a raging thirst; I think the sweets consumed had a very high salt content. My back was also nagging at me. I did not sleep very well.


**Day 9 – Sunday** 15<sup>th</sup> July 2018. Rongen Farm, Bolstadoyri to Lom. Leaving time – 08:00; temperature range – 19°C to 31°C; distance ridden – 287 kilometres;

I had a special treat for breakfast this morning, rice cakes and jam. As I loaded my bike in the tranquillity of this stunning Norwegian location, Torsten came out to bid me farewell; he's a fine man and I liked him a lot. Food apart, I had loved staying here and wished I could have stayed a few days more.

I would love to return one day for a longer holiday. I had planned routes for a little sight-seeing over the next few days and wondered if I was cutting into the challenge ride too much by doing so.

Because of my somewhat confused day yesterday my route to Rongen had become a spur rather than a looped route via Bergen as I had originally planned, so I was retracing my ride back to Voss to pick up on my route north. I was 26 kilometres on and back at the lakeside stop trying to find a breakfast (the kiosk was closed) when I realised that I had left my posh gel water bottle, the one which Liz had bought me, in the kitchen back at Rongen.

I seriously contemplated going back for it, but was concerned, with an unknown day of riding ahead, that a round trip of some extra 50 kilometres would take too much out of the day. This was not a good start. It didn't get much better when I stopped at a large filling station in Voss.

It had a large café area, which was empty, yet promised much with one of those over-counter menus showing pictures of the fare on offer. Most of the meals had a sausage of some sort in them. The woman who took my order at the large counter had no English, which thus far in Norway, I found unusual.

By a system of pointing and thumbs up we arrived at an agreement on what I wanted. She grunted at me and pointed to a small screen above the cash desk which should have been displaying the price but was totally blank, much like the look I must have given her. I shrugged my shoulders and she pointed again to the screen, a little more aggressively the second time.

I looked straight at her and held my hands up in a gesture of helplessness. I think she thought I was being awkward, so in an act of annoyance she swivelled the screen toward herself and her assistant, who had wandered across no doubt to help her deal with this wayward foreigner.

When they saw it was blank, there was much discussion in Norwegian (I think) and then suddenly, they were quite apologetic as they realised I was not in fact being troublesome. They indicated to me to pay at another desk.

When the meal arrived, it was pretty dreadful but because I was hungry, really hungry, I ate most of it. Had I known quite how bad the food was going to be, I would have walked out or, rather more accurately, I would not have walked in. I bought a small bottle of water; once emptied, this bottle would be refilled and it would serve as a very cheap replacement for the expensive one I left behind at Rongen earlier.

I sat sipping my coffee afterwards feeling quite low. My night's rest had not been good, my day had started badly in more than one way, and I was sensing it did not bode well for the rest of it. I could not have been more wrong. What followed was to be one of the best day's riding I have ever had on a motorcycle.

From Voss, I followed the E16 north for a while and kept to the expected 80 kph and then turned left onto road 13 again. But unlike the 13 south of Voss, here it was simply a rider's dream, a brilliant grippy road surface, no potholes and bend after beautiful bend, taken in bright sunshine with stunning backdrops and, being a Sunday, there was virtually no traffic on it at all.

The 80 kph limit just went out of the window; I rode the 13 north as it was meant to be ridden with enthusiasm and gusto and if a speeding ticket was to be the outcome, well so be it. My bike has 2 riding modes 'sport' and 'touring' either of which can be engaged easily on the move via a switch on the left handlebar. If ever a road was 'sports' mode territory it was this one, but I found it made the throttle responses just too snatchy and unpleasant so it was discontinued.

You can smell the mountain sections way before you get to them (in a car you wouldn't) from the unmistakable scent of over-heating brakes. I stopped before the first true mountain pass and watched the few vehicles on it snaking their way up and down.

This was a much steeper section of road than I had experienced so far and, as I approached the first of a series of hairpin bends, I downshifted to second gear but found it a little too high for the steepness and the acuteness of the inclines so I balanced the throttle openings with the clutch to smooth the whole thing out.

As the hairpins became ever steeper I found that first gear was more suitable for the rest. Even so one had to be mindful not to feed in too much power coming out of these corners because when leant over on a steep camber in first gear it would be very easy to give too much gas and have the back end step out on you as a result.

At the top of my first true mountain road I stopped at a viewpoint, once again stunned by the beauty of the scenes before me stretching in every direction. For the first and only time on the trip I entered the car park on the wrong side of the gravel entrance, causing the driver of an exiting RV to give me, quite rightly, a hard look.

There were 3 motorcyclists riding high power sports-bikes that were just about to leave the car park. I nodded as I rode in but they ignored me completely, and as I have said, this is really quite unusual amongst true motorcyclists. All the way through Europe approaching motorcyclists waved to you, sometimes being a bit of a distraction because there could be a lot of them on some sections of road. I responded in kind as we are, after all, kindred spirits bonded by our unique way of travelling. But, as in all walks of life, there are also the poseurs with 'all the gear and no idea' which, unkindly perhaps, is what I thought this trio might be. I was trying not to be judgemental but their lack of friendliness was a bit of a clue.

In a spun-up cloud of dust they were gone, their noisy expensive after-market silencers giving me an aural clue as to the nature of the road ahead. No long straights obviously.

I followed on about 10 minutes later and the road started to drop off the mountain into a lovely Norwegian village, Viksoyri, dominated by a large church, which seemed eerily deserted. Very shortly afterwards, the road ended abruptly at large quayside and ferry docking point.

Sognefjorden, my very first fjord crossing. Here, I was faced with 2 choices of ferry destinations and check carefully that Hella, not Dragsvik, was the one that I wanted. Of course, Emilie had sort of indicated it, but I did not quite trust her so I doubled-checked on my map. As I did so, the 3 Sunday riders pulled in behind me which was a surprise, perhaps having stopped for a coffee, or fuel, in the last village. They did not make any attempt to engage with me.

As we waited for the ferry it started to become uncomfortably hot on the quayside and, being concrete, the glare became savage on the eyes too. I walked over to a large information sign printed in four languages, saying that Sognefjord is a UNESCO World Heritage Site, the longest fjord in Norway, has the highest surrounding mountains and the biggest glacier (there were 6 of these in total) and it also had 6 waterfalls pouring into it.

I wondered naively if any of these might have dried up in this heat wave. I looked into the clear depths along the quayside; it was clearly a very deep fjord too. Fjord ferries, I was to learn, are heavily subsidised because they are an essential part of linking the road networks so I was pleasantly surprised at the modest charge they made for the crossing.

I was first to board the ferry for Helle, the other 3 motorcyclists following on behind the few cars that were also crossing. I made my way to the upper deck and relaxed in the sunshine; naturally the scenery we were passing through was incomparable, and I was once again enthralled by it. I looked down and noticed one of the other riders slowly sauntering over to inspect my bike.

I wasn't sure if it was acknowledgement or disdain as he gently tapped my rear tyre with the toe of his boot; certainly my rear tyre, scuffed right to the edges, would perhaps be indicating something to him. Their bikes were 4-cylinder high performance models and one, a BMW S1000RR, was brand new. They were all wearing top of the range riding clothing, Alpine Stars leathers Arai helmets and such and had expensive but unscuffed boots.

By comparison my bike and I looked a little dull, lived in and dusty. I assumed they were Norwegian riders and I was again a little disappointed they did not speak to me on the ferry, but as so often in life, the effort has to come from you sometimes and not them. I confess I am at times quite a shy man, so I do not judge them too harshly, but they never once said hello or held a hand up in friendship.

At Helle, I was first off the ferry and I heard the cacophony of revving bikes behind me as I rode off the ramp. I anticipated they would soon be past the couple of vehicles in front of them and then were going to give me a hard time on what proved to be a very tight, twisty and challenging road along the fjord side to Sognal, much more suited to their kind of motorcycle than mine.

So, buoyed up by my wonderful ride from Vosso earlier, I decided to go for it and make catching me a bit of a challenge for them. They were, after all, riding much faster bikes and were wearing all the right gear and they were clearly 'day out' and not visiting touring riders so, unlike me, I suspected they would know this particular stretch of road and soon catch and pass me.

Apart from a brief glimpse of their headlights in my mirrors early on, 36 kilometres later at my turn off point there was not a sign of them, and my initial assessment of them in the car park was probably correct. I reflected afterwards what they must have thought of the old mad guy riding a lardy Yamaha traillie, festooned with peculiar stickers, who had left their posh super-bikes for dead. I shall never know. However, the situation was to be reversed on me a few hours later.

Route 55 from Sognal to Lom (my destination for the day) includes the Sognefjell mountain pass, which, I was to discover later, is classed as a 'dangerous road' and rises to 1,437 metres (4,712 feet), the highest in Europe. At the time I did not know this, having chosen the most direct route to Lom along an innocuous looking grey ribbon of road on my map without realising then its fearsome reputation.

The first section of the 55 is comparatively gentle and skirts a fjord, but once again, it was along another simply stunning section of eminently ride-able Norwegian road.

With its superb bakery and café, the little village of Luster promised a welcome relief from the heat (for by now it was torrid) and, judging by the fullness of their car park for a Sunday afternoon, business was doing well. As I stood in the queue waiting to be served, I was looking at a mouth-watering selection of pastries on the serving counter and had mentally made my selection.

In front of me, a large blonde woman was being served and I watched in utter disbelief as almost all the pastries on the counter are swept into 4 large brown paper bags. I ordered a coffee and the lone cinnamon bun, which was pretty much all she had left behind, and sat at a table inside, munching it in sullen silence.

After my appalling breakfast, something I had really fancied eating ended up in someone else's bag! Through the window I enviously watched her outside distributing her booty to a group of equally large adults, all of whom looked as if fewer visits to the bakery might be the healthier option for them. It is not easy to exercise grace sometimes.

Shortly afterwards, back on the 'grey ribbon' soaking up the riding and the unrivalled scenery, my riding enjoyment was marred by an incident that gave me another opportunity to exercise my waning skills in the art of being gracious – but one which I failed.

Legend has it that Norway has bridge trolls and I was to meet one head on. Dropping down into a steep valley the road narrowed to a long river bridge which was wide enough for just one vehicle. I watched in total amazement as the driver of a very large RV comes down the hill opposite and straight onto the bridge which, I should add, already had me three quarters of the way across it.

I was forced to stop and for an anxious second or two feared he might not! I breathed a sigh of relief when he did, a car's length or so short of me. I will be kind and say he possibly hadn't seen me initially but if so, with my headlights and auxiliary lights on and positioned smack in the centre of the bridge, his powers of observation were somewhat lacking wouldn't you say.

On the other hand, perhaps he was just trying to bully me to move aside, in which case, where exactly he was expecting me to go can only be speculated on. You may have picked up by now, I am not easily intimidated. I looked up at him towering above me and slowly shook my head but he had his gaze fixed firmly ahead and, not for the first time today, I was totally ignored, as if I was not there.

A spectator might have been struck with the comical absurdity of the unequal David and Goliath stand-off. He, in his mobile block of flats versus vulnerable little me, on my puny two-wheeler. I thought of being awkward by forcing him to reverse but decided on this occasion to allow him to win. However, I was not going to get off the bike and walk it backwards along the bridge for him and I was certainly not going to try to do a multi-point turn.

I calculated that if I pulled over hard to the very edge of the bridge tight against the fence there was just about enough room for him to squeeze past me. It was really the narrowest of gaps and I did not make a big thing of it but as he slowly edged past, I think he must have sensed what I thought of his bad driving.

He did not even give me a thank you wave, at which I gave him a tut. I was more resigned than angry because my riding had been too pleasurable to allow a rude and unthinking road user to spoil it. I sensed the other bridge trolls were sniggering as I rode up the valley the other side.

Shortly afterwards, the 55 became the Sognefjell mountain pass proper and it was more steep climbs and hairpins. I was starting to feel a little tired now and treated them with perhaps undue caution for at that moment a BMW rider (unmistakable 'boxer' engine) slipped past me. I tailed him for a while, very impressed with both his riding ability and his obvious knowledge of this road.

However his riding pal could not get by me so easily and I split them for a few kilometres but, on one hairpin in desperation with his knee down and on a wider line, he did. Respect. These were technically two very good riders, certainly not part of the group of three from earlier, and I sensed this was a regular run for them and who could blame them, for it was clear these boys knew this road intimately.

Their pace was hot but for the sheer fun of it I stayed with them over the next open section of road as my bike was as quick as theirs, until the next staircase of steep upward hairpins that is. Then, with my jaw dropping, I watched them as they made a series of late insane overtakes on cars whilst approaching blind corners.

Clearly these were riders with physic powers, there was no way some of the overtakes witnessed were safe, and in fact, as I noted in my journal for that day, I felt they were just suicidal. I was not going to emulate it just to prove I could keep up with them. I slowed up, relaxed and let them go, accepting I had just met my match.

The ride across the mountain plateau, stopping from time to time to take in the distant glaciers and related scenery, was almost beyond description in its beauty, and as the road dropped down off the other side I followed a series of fast flowing turquoise coloured snow melt-rivers.

Cascading down a neighbouring mountain a high white waterfall was falling through the forested slopes into one. I began to run out of superlatives for the beauty of the Norway scenery. I thanked God for the privilege of seeing it.

Arriving at the Fossheim hotel in Lom, I was brought back down to earth a little with practicalities like where to park the bike securely. There were other motorcyclists here, not our errant riders from earlier I noted, but serious touring riders like me, mostly on BMW GSs and a lone Honda XL1000V (I had a number of these as Company demonstrators back in the day – a good bike).

I would rather my bike was not obvious from the road but the car park was quite steep further back, making parking more of a challenge, so I decided to park where they were. They had every security device known to man on their motorcycles, I had none, but at least there might be safety in numbers, I thought.

The young woman at the reception desk was on the phone. Even given the language was Norwegian from the tonal inflections, it was very obviously a private call and she made me, and another customer, wait a good few minutes before she decided to terminate the conversation.

This was my most expensive accommodation of the trip and, so far, first impressions were not good. I have spent most of my working life advising businesses on the value of good customer service and this was not a good example and it annoyed me a little. She must have realised for, as she checked me in and handed me my keys, it was with a smiley charm offensive and, I confess, it worked.

I opened the door to my room and was immediately disappointed. From my notes, I described the room as '*tiny, like a monk's cell, and very hot, facing the sun.*' It did not offer much by way of luxury either, especially for the price charged. However, it was front-facing which pleased me as I could see my bike.

Lom is a very popular tourist destination. There are few hotels there so market forces dictate the prices; essentially you pay five-star prices for three-star accommodation and have to accept it. I showered and went for a walk in this rather pretty bustling town.

A glacial melt river was crashing in full flow just off the centre and was powerfully beautiful of course, but you certainly would not want to accidentally fall in. I found an excellent little supermarket with friendly staff and bought my provisions for the next day.

I began to start thinking about presents to take home with me and back at the hotel there was a museum and a shop selling fossils, jewellery and rocks, for which the area is famous I later learnt. I never actually made the museum.

The shop assistant, and I use the term loosely, was a woman who must have been in her eighties (do not jump to conclusions here, this is not about ageism) and was in full sales flow with a lady customer who bought nothing.

It was not long before she diverted her attention to me and started her pitch again in Norwegian. I smiled and gently pointed out that I was English at which she switched language and went into some half-hearted sales spiel about the famous Norway stone, the notoriety of which had clearly escaped me.

Then, and I can scarcely believe it even now, she abruptly and rudely informed me to hurry up because she wanted to close. Turning on her heel with a dramatic flourish that would not have been out of place in some gothic theatrical production, she disappeared behind a black curtain into the museum section, where presumably her supper, a bowl of congealing blood perhaps, was waiting. Needless to say, I obliged with her wishes and closed the door rather firmly just to make a point.

I went to reception to inquire about hotel laundry amenities and once again I was made to wait, for a longer period this time, because the receptionist was engaged in another nice private phone conversation with her kids, it seemed. Given my experience earlier, and at the shop, I found this casual attitude to paying customers really quite surprising and I did not come across it anywhere else in Scandinavia.

After what seemed an age, she finished and, sensing my irritation again, gave me her full Norwegian smile, but it didn't work a second time. She received 'the look' which she totally ignored and informed me sweetly that they had no laundry facility. In many ways, this hotel seemed typical of a business that, having an ever-uninterrupted pool of customers, had forgotten the value of something fundamentally important…them!

It was as if they felt they didn't really have to try anymore. Back in the room I hand-washed my smalls then, like a Brexit protester's flag in front of Westminster, I hung them out of the window to dry in a small act of protest.

People walking by or in passing vehicles I hoped would have noticed and smiled perhaps.

The service in the restaurant, by contrast, was superb and at least in this regard, I was not to be disappointed. The prices were very expensive but, at this halfway point of my challenge, this particular hotel and this meal was my treat to myself, so I ordered the highly recommended klippfisk cod special and paid over £10.00 for a glass of Heineken.

Johanna, my waitress (she looked like a young Doris Day and that statement clearly dates me) told me she was Swedish and she was working in Norway because there were more opportunities for her. I gave her my challenge post-card and she couldn't quite grasp the enormity of what I was doing. She kept looking at it and then at me, but perhaps she was thinking I was quite mad. I couldn't really blame her.

If a hotel was really busy, as the Fossheim was, I would pay for my room and extras the night before to avoid the inevitable check out queues at the desk in the morning. It is a habit I acquired after years of working away from home. It meant next day you could just drop your key and go as early as you liked.

The receptionist who, for once, was not engaged in a private phone call told me, 'You are wise to be away early tomorrow.' 'Oh, why?' I asked. 'Well, the cruise ships came into the fjord last night, there will be tour buses and people everywhere.' 'What time?' I asked. 'It will start here around 11:00,' she said. It was my intention to be long gone by then.

Around 22:00 I went to bed, it was still bright daylight outside and in spite of my failure to be more gracious than I ought to have been today, I slept very well.

**Day 10 – Monday** 16th July 2018. Lom to Malvik (north of Trondheim). Leaving time – 07:15; temperature range – 16°C to 28°C; distance ridden – 528 kilometres.

I woke up fully refreshed and ready to go and fortunately remembered to retrieve my washing; it was still a little damp but it would dry on my journey. No, I did not string it out behind the bike (I did think of it at one point) but lovingly placed it inside the top of my luggage bag. At 06:45 I was first down to breakfast and, whilst expensive it may have been, it was excellent and I felt well set up for the day ahead.

I fuelled the bike up in Lom itself and, to my surprise, there was a Triumph motorcycle with UK number plates opposite and I exchanged greetings with the guy as he mounted his bike. Looking at the stickers on it, he was clearly ex-military and I wondered what adventure he was on. He rode off the way I had come in yesterday, so I will never know.

Today was deliberately to be a day of sightseeing, albeit in an ever-northerly direction. I had carefully woven a route to take in the 3 things I really wanted to see and experience in Norway, Geiranger Fjord, the Trollstiggen mountain pass and the Atlantic Road. I did not, however, refer to my map this morning trusting in Emilie to guide me to the points I had programmed in; it threw up a couple of surprises.

The first surprise came as I rode out of Lom towards Geiranger following what I thought was the fjord the receptionist was referring to. There were, of course, many Norwegian fjords that did indeed stretch far inland and I thought this perhaps was one of them. A quick check of the map would have told me it was, in fact, a very long narrow and deep lake, Vagavatn.

I mean, it could have been a fjord. In fairness to myself, it was early and I was enjoying my ride and not really thinking it through. I rode along the lake road looking for the cruise ships, but eventually it narrows and shallows into reed beds and I realised my mistake and laughed out loud about it.

Of course! She meant Geiranger Fjord, the place I was riding to. And the ride itself was just fabulous, 75 kilometres (I checked as I went past it) before I overtook my first car. Can you believe that? Where in the UK would that be possible anywhere at any time of the morning?

I stopped at a viewpoint and was blown away by the sheer splendour of the scene before me. A distant snow specked corrie above an icy blue tarn from which crystal clear streams ran into another small glassy lake.

As I rode back onto the road, I noted a fast-approaching Audi and, as I really did not want him in front of me, I accelerated hard to stay ahead. I did not cause him any bother and he settled in behind me some fifty yards or so back. Soon, I could smell burning brakes again, so I knew exactly what was ahead.

The ensuing mountain section of road, where the Audi driver tried to push me a little, brought me to a spur road leading up to the Geiranger viewing point which I knew I just had to take. I chatted with the young man in the toll booth. We talked of the beautiful day.

'It is crazy here some days though,' he told me, 'the winds can get so strong that you think the toll booth is going to be blown down the mountain.' It never occurred to me, but of course he was right; it was a high and very exposed place. The road up to the viewing point was a challenge in itself, the steepest yet ridden.

I met a tour bus making its way down on one of the very tight hairpins and it proved a lesson to me. Buses need a lot of swing out room on these corners and I did not quite allow for this. Not the driver's fault; mine for not anticipating it. It was awkward for a second or two but I did have enough room to get out of his way and noted it for the future.

At the top, I was amazed how many vehicles there were up there already. As none of this crowd had been on the road from Lom it was obvious they had all come up from Geiranger and there were quite a number of tour buses amongst the throng of people there. It was a taste of what awaited me.

The view down to the fjord was, well, have I used this word before? Spectacular! I wanted particularly to see Geiranger fjord because my research told me it was breath-taking and there can be little argument in that regard. It was a deep and narrow fjord cutting far inland, surrounded by the steepest of hillsides with waterfalls cascading from them.

There were two cruise ships in the fjord and, from this height, they looked like little toy white boats bobbing about in a play pool. But I noted two things that were to take the shine off my delight. The first was the pall of diesel fumes from these two ships that was actually filling the valley of the fjord. Clearly visible even from this distance and height, my pictures of the fjord were ruined because of it. The second was the train of 'match box' sized tour buses I could see making their way from the town of Geiranger up the mountain roads heading here, then ultimately for Lom. Time to move on, I thought.

The way down from the viewpoint was treated with respect; gravity apart, there were now many tour buses on the road up to the viewpoint. I was pleased to wave to my friend in the toll booth on the exit. The road zigzagged ever downwards to Geiranger and I was slowed very much by a blue Volvo estate car behind a tour bus heading perhaps to pick up passengers for the day from one of the ships.

The driver of this car tried to undertake the tour bus on the inside as it swung wide on one of the hairpins. Whether he thought the bus driver was pulling over for him to pass or not I don't know; what I do know is I was on the brakes immediately because I could see a crash unfolding right in front of me.

He was actually alongside the rear section of the bus before it dawned on him the bus had moved over to take the bend and was now moving back. Tyre smoke!

He was very fortunate indeed not to have been taken out; another few feet further on and the bus would have hit him and who knows where his vehicle might have ended up.

That was the really scary thing because the drop off on some of these corners, well, you can imagine. I decided to hold back away from this driver as we continued our slow and tortuous progress down.

About a kilometre out of Geiranger on the ever-steep descent down to the town itself there was a service area and, as I needed to use their facilities, I stopped. It was absolutely heaving with people and I felt the atmosphere there was quite tense. You had bus drivers trying to find a slot to park, car and RVs trying to make their way up, and tour buses trying making their way down to pick up points.

Tour guides with their little flags were leading groups both up and down. Perhaps there was some order to it but to me it seemed utter chaos. In Geiranger itself it was even worse. I was halted by a man in the road centre who proceeded to assist a huge bus in backing out. I looked down the side street; the bus was one of very many.

There were by now an amazing number of tourists milling about and it was just not very pleasant to be there with cars, RVs, cyclists, walkers and a lone Englishman on a motorcycle trying to find his place through the mayhem.

I had planned to stop for a coffee in Geiranger but had no idea it would be like this. It was just too stupidly busy. But what a magnificent setting and I was so sad not to be able to appreciate it more fully.

If you zigzag down then guess what? Going up and out of the village was no different. I stopped at a viewing point and miscalculated just how much camber there was on the parking area. As my bike went over onto the side stand much further than I liked, I groaned because I knew it was really going to be a struggle to get it upright which normally I would do astride the bike.

The bike was now too leaned-over to do this easily and safely and my concern was what might happen if I put too much effort into getting it upright and over balanced the bike the other way. I ignored it initially and took the customary pictures looking back down into the fjord but my heart was not really in it and once again I was absolutely surrounded by people from the descending tour buses.

I manage to indicate to a very kind man, who I think was Spanish, that I needed just a little help to get the bike upright and he was delighted to help me. The day had, by now, also become tiresomely hot.

Following route 63 out of Geiranger soon had me descending again down to Storfjorden fjord ferry and, once across, I was climbing again towards the Trollstiggen (Troll's Ladder) Pass which is another trans-mountain route. I had read much about it; only open in the summer months it has an incline of 1.12 with 11 hairpins bends.

I even watched a YouTube video of the pass which, taken from a car window on an inclement day, made it look much worse than it proved to be. As I said, I had not consulted my map that morning and, as I rode across the mountain plateau and past the huge car park there, rangers waved me through.

I realised they were controlling the number of vehicles accessing the pass and they were using drones to assess the traffic flow. My imagination of riding the Trollstiggen for months had been that I would be riding up it; however, a few hundred metres on I was a bit bemused to suddenly realise I was going down the pass and for the second time today, and I laughed at my silly mistake.

But it did not disappoint and in fact proved to be a very good thing indeed. I stopped half way down and I do not think I have ever seen a more incredible view ahead anywhere in the world. Calling it a valley would be rather like calling the Grand Canyon a gully; it was on a scale quite unlike anything I have ever seen, so vast and so far-reaching.

I was just by the Stigfossen falls, a powerful waterfall crashing off the mountain side and under the road which was very atmospheric, and the clarity of day just made it perfect. I was so grateful. I wondered how many days the views would have been as good as this; not very many I think.

The rangers were relaxed with my presence. On a bike, I had enough room to park in the small stopping area and was not in the way, but they were waving other vehicles on once it filled up.

Dropping down the pass, I met the inevitable tour bus coming up on a tight bend of course, but this time I had anticipated it and the driver gave me a friendly wave as I stopped to allow him to swing around. I did not see any trolls, but they may have been lurking nearby.

I rode down into a small town called Andalsnes, another place with a fine setting under towering peaks and, after passing through a long and cooling tunnel, I followed the shores of Romsdalsfjorden turning right off the E39 and another ferry crossing (Moldefjorden) to Molde. This one proved to be a longer crossing and it was uncomfortably hot on the ferry, but I was tired and I dozed whilst leaning against my bike.

From Molde, I rode towards Kristiansund, where I was meant to be stopping overnight, ensuring that I took in the famous Atlantic Highway (Atlanterhavsvegen) on the way. It was supposed to be one of the defining moments of the trip, the road everyone who visits Norway wants to drive or ride.

It is indeed an incredible piece of highway engineering. For just 8 kilometres along the coast, indented with numerous inlets and rocky promontories, riding twisting causeways and over one particular and wonderfully steeply arched bridge, on a road that at times is just metres above the sea itself.

I had seen videos of people driving it in a storm which made it look simply exhilarating, but today it was flat calm. I was frustrated also because I really wanted to stop to take a picture of that iconic bridge but there was nowhere I could stop, well not safely anyway.

Maybe because the sea was so benign or perhaps because I was over-tired, I was just a little bit underwhelmed by it to be honest. Also, I did wonder if I was on sensory overload after all I had seen over the last few days.

Kristiansund, a town of some 24,000 residents and built around 4 islands, was busy when I arrived with lots of traffic on the roads. I noted a large harbour and lots of small industrial sites, parts of it reminding me very much of Plymouth.

Emilie was busy guiding me to my overnight accommodation booked and paid for in advance via Airbnb. As I arrived in the area, and eventually the street where I was supposed to be staying, alarm bells were ringing in my head.

What I had not checked in advance was the parking situation for the bike and it was clear this area was on-road parking only. It also appeared that my accommodation was in a second-floor apartment. Stupid, stupid, stupid! I should have researched this with more care; the whole area had a kind of run down look about it that made me feel uneasy.

I stopped astride the bike, leaving it running to further assess the situation. As I did so, a hoodie with his mate in tow rode up to me on BMX bikes two sizes too small for them. Clearly he had noted the UK number plate and greeted me with a 'Welcome to Norway.' He was a young man, in his 20s I guessed, and having worked as a volunteer in a drugs rehab for four years I had the mark of him, that gaunt haunted look of the addict.

I thanked him but managed to appear so distracted looking down at my phone there was no further dialogue; afterwards I felt a little guilty about it. Actually, I was fretting and their sudden appearance did not help. I rode around the corner and sent my host Anne an e-mail from my phone (isn't modern IT just wonderful?).

I told her that my travel plans had changed and I was making my way directly instead to Trondheim for an overnight stay. She'd been paid anyway, so for her it was an easy earner. There was no way I was going to risk an unsecured, or even secured motorcycle, overnight parked on the streets in this neighbourhood.

As it was by now too late to secure a refund I decided I would rather take the hit financially than jeopardise the challenge by a bad accommodation decision and a missing motorcycle.

So, wearily, I made my way back through the town the way I had come in. I had already ridden over 300 kilometres this day and the route had been challenging at times and I was not now as euphoric over the day's riding as I ought to have been. I picked up the E39 going north to Trondheim, it was now early evening, I had the complication of having nowhere to stay overnight, but I was ever trusting.

Soon I was facing another ferry crossing, the third today, and I had become very fatigued. Looking at the map now post-trip, I am amazed I took on that ride up from Kristiansund to Trondheim so late in the day. Apart from a indistinct recollection of the ferry and a huge traffic island close to Trondheim itself, I do not have anything other than a vague recollection of riding that road. I just kept on going. I think I must have been like some motorcycling automaton and it chills me to write of it now. Later on, checking Google maps, I was shocked to find I rode 211 kilometres that evening from south of Kristiansund to the hotel. Obviously I was riding safely, but not to remember it? That concerns me somewhat.

I do remember that I did not want to ride into the city traffic to find a hotel so joined the E6 north and, once past the city area, I stopped and did a Sat Nav search for a hotel, one which I hoped would be close to the highway. There was one, a 'Best Western' hotel at a place called Stav, just north of the airport.

As I pulled into an almost empty hotel car park there were a few motorcycles parked, a very good sign. However, the car park itself was on the opposite side of the dual carriageway from the hotel and accessed via a pedestrian bridge which gave immediate concerns about bike security.

I parked next to the other bikes and pretended to secure my bike with the faulty disc lock. Thankfully the hotel did have a room available. The young man on reception could not believe I had ridden all the way from the UK (just at that moment, I couldn't quite believe I had just ridden all the way from Kristiansund) and he was very kind to me, not only giving me a reduced room rate, but also finding me some hot food, even though the restaurant was shut. Provision.

I used the time before sleeping to try 'Booking.Com' for accommodation for the next night in Mo I Rana and I found a reasonably priced hotel, but there was to be a slight sting in the tail here also as we shall see. Having completed my excessively busy riding day I had no problems in falling into a deep sleep.

My publicity picture. It could have been worse but let's be honest, it still looked more Shropshire than Scandinavia.

Day of departure 7 July 2018. Over-dressed, over-geared and over awed.

Tim and Catherine Wilson, Great Chart. Kindness personified.

Day 1 in Europe and the heat was already kicking in.
Trying to cool off near Antwerp

Relaxing with my ex-Honda buddies, Franklin and Eddie. Sadly, it would prove to be the last time I would see Franklin.

Norway, dramatically and wonderfully different.

Forest fires off the E9, a day that so easily could have spelt disaster.

Trollstiggen Pass, beware of the tourist buses!

Gateway to the North

The Arctic Circle. It didn't feel this celebratory if I'm honest

Hammerfest. Technically the challenge completed

Some have unkindly said I look hung-over in this shot. No, I was just knackered

Nordkapp, the northernmost point in Europe. A hauntingly beautiful place

Goodbye to Hammerfest – a town that had captured my heart

My commemoration left at the parish church of Hammerfest

My reindeer friends had gathered to bid me farewell

Coming home – the tundra road to Alta just after seeing the wolf.

Finland and the Arctic Circle crossing coming back

Home, 27 July some 18 days and 5,907 miles later

# Chapter 8
# North Norway and the Arctic –
# the Serious Stuff


*'Our brothers and sisters around the world are supporting us, and also the most important thing: Jesus is with us.'* – **Father Daniel who is serving Christian refugees in Iraq**.


**Day 11 – Tuesday** 17th July 2018. Stav to Mo I Rana. Leaving time – 07:45; temperature range – 22°C to 34°C; distance ridden – 470 kilometres.

I looked out over a calm sea as I grazed on my breakfast cereal; the reflected sun was very strong making the water look almost mercury like, and quite painful on the eyes. Again, there was not a cloud in the sky and, as I was not anticipating riding at higher altitudes today, I sensed it was going to be very hot on the bike.

I walked in a rather ungainly fashion across the bridge, balancing luggage, crash helmet and the tank bag. I was relieved to see the bike was safe and sound. By making this extra trip to Trondheim and beyond, taking in the Atlantic Highway yesterday instead of today as originally planned, I had gained a day on my itinerary and was now making for the nearest Norwegian town to the Arctic Circle, Mo I Rana.

Initially, I started my day riding on a dual carriageway. I was now on the E6, the major Norwegian highway north, and it was not quiet. The next large town was a place called Steinkjer (which immediately in my mind became Stinkjet), with the normal commercial traffic being further swelled with tourist vehicles, most of them heading north it seemed.

Unlike yesterday, the scenery here could not be described as spectacular and I noted there was quite a lot of industry in this coastal plain north of the city; it was the first real evidence of this seen in Norway to date.

Reaching the end of the dual carriageway at Levanger, I was resigned now to the limitations of the 80 kph speed limit for a very long way. However, at Verdalsora, a few kilometres later, it dropped further to 70 kph for no obvious reason since it was not a particularly urban area.

I saw him immediately, there was a marked police VW van parked, not very inconspicuously, in a lay by ahead and, wouldn't you know it, he selected me as the vehicle he was going to tail, pulling out directly behind me. He had seen me approaching of course and riding a motorcycle naturally I was much more likely, in the eyes of the police, to be that potential speeding law breaker (me?).

If not, he was certainly intent on testing my patience, endurance and my ability to ride without committing some other traffic misdemeanour. I was certain also, with ANPR (Automatic Number Plate Recognition) systems now being commonplace throughout Europe, that he would have run a vehicle check on me because it is what the police do.

What followed was the most tedious riding of the Norway part of the trip because I swear this 70 kph limit stretched for 30 kilometres or more. Some 15 kilometres into it (I was seriously fed up by now) I was relieved to see the police van pulling into a police vehicle park, but my joy was short lived and there was no relief for me.

There was clearly a relay operation going on because he handed over to his mate in a marked Volvo who, ready and waiting, pulled out directly behind me to take over where he had left off.

They were playing games. From experience they know motorcyclists often tend to go faster than most other road users and, as such, are often flagged by the police as 'people of interest.'

It used to be so in the UK too. I lost count of how many times over the years I was followed or occasionally stopped by the police when riding. These were the days before successive Home Secretaries slashed police numbers and budgets so drastically, rendering UK roads policing all but redundant.

I know a little about the police, not from any criminal activity I might add, but operationally having been involved with supplying them with motorcycles over many years. However, being a vehicle supplier to the police can be fraught with difficulties, particularly if there was ever a suspected product issue, which as you now know, sadly in my final years at Honda we were having to defend.

I have some sympathy for the role of the police and know what a difficult and thankless job they have at times. I know only too well the effect the years of austerity have had on police morale and their operational ability in the UK. The legacy of cut backs and under spending continues and all aspects of efficient policing in the UK have been affected by it, especially road policing.

But in Norway, there were no such issues; they had an operational roads traffic operation going on and I was the focus of it. Was I pleased that the Norwegian police had the resources to actually conduct targeted road policing? No, just at that particular moment in time, I wasn't.

I felt they should be elsewhere doing far more important things with their time and resources than just sitting pointlessly on my tail. If they thought I was going to risk making progress away from them and picking up a ticket they were going to be very disappointed. My bike had cruise control and it was firmly set at 70 kph. I tried to relax but it was intimidating, annoying and wearisome.

After Steinkjer the police vehicle, along with the 70 kph limit, just seemed to evaporate, but the event had rattled me. I would rather not be on the E6 at all but, after my sightseeing days, I was now resolutely set on reaching my challenge goals and it represented the most practical route north.

I did consider taking, and now wish I had, highway 17 from Steinkjer, but it would have involved 3 ferry crossings, one of them long and possibly expensive, and in reality it would have been a 2-day ride. The E6, as expected, was policed both by traffic cars and, as my Sat Nav was now indicating, many speed cameras.

It warned me well in advance of the major ones but I was more concerned about the sneaky ones hidden in vans or behind traffic signs and trees. I kept to the limit, mostly, and a number of motorcyclists and indeed the odd car came past me, which had me wondering if they knew something I didn't.

Not far north of Steinkjer, one could not fail to notice a large and imposing arch over the E6 informing me that I was now officially in North Norway. This archway is a beautiful design, an artistic representation of the northern lights.

There was a café and a large car park which inevitably was almost full of RVs and tour buses. I stopped only to take a picture of the archway, people were queuing for the toilets and the café looked full to overflowing, so it was not a place I intended to linger.

Re-joining the E6, a guy riding an old dark green BMW motorcycle became my riding partner for many a kilometre and we became road buddies even swapping the lead a few times. It was all genteel and gentlemanly stuff since we were only riding at 80 kph or thereabouts, hardly a race.

As I pulled in for fuel, he rode on and held his arm high in salute; I do wish he had stopped for a chat. But this day became a 'head down, means to an end' sort of riding day up to Mo I Rana. Where the road was completely clear visually, I did squirt the bike over 100 kph occasionally to relieve the boredom but knew that to hold it there would only end up with a speeding ticket sooner or later. The route became very pretty again as I rode along lakes and rivers.

It became uncomfortably hot riding the bike as the day wore on; the outside temperature was again hitting 34°C by mid-afternoon. There was no respite; all I could do was stop often and drink lots of water from my frequently replenished plastic bottle; so hot was the day that after a few hours in the top case the water was always warm; in fact I have often drunk colder cups of tea!

I set the cruise control for 80 kph and learnt how amazing it is that you are always making subtle adjustments, sometimes almost unconsciously, when riding normally. I left the cruise control set up hill and down dale on the now quieter sections of road approaching Mo I Rana.

Being brave, or more accurately, stupid, I did not disengage the function (easily done by snapping the throttle forward or a quick dab on the brakes) when entering quite a sharp corner and barrelled into it a tad too fast only to meet a huge truck coming towards me travelling itself just a little over the speed limit.

I mention it not because there was any real danger but because suddenly I did not feel 100% in control. Ordinarily, I would have just trimmed a little off my speed entering that particular corner. From that moment, cruise control bravado went out of the window and only used on sections of road where a set speed was always within completely safe riding parameters.

In the isolation of this ride, I began to take some comfort in the artificial intelligence through the Sat Nav and the very English voice chirping at me from time to time. Yes, naturally it was a one-way conversation, and I had not become that deluded in my loneliness to think that we had any sort of relationship.

But Emilie slightly failed me at Mo I Rana, a bigger town than I expected (pop 19,000). She correctly guided me to the hotel which I could see but could not get to because it was across a now newly pedestrianised square. Not her fault and I forgave her but going round the square and locating the correct street the other side of it proved a bit of a challenge and involved at least two circuits of a large traffic island.

Eventually, I stopped directly outside the hotel and was dismayed to discover there was no obvious parking area. I got off the bike and walked around the hotel block and found a minute car park (staff only? I couldn't understand the sign) up a very steep ramp and parked the bike up there well out of everyone's way. It proved to be a fruitless exercise.

I was sweltering, dusty and no doubt not a pretty sight as I stumbled into the hotel lobby.

'Hello, you have a room for me I think?' The receptionist checked my booking reservation number. 'We do,' she said, 'but you are not here, you are staying in the barracks'; I blinked at her in a moment of complete and utter confusion. She explained, 'We have two sites and we are fully booked at this site; your accommodation is a few blocks down the road, though you still come here for breakfast tomorrow,' as if that suddenly made it alright.

She gave me my key. 'Was it very hot riding today?' she asked. 'Very, just look at me' I said. 'Ah', she said knowingly; the dishevelled state of me did not really need further comment. She looked up at me and smiled. 'Sorry to tell you this but they have forecast 40 degrees for tomorrow!'

Now just consider this for a moment. Here was I, 2,000 miles (sorry, yes miles, just making a distance point here for those who still drive in the old currency) north of home and just 60 miles or so from the Arctic Circle and the temperature was going up and not down! This was clearly not normal for this region even in midsummer and I was becoming ever convinced as my ride went on that global warming is no myth.

She explained how to get to the other site and told me that there was ample parking down there. What could I do? The booking was made and paid for. I trudged back to my bike and rode down to the site. It was indeed a three-story barracks, cheaper accommodation for the 'Norwegian working class' and just at that moment I felt like I was entering 'steerage class' on the Titanic.

The room was actually okay, basic but okay, and in fairness it was not expensive and as a welcome bonus, being late afternoon, it was in shadow and relatively cool. I was grateful too that it was on the ground floor because once again secure bike parking was an immediate concern; it was on a busy back road.

I showered and lay on the bed with the windows fully open to cool down and naturally, I fell asleep. I awoke to some fellow guests drinking beer, young men, construction workers I think, sitting at a picnic table right outside the bedroom window and they were getting progressively louder. I didn't remonstrate with them, it was only early evening after all, and got up and walked into the town glancing back at my bike and thinking it looked a bit too conspicuous to passing traffic.

Passing a dockland area, I noted there were huge mounds of felled timber waiting to be shipped, one of Norway's most natural resources obviously. I found Mo I Rana town very modern and quite familiar as a result. The people were very friendly. I strolled into a mall and in one large shop there was a sale and I bought 2 very cheap T-shirts to supplement my clothing as my 'not washed' pile was getting a bit too high.

Both T shirts had a very tropical theme which was a bit of an odd design to be selling this far north I thought, but the way the weather had been shaping up perhaps not so strange after all. I grabbed a late sandwich and a coffee at a small local café which was close to closing.

The waitress misheard my order for an americano and brought me an espresso instead. I was just too tired to change it. The owner was fascinated with my story and promised to pledge a donation. I wandered back to the barracks and there were enough vehicles parked now for me to move and hide my bike behind a row of them making it impossible to see it from the road With the bike now being hidden from view I could now relax as I went to turn in. The early al fresco drinkers had also gone from outside the room and it was now quiet, which was more than could be said for my night.


**Day 12 – Wednesday** 18th July 2018. Mo I Rana to Narvik. Leaving time- 05:30; temperature range – 22°C to 35°C; distance ridden – 433 kilometres;

My alarm was set for 5:00 am but I had been awake already for 20 minutes. In fact, I had been awake most of the night, having at best about 4 hours sleep. The sleep deprivation gave rise to concerns about the trip, how far yet to go, and the long, long journey back home. Once in that mind frame sleep never comes easily, but that espresso must have contained enough caffeine to keep an elephant awake for a week! I decided to forgo breakfast, which would have had me hanging around for another hour, and just drop the key off at hotel reception and head for the Arctic Circle.

Some facts about the Arctic Circle. It is a geographical line around the Earth at latitude 66.5 degrees north, and, as I have alluded to, in the extreme north there is a period in midsummer when the sun does not stray below the horizon even at midnight. It is literally the land of the midnight sun.

Conversely, in mid-winter this phenomenon is reversed and the area is subject to the polar night, a period of constant darkness. Again, the further you go north of the Arctic Circle the longer this lasts. It is a place that has always held a fascination for me.

I was on my way and had a very pleasant ride out of Mo; the morning sky was particularly beautiful with a few clouds for a change, and the roads were completely empty and surprisingly, in some places, a little damp, but there was no doubt at all, it was going to be another very hot day. Having not slept much I was already feeling the effects of that and hoped the mild fatigue would pass as the day progressed, with a gentle unhurried ride.

The road began to climb steadily towards the Arctic plateau and 84 kilometres from Mo I Rana I pulled into the Arctic Circle Polar (Polarsirkelsenteret) Centre. The centre building is not exactly attractive; give it a few metal fins and it would look like some recently landed UFO.

The overnight parking area, unsurprisingly, was filled with RVs. At 07:30 the centre itself was not yet open and, having read about it, this did not bother me in the slightest. It was very much a tourist trap apparently and I did not need to pay 'x' amount of Krone for a 'Polarsirkelen' certificate to record I had actually been there.

I tried to take some pictures from my phone using what was to become the somewhat superfluous item, the selfie stick, but they were not very good. I even tried to look victorious in a 'punching the air, I've done it' kind of pose, which now, on later examination, looks just a bit ridiculous.

The truth is I did not feel particularly victorious at all. I am not very keen on the phrase but it was one 'off my bucket list'. I was here; one of my personal goals had indeed been achieved. I had ridden from my home to the Arctic Circle, but suddenly it was a lonely feeling without someone, Liz, or my kids, to share it with.

I was not exactly sure what I expected but certainly not the feelings that had surfaced. The Polar Centre and its surrounding car parks were, well, too civilised, too commercial I suppose. When you think Arctic, you think wilderness where this had the feel of an upmarket truck stop.

And wasn't I supposed to have a certain emotion or feeling having achieved my 'dream' to ride to the Arctic Circle? I did not feel very jubilant, it was all a bit matter of fact, an anti-climax and it certainly did not feel Arctic being already far too hot for that.

My lone motorcycle parked in the massive public parking area looked oddly out of place against the backdrop of all the white (do they actually make them in any other colour?) RVs which were showing no signs of life. Just at that moment in time, it was serene and quiet and I felt like I was the only living being on the planet.

I walked across to look at the stone memorials to the side of the centre building, already knowing what they were, a moving reminder of more savage times. Erected to commemorate some 13,000 Yugoslav and Soviet POWs who laboured for the Nazis in appalling conditions to build their Arctic railway, they stood grey and forbidding in stark contrast with the bright sunshine of that morning.

With me alone standing there giving my silent prayers for the pain visited on this peaceful region just a generation ago, it was these memorials rather than the appalling Arctic Polar Centre which became my lasting memory of crossing into the Arctic Circle. Multitudes died as they struggled to build this railroad north from Mosjoen to the port of Narvik.

The German military objective for the railway was to allow safer movement of essential war materials and equipment from their ships which were plying the dangerous waters along the coast. It was never actually completed and only in 1962 did the railway eventually reach Bodo, still a long way short of the Narvik war objective.

It was yet another poignant reminder of a country that had suffered greatly during the Second World War. There were to be others before my trip was completed. I wondered how many tourists actually made the effort to visit this spot. I am certain it was easier and safer for most just to get a Polar Circle certificate than to reflect on the very real suffering that took place so close by.

In our pleasures, we often live in denial to the reality of our human condition, that we are slowly destroying the planet and, often rather more quickly, each other. The memorials became a forceful reminder of why I was really undertaking this challenge.

Back at the bike, very much in reflective mode, I observed signs of life over at the RV car park. I wanted to be well on my way before that army hit the roads. It was 08:30 and I flicked the ignition on my bike and was shocked to note the outside temperature already showing 28°C!

I rode on into the arctic tundra and now I was captivated by this strange landscape. Some might see this place as terra nullias, a nothing-place, notable only for its emptiness and unremitting sameness. But for me, this was something very different. It was a kind of scrubland, the stunted trees, mainly birch, covered in sphagnum type mosses of various hues some grey, some bright green.

There were myriads of lichen-covered rocks and, despite the drought conditions, many glacial-fed streams ran crystal clear close to the road and it was surprisingly green. This was a unique topography to me; I had never experienced anything quite like it, even in remotest Scotland. I loved it.

In the far distance, I could see the mountain ranges and unthawed pockets of snow on the nearer hills. I felt at peace and very happy to be away from the sadness of memorials and the fripperies of tourist centres and car parks. This is a natural landscape fashioned over aeons of time and I felt hugely blessed to be able to move through it and experience it.

I stopped by a river and dismounted because spanning it there was a rope bridge which swayed in a pleasant manner as I crossed it. The river was wide and shallow, as clear as glass, rocks of all sizes and different colours littering the bottom, some red, some dazzling white (quartz perhaps), some even pink. The ground was springy underfoot but not boggy; I think under more normal weather conditions it would have been.

I sat on that opposite bank and drank it all in. This arctic plateau was the starting point for many of those huge western Norway rivers such as the Gaula and the Vosso and I wondered which one this became. I did not want to leave, but as ever, my next destination dictated my time and I wanted to ride ahead of the coming RV armada.

Dropping down off the plateau the panorama ahead of a huge sweeping valley encased by mountains was magnificent and the scale of it quite breathtaking. It was not too long, however, before I needed fuel. Normally, I would not record this event as it was a thrice daily (average) necessity, but at a village called Storjord my credit card was declined at the pump terminal and for obvious reasons it became an immediate concern.

The particular credit card (Halifax) was being used because they did not charge for foreign currency transactions; this proved quite a saving for me. I tried my other credit card and it was immediately accepted and, just to illustrate the saving they later charged me a cool 0.50p for this single small £17.00 transaction alone, which I just happen to think is extortionate.

Multiply that by the number of times I used my credit card on this trip and the currency transaction fees, had I been using their card, would have accumulated to a considerable amount.

A few kilometres on there was a nice café, I stopped and sitting at a bench in the sunshine I rang the emergency customer services number on my card, because obviously, if they had put a 'stop' on my card I wanted to know why. Again I just want to record that I marvel at the technology at our disposal nowadays.

Here I was in the middle of wilderness Norway using a device small enough to fit comfortably into my back trouser pocket and talking to a guy in the Halifax office in England and the call was as clear as if he had been in the next room. I don't know about you but I am old enough to think this is simply incredible.

After the qualifying security questions, he told me there was no problem with my card, that it was simply that particular pump terminal did not like it. We had a chat about my challenge, because the guy was intrigued at what I was doing; it was a concern that turned into a very pleasant conversation in the end.

I bought some food and a drink in the café and paid by the favoured credit card which was accepted as normal. I was relieved.

My ride up to Narvik was memorable, however, for one other particular thing that day. Once again, it was the heat of riding and the draining effect it was having on me. By now, I had hoped that I was acclimatising to it but even if I was, this day seemed to push my physical adaptation and endurance by being even hotter.

I would remind the reader yet again that I was now above the Arctic Circle heading north and yet it was getting hotter by the kilometre. Once past the small towns of Rongen and Fauske it became a real battle. I stopped by a small harbour at the end of some nameless fjord to try to cool down, hoping the marine environment would afford some relief, but found it worse than actually riding, where at least the air flow offered a little respite.

Stopping often, both to drink and replenish my water supply, the heat this day was sapping my energy at an alarming level. The chilled chocolate milk drinks I bought were not just for the taste, for I knew milk, in particular, worked better at replenishing spent energy than some of those well-known caffeine-laced drinks.

It seemed to help, but words cannot adequately express the oppressive nature of the ride that day with temperatures as high as 35°C. The E6 terminated briefly at Bognes for a ferry crossing, which provided free passage.

It was a long and wonderfully cooler cruise over the depths of the fjord, but when I got back on my bike on the other side I was not in good shape and even though I was not feeling quite right, I knew I just had to push on. I could not stop. Had I done so, I am not sure how my day might have ended.

I rode into the outskirts of Narvik, stopped, tapped the 'lodging' icon on the Sat Nav and made for the very nearest which was the 'Thon' hotel. I was now feeling quite unwell and beyond the point of caring about room prices, I just wanted to lie down.

I was not even pleased to see a few motorcycles in the car park. It was an effort to enter and inquire but thankfully they did have available rooms and, mercifully, they gave me a good room rate. I dragged myself and my luggage to the room, passing the cheerful motorcyclists having a drink at the bar who must have wondered why I did not engage with them.

I was suffering from heat-induced exhaustion and on the verge of a bad migraine headache which I knew from many years of experience could down me for a day if it developed beyond a certain point. Worst of all, I was just not able to get my body temperature down.

In the room, I literally dumped my luggage on the floor and threw off all my clothes, took a cold shower and downed litres of water and 2 very strong pain killers (which also helped lower my body temperature) and lay down 'in a darkened room.'

Thankfully, I was so dog tired I did sleep for a few hours and came to feeling much better. For the first time this ride, I took a dioralyte drink for the effects of severe dehydration, replenishing the essential salts and minerals that my body had excreted through sweat. After a much-needed rest, I decided I was recovered sufficiently to walk down the hill into the town. Although evening, it was still very warm.

I found a small pizza restaurant and chatted with the friendly waitress. I asked her about the weather. She gave me a concerned look and told me she had lived here all her life and had never known such a hot day as today. I really should have taken a taxi back up to the hotel, and I was hot and sweaty again by the time I got back there.

I realise now that this day had been made far tougher because of the lack of sleep the night before and I wrote this in my journal before sleeping, which perhaps captures exactly what was going on with me at that time.

*'Too hot'!*
*'Too hot'!*
*'Too hot'!*

*'So how is it going? What has changed? I have been surprised at how determined I have become. Yes, I have always had an awkward streak, but this is something different. After telling someone I met on this trip about it and my heart surgery they said it changes you, they said that their father acted much the same after his heart valve was replaced. But it is more.*

*Over the last few days, in the appalling heat on the bike, I have lost sight somewhat of why I am doing this challenge. The persecuted church and Open Doors have taken something of a back seat in my mind due to the sheer physical and mental demands of the daily ride.*

*By nature, I can vent my frustration negatively at times, and whilst that still surfaces, I seem to be in a process of change – I do hope so. And God is definitely with me; even in the hottest day He is helping me make the right decisions.*

*But I am sooooo grateful for the ever-present sense of His hand over the trip. And now, over half way but still a long way to go, my natural mind quails at the thought of the reversal of the trip. The huge distance I have to go to come back. But He says 'trust me' and that has to be enough'.*

I 'secured' my bike, showered again and slept the sleep of the righteous – mostly. But at some point in the still light night, I was awakened by high winds flapping the curtains madly at my open window. As I shut it, I caught a flash of lightning and heard rain and thunder.

**Day 13 – Thursday** 19th July 2018. Narvik to Hammerfest, leaving time 06:30; temperature range – 22°C to 30°C; distance ridden – 670 kilometres.

Despite the interruption to my sleep, I awoke feeling much better and stronger than the day before but knowing I had to make a major decision. I was up at 05:00, there was not a cloud in the sky and I was pondering long over the map. I knew sensibly I should not really be attempting to make Hammerfest from

Narvik in one day. But then I reasoned it was better to leave early and endure one day riding in the heat, rather than 2 to get up there.

Given the ride yesterday, this may seem like a perverse argument but there was another reason; there proved to be no major town half way between Narvik and Alta to find accommodation and Alta itself was too close to Hammerfest to break the ride so…it was going to be a big riding day today, the biggest of the trip so far and I mused on the fact that I would be exposed to a different kind of Scandinavian sauna than the one normally experienced.

I was down to breakfast at 06:00 along with all the early working crews who were busily filling their plastic bags with food for their lunches; this phenomenon was no longer a shock to me. Yes, it was indeed the expected buffet breakfast, and a very good one I have to say.

There was a young, waif-like, oriental waitress serving coffees at the tables. One large, ugly (and, sorry, he was!) ogri of a man was giving this girl serious verbal abuse. I did not have the language but nevertheless got the gist of it.

He was moaning and waving his arms around because there was no ketchup. But there was something else in his obnoxious attitude; he was going out of his way to intimidate this poor girl, maybe because she was a recent immigrant, who knows?

Bless her, she was made of sterner stuff and did not need my intervention (I was at the point I can tell you). She shrugged and just steered the troll to a small table where all the sauces were. Did he grunt in appreciation? No, of course not, ignorant rude man that he was. As she served me, I thanked her, discreetly pointed towards him and did a small throat cut gesture with my finger and she laughed richly.

Perhaps it had been the fatigue but exactly why this had not occurred to me before today I cannot say, but suddenly a way to increase the airflow through my riding jacket came to me and I am almost embarrassed to admit to it. It is a force of habit over many years to ride with my jacket sleeves tucked inside the gloves.

The reason is eminently practical; in the event of rain, the water would run over the gloves and outside the jacket sleeves not up them. From now on, I rode with the jacket sleeve outside of the gloves and opened the adjustable sleeve cuff wide to allow as much air as possible to flow through the jacket and up the arms.

Of course, this would be the last thing you would want if it did rain but anything to help dissipate the heat was welcome and it did make some difference.

Naturally, if it had come on to rain, I would have to stop and quickly reverse the situation.

This morning, I was away and riding by 6:30 and after an hour of droning along at 80 kph, I decided to ride the E6 at normal riding speeds and not subject myself to the ridiculous limit. I did not care if I picked up a ticket, I had a very long ride today and needed to get it done in good order, and as a result it proved to be a fabulous day's riding.

I respected and slowed to the correct speed limit in the urban areas, but outside of them I just rode naturally through the magnificent Norwegian countryside. The E6 was much quieter now north of Narvik and there was less police presence also, well at least on this day.

My Sat Nav was pinging warnings anyway at the fixed and mobile speed camera sites and naturally I heeded these. My riding was quick, but certainly not dangerous.

I stopped from time to time to take pictures which had me overtaking a grey Mercedes car a few times as they, in turn, came past me each time I stopped, as much an annoyance to them as to me no doubt. At a place called Odden, the huge and striking recently built road bridge ahead was not yet open to traffic so I was forced to take the long and, I have to say quite splendid, ride around the Kafjord.

On the other side, I came across the first of the brightly painted fishermen's huts; most of them have turf roofs and also have the whiff of the drying fish hung out close by on the large wooden airing racks. The scent of these in this region became very familiar to me over the next few days.

The ride along the now Arctic shore to Alta is a dream for a motorcyclist on this fabulous road, through stupendous scenery, with few vehicles and no police disturbances. I stopped and took a small side road to look and photographed some of these fishermen's huts.

The distant high mountains way across the fjord were still pocketed with snow and the fjord itself was an almost unreal inky black-blue in colour, which to me indicated it was deep indeed and very close to the shore too.

I looked through the window into one of the huts; there, poking out of an enormous plastic bin, was a dried head and skeleton of what was once a halibut, a big fish, but, as halibut go, only average. A really big one would not have fitted in the hut.

The shed was filled, as one might expect, with lots of fishing accoutrements, nets, ropes, brightly coloured buoys, oars and the like. Outside of all of the huts there were many fish drying racks but these had no fish on them at this time. I sat on a large rock and relaxed for a while.

It was a very peaceful time and once again I drank in a stunning vista across the fjord which I noted was cutting up rough in places with many white horses. There was not a boat in sight and I wondered if this was a seasonal base for the fishermen used only at certain times.

It was pleasanter riding today as it proved a little cooler and I was grateful for this after the rigours of yesterday's marathon. Pushing ever northward and sensing not to get too blasé about the police, as I came into the outskirts of Alta there was indeed a speed trap.

Here, coming into an urban environment on a dead straight road and riding within the 50 kph limit, I spotted the police car. It was stationed just by a traffic island and there is no doubt the location would be very productive. I did wonder if he might pull out behind and tail me, but noted he was intently looking down into his speed detection device and seemed not to notice my passing.

From Alta, the E6 went into tundra again and the road perspective was clear for very many kilometres, and with long and very straight sections I confess the bike here was really given its head.

I did slow down though for what I thought was a broken-down motorcyclist with his mate, but with a thumbs-up and wave he indicated the situation was in hand. It's normal that motorcyclists look out for each other, unless of course if you are boarding a Hirtshals ferry!

At a point where a wide shallow river ran under the road, I took a break. It was by a Sami camp of some sort but not a soul was around. There was a skeletal framework of birch poles that I thought would be covered by skins when in use, much like an Indian tepee. But I suspected this was a winter camp for there was no sign of life.

The Sami are a nomadic people and they are the famous reindeer herders who follow the seasonal movement of the animals. Once this area of northernmost Norway, Sweden and Finland, and part of Russia, was known as Lapland and the indigenous people of this region were called 'Lapps' but this name is no longer used and they are more commonly known now as the 'Sami'.

There were no reindeer anywhere to be seen here; in fact the absence of any kind of wildlife in Norway on this trip, apart from the suicidal lemming, I found a bit odd. No fish in the river either. I looked.

Very soon after this stop, I said goodbye to the trusty E6 and turned left and north west onto highway 94 to Hammerfest. The 94 soon runs across a beautiful river and, for the first time, I saw some salmon fishermen trying their luck in the estuary and a couple more on the river itself.

With weather like this I doubted they would have much success but 'hope springs eternal' as they say. The river, I sensed, was the same one I stopped by earlier on the tundra. I doubted salmon would be trying to run up it in these conditions; I was enough of a game fisherman myself to know this.

I suppose there could be a possibility of tempting a fish that might have come up the river waiting to run further, but this close to the fjord when they had the option of going back downstream to wait until better higher water level conditions? I think there would be very few holding in the river, if any.

I was now very close to my destination. Hammerfest is actually on the island of Kvaloya and there is a bridge across the narrow fjord to access it. As I rode onto this bridge there were about a dozen reindeer just quietly standing or lying in the road as the local traffic negotiated respectfully around them, as I did.

The island on the other side was very rugged and I quickly became aware of the danger the reindeer could pose. Rather like the errant roaming sheep on the Shropshire hills near my home, they wander out into the road willy-nilly and without any warning.

I stopped on the outskirts of Hammerfest to take a picture of the town sign with my bike in front of it, but the road was not very wide, the verge even less so. I did it but not that successfully. I pulled into a tourist information area and took a selfie in front of the town map using the stupid camera stick with even less success. But I had made it here!

It was 16:30 in the afternoon. I had made the epic ride up from Narvik in one day and just completed my challenge. I had indeed ridden a motorcycle from Highley to Hammerfest for Open Doors and the persecuted church.

There was not such an anticlimactic quality as arriving at the Arctic Circle and I actually did have a strong sense of achievement at that moment and even breathed a sigh of relief I think. I had done it!

But practicalities had to override any sense of relieved arrival. I needed a hotel. Riding into the main street I found a charming little town which was quite busy and the main hotel was there on that street. But again, as I investigated, I was not comfortable with leaving my bike in an open car park right so close to the main road. I decided to ride on a little to investigate what else might be available. Just on the town limit, I saw a little sign right for the Skytterhuset Hotel. It was a small insignificant sign easy to miss. I decided to go and have a look.

I rode around a lake and up a hill; the hotel itself looked unpromising from a distance, not very pretty, stark purposeful buildings appearing almost like they had just plonked themselves there of their own accord and were much unfinished with lots of work going on around it. As I rode into the gravel covered car park, (not again!) there were motorcycles, always a good sign.

I talked to one of my fellow bikers outside, a big friendly guy who was having a smoke and relaxing in the sunshine. He was Finnish, and a BMW rider, a GS of course (for the unenlightened reader GS stands for Gelande/Strasse, German for off-road/on-road). He told me they did have rooms and that accommodation was basic but good. My hopes were raised.

The reception area was new, modern and really quite nice, except there was nobody staffing it. Eventually, after I rang the desk bell a few times, the cook, still in his apron, wandered over wiping his hands. He was big, round and an amiable guy too, but his English was at best rudimentary.

He reminded me of a Ronnie Barker character, but he proved very helpful and was doing his level best. I gave him my post card and went into my 'I am riding for a Christian charity; can you give me a good room rate for 3 nights?' spiel.

He stared at the card for a long time before turning it over to read my message about the trip. 'I make a phone call' he said' He spoke Norwegian to the boss for a long time, returned to the desk, 'This price for you' he said and writes me a figure down, which was Kr1,770.00, about £150.00!

Holding up 3 digits, I said to him, 'No, no, for 3 nights please,' he nodded firmly and pointed again to the figure and told me it included breakfast and dinner. I could not quite believe it. After all, this was expensive Norway, I cannot think of anywhere in the UK I would get 3 nights including meals for that price.

He gave me a room key and I dragged my gear down a level to a room I fully expected to be less than basic. It was perfectly acceptable in every respect and very quiet to boot. God's providence once again.

There was a set time and routine for dinner and now, as I queued with my fellow guests at the serving hatch, the penny dropped; this hotel was primarily a working hotel for the gas and oil rig crews and therefore the prices were subsidised, possibly by those industries or the government itself.

The rather stark buildings were barracks for these workers but the hotel clearly did have other guest rooms like mine. It was a buffet meal but on a rather industrial scale and there was a good offering of dinner choices and desserts.

There was a set routine also for stacking plates and cutlery after the meal which I picked up quickly by watching my fellow guests. It was a large canteen style restaurant but with only a handful of worker diners; obviously given the size of the room at other times there must be many more of them than this.

Again, it was all perfectly acceptable, it was immaculately clean, the food was good without being excellent and the ambience was friendly. I was a happy man, so happy I risked the equivalent of £9.50 for a can of Tuborg lager before retiring. I slept very well.


**Day 14 – Friday** 20th July 2018. Hammerfest to Nordkapp and return. Leaving time – 06:30; temperature range – 12°C to 22°C; distance ridden – 430 kilometres.

It seems I am a slow learner. How do you ride big mileages in Norway and what predetermines your ability to be able to do this better some days than others? Well, a good night's rest helps and an early start the next day before the heat really kicks in.

As you ride, try to forget the distance you are going to put in and just ride. That said, I awoke at 04:45 somewhat depressed and concerned again at the thought of what lay ahead in going home. I shrugged off the negativity, for today, I was off to Nordkapp, the northernmost point of Europe that can be reached by road.

I was excited and, if I am honest, a little daunted after reading some of the misadventures of other motorcyclists who have ridden up there. I had already enjoyed the early start buffet breakfast; my bike was fully fuelled up yesterday in readiness. I was set.

There was an audience of early shift workers outside having their fags as I prepared my bike for leaving and, as it was another blasted gravel car park, extracting it and turning it around became a bit of a pantomime. I like to think I looked relatively competent and indeed there was no sarcastic reaction from the observers.

They gave me a friendly wave through exhaled smoke as I left at 06:30 to avoid the mêlée of the RV swarms (I had been warned about them particularly on this Nordkapp run) and it felt positively cold compared to my starts on other days of this trip so far. It was 18°C on leaving but I was suitably layered up and it was not unpleasant at all.

It was very quiet as I rode out of Hammerfest. A lone baby reindeer wandered across in front of me; they seem less road savvy than sheep even and that is saying something. On the fjord bridge there were no reindeer this morning but you could certainly see where they had been, droppings everywhere.

I briefly re-joined the E6, ever north naturally, and rode through some rugged foreboding scenery like a disturbed version of Rannoch moor, which was certainly bleak. I turned left going due north now onto the famous E69, made so because it is the road to Nordkapp, to follow the coast for the 140km run up to my most northerly destination. I switched on the heated grips to take the growing chill off my hands and it actually felt like the extreme north for the very first time.

The beginning part of this road was very narrow and my first road tunnel today (there were 2 more) was one of old type, badly lit, and, bang on cue, as I entered it, a massive truck was coming towards me. This was the first commercial vehicle seen that morning and I had to meet it there!

For a long distance following the road was a causeway cut into the rock face, the boiling, steamy sea was way below me and to my right. I understood immediately what riding this road might be like in really adverse weather, which thankfully was not today.

Nordkapp is on an island (Mageroya) and the road widened and ran pleasantly inland a little at times as I got nearer. Now, alarmingly, I was riding into thick sea mists which dropped the outside temperature like a stone but they were not constant, one minute with dense thick fog, the next bright sunshine again.

Riding out of a mist cloud, I entered the relatively new North Cape Sea tunnel, an amazing piece of engineering at 6.9kms long and dropping to 212 metres below sea level. I rode out of it into the sunshine again; soon, after another tunnel I was approaching Honningsvag, the main settlement on the island.

I had a vision before this trip of the petrol station here being like those I encountered years ago in some of the remotest parts of Ireland, staffed by a lone man in a wooden hut with a few rustic buildings around it. Did I really expect a single pump, queues and rationed fuel in this last outpost of Scandinavia?

My imagination failed me completely for the harbour town of Honningsvag was charmingly Norwegian (surely this is the northernmost town in Europe, not

Hammerfest?) and not rustic at all, with a service station as modern as any so far in the country.

I was relieved, for refuelling had become a bit of a concern in my mind for the return journey back to Hammerfest. I took the opportunity of filling up and found the most northerly service station in Europe was more modern and better equipped than many in the UK and did a wonderful selection of food also. I could not fail to be impressed.

On the other side of Honningsvag the road rose steeply and the mists still rolled and, as I rode, I was concerned about getting decent pictures at the cape because of it. The road was good here, but by now there were lots of tourist buses heading towards me, going back to wherever; presumably they had done their cape visits yesterday had stayed overnight up there.

The road climbed and then undulated as I approached Nordkapp. I stopped and took some pictures of the mists rolling in. I paid the massively excessive kr275 (about £25.00) charge to a pimply youth in his kiosk to enter the visitor centre and the car park and immediately regretted it.

I had an unsettling feeling about it and at this price I was already certain it was a rip off. The car park itself was absolutely full of cars, RVs and tour buses and the whole area bustling with tour groups and kids running about. I parked the bike carefully because it was, yes, you guessed it, hadn't you? Another gravel covered car park.

I dismounted and began my explorations. I was here, Nordkapp, the roof of mainland Europe. I waited ages for a man and his daughter to stop playing on and in 'The Globe' described in the given leaflet as,

*'This monument, erected in 1977, has become the symbol of the North Cape. For the sake of safety, we would like to make you aware that it is not permitted to climb on the monument.'*

So much for rules, I thought. I managed to take a selfie at this North Cape monument. I look at that picture now and realise just how much the trip had taken out of me. I looked haggard and tired, and some have unkindly said hung-over. I walked around the site taking some very nice pictures of the area and the cliffs.

I never really knew how far down the sea was (307 metres I discovered later) for the mist was holding over it, but it made for a couple of wonderful pictures and, away from the crowd, it was hauntingly beautiful. Here, I discovered I was closer to the North Pole than to Oslo, a place where the sun truly never drops below the horizon from mid-May to the end of July.

It was 10:00 and the upper floor of the visitor centre was only open for the toilets and the exhibitions. I say again, it was 10:00; if you wanted a drink, snack or, as I did, a commemorative T shirt and a sticker, there was no chance. Plenty of staff were milling about chatting with each other and doing absolutely nothing. I was seriously unimpressed. £25.00 for this?

I know instinctively when customers are being taken for a ride and being used as a commodity rather than the asset they are. Bored staff doing as little as they can because they know once people come here they have a captive market; the customer has no choice but to accept the situation.

The place was getting to me; the gift shop and coffee shop area were barricaded and soulless, completely at odds with the natural beauty outside and it became an anathema to me that they had opened such facilities there and I resolved I was not now going to give them another kroner of my money.

However, in fairness, I found there was a little more to the centre than this. Out of interest, I did walk around the exhibitions which led you ever downwards through a large tunnel (well-lit in this case) into the rock core of the ground underneath and I admit it was very cleverly done.

There were some very good 3D exhibits about the history of Nordkapp including a touching reminder of the wartime Arctic convoys that sailed past this point. How many ships were to be lost to German torpedoes out there, I wondered? Again, it made me think deeply about the sacrifices that were made to bring relief to others.

Further on, I found myself in St Johannes Chapel, an ecumenical/interdenominational place of worship. With the natural rock walls, cobbled floor and simple but modern seating it was, in its way, really very striking, but also completely spoilt.

It proved not to be the quiet and dignified spot it should have been but was ruined by the endless looped music playing, the kind that never goes anywhere, more fitting to some New Age shop in Glastonbury than a Christian chapel. I sat and tried to 'be still' for a while but the constant noisy intrusion destroyed it as a place of meditative reflection for me.

I had brought a commemoration specifically to leave at Nordkapp in an appropriate place, a palm cross on which I had carefully written in purple ink (the Open Doors colour) *'Highley to Hammerfest Challenge for Open Doors, July 2018, riding for those who have no voice.'*

I wanted to leave it at what I thought was the zenith of my trip, the North Cape, and the chapel should have been it, but it felt wholly inappropriate. My deed of respectfully leaving this little commemorative cross was important to me, symbolically marking the end of my challenge. I wanted it to be an act in keeping with my ride and my heart for the persecuted church. I knew that no one else might even look at it, or a cleaner might just throw it away as rubbish, but it represented a culmination of all I had worked for and sacrificed over the last 9 months and I wasn't leaving it here.

I did not linger in this chapel and walked ever downward to the final exhibition called the 'Cave of Lights', *'a journey through the seasons by way of sound and light.'* It felt almost pagan. I wondered what messages they were trying to give here. We offer something to everyone…except if you wanted a sandwich and a coffee.

Enough, I had just enough of it. Returning to the shopping area, it was now 10:45 and still absolutely nothing was open and even more people were roaming about now looking lost and bemused that they could not be parted with their money. It was a disgrace.

Back at my bike, I had to confess to feeling quite poignant. Was this how I should feel? I ought to be congratulating myself on my riding achievement, but because the final act of commemoration had not been completed, once again I had that hollow feeling. I was disappointed as if I had been cheated or as if somehow I hadn't quite done it or planned it right. I was now feeling very tired which was not helping.

I looked up and said a little prayer of thanks, thanks that I had really done it and my mood immediately lifted. Looking around Nordkapp it was still hauntingly beautiful, and just at that moment, very peaceful with the wild flowers, mists, sea birds and the reindeer grazing in the distance. It was not quite finished yet.

I had noted the shop on the road on my way into Nordkapp, a Sami gift shop, so riding back I stopped and went inside. This was the real deal, not full of tacky touristy items (well a few perhaps) but lots of handmade quality objects. The old lady who ran the store lived opposite and she came across to serve me.

I asked her about the visitor centre shops, at which she smiled knowingly and said, 'They never open before 11:00, lots of people come here and complain about it.' I asked her what she thought about the summer weather. She looked thoughtful for a moment and then said, 'It is not right, it is too hot, it is a big problem for the animals', and she told me there were around 30,000 reindeer on the island owned by 10 families.

That many deer would need a very good food source and, in this drought, I did wonder how they might all survive. I bought some nice presents to take back home, genuine Sami made items, more fitting than anything the Nordkapp centre could offer I felt.

As I prepared to leave, I spotted a nice newish Audi parked in her driveway, so business could not be too bad. I thought the 11:00 opening time up the road was not doing her business any harm at all and I felt happy about that.

Back at Honningsvag, I had my lunch in the small café at the service station there. I felt drained both physically and mentally. On the road coming off the island, my fatigue led me into making a less than desirable overtake of an RV. It was a riding error for I misread the road ahead slightly, and whilst experience got me through, it was another wake up call for me about continuing to ride when very fatigued.

Once through the sea tunnel, I stopped at a delightful car park by a shingle beach. It was a popular place. I walked down to the beach area. Using a steep sided gravel bank as a back pillow, I slept for about an hour. I awoke to the sound of children playing and watched people making stone structures with the large pebbles. It was a pleasant and peaceful scene.

Across the calm little bay, I noted a fisherman had beached his small boat. There was something quite odd about it. He tossed some seagulls a few tit-bits of food and then proceeded to pull his boat up the beach whilst in a sitting position. Once he was satisfied he had secured it, he shuffled along on his backside using his arms as propulsion.

This man was clearly disabled. I lost sight of him behind a parked van but then he appeared in the driving seat and away he went. I did not think anyone else witnessed it and I marvelled that this man had the skills to even go fishing despite his obvious physical issue. I wondered how he had got into his van, or even launched his boat in the first place. A small thing to witness but one I will never forget.

The E69 was now quite busy, mainly with RVs, so there was much overtaking; I was fresher and more sensible now. At a little hamlet called Normannset I stopped to take some pictures of fish heads drying on one of the wooden racks. It was a macabre sight and I wondered why only the heads of were being dried and not the whole fish.

I was to discover that Norwegian fishermen waste very little; whole fish are dried separately but there was also a market for these dried heads and, ironically, Nigeria was one country where they were in high demand as a food source. Nigeria has become one of the worst countries in the world for the murder of Christians, many thousand lose their lives every year.

I smiled as a small troupe of reindeer invaded the garden of a close property. Clearly, these were animals that were not going to be deprived of food in a drought; they took absolutely no notice of me and were munching on the garden plants as I remounted my bike.

On the road back to Hammerfest, I stopped at the river. The road bridge was new, but the older one still survived alongside it. I rode onto it and parked. I watched the salmon fisherman downstream, nearer the fjord shore, casting and casting in hope, and another man on the river section above me.

They were locals so they must know, yet I stood on that bridge looking into the river for a very long time and being an angler of many years standing, I am an expert fish spotter. The water was so incredibly clear I saw the smaller fish, trout mainly, but I did not see one migratory fish run through, not one. I remain convinced those anglers were just labouring in vain.

The reindeer were back on the fjord bridge, many more of them this time. I had worked out why they came here. That bridge high over the fjord was the coolest place around for them and the day had, by now, become very hot once again.

As I approached Hammerfest town, there was a reindeer smack in the middle of the road; no problem for me as I slowed down and rode around him. Then I noticed a green van filling my mirrors which had come up on me very fast and was extremely close to hitting the back of me.

A driver of little discernment with a deprived sense of observation had, I think, decided to try to overtake me in the 60kph limit and at a dangerous place and clearly he had not even seen the deer. Around the next corner, I pulled over and angrily waved this madman past.

I then watched as he came up behind 2 cyclists, overtaking them on a downhill corner and in a positively dangerous fashion. I noted his plate was German and he was driving like a drunk. As he turned off left at the brink of the next hill, I blasted him on my horn. It was one of the worst pieces of driving I was to come across in the European leg of my trip.

I was unloading my bike outside the hotel as an old, and somewhat rattling, red BMW R80RT rolled up and an old guy got off it.

'Hello. I'm Eric,' he said offering his hand. Greeting me in English meant he had obviously seen my GB number plate.

'Do you think they will have any rooms?' I told him that almost certainly they would.

'Ah, gut, gut', he said, 'because I am over a day late in getting up here.'

'Was there a problem then?' I asked.

'Yes, forest fires in Sweden, everywhere; I had to keep turning around trying to find other routes.'

'And this,' he said wafting his Garmin Sat Nav at me, a more modern version than mine, 'is not working correctly.'

'Where have you ridden from?' I asked him. 'Switzerland,' he ventured, 'I live there.'

I was immediately concerned by this piece of information about the forest fires. It was my intention to be riding back through Sweden and I did not want to lose days making long detours to avoid them.

I wanted to know more and we arranged to have dinner together. Back in my room, I Googled it. The fires seemed to be striking up everywhere, but none were noted near the E4 the route I was taking. But the information was at best fluid and I was uneasy about it.

Eric proved to be a bit of a character. Over our meal, he told me he was 70 and had just sold his business in Lucerne. He complained that since he retired his wife had been pressurising him to move to the country but he told her no, he was not giving up his large garage.

Clearly, in spite of riding an old BMW, this man was well heeled, for he then reeled off a list of classic BMW motorcycles he owned, some very rare ones, and once more on this trip, I was a little envious of people I met who had such wonderful bike collections. Sadly, I have neither space nor the finances for such indulgences. He handed his Garmin to me.

'Have a look at this for me please Mervyn, it's not right'. I looked at it in an attempt to sort it.

'But Eric,' I tell him, the guidance notes are all in German, I cannot really help'.

'Hmm,' he said taking it back, 'my phone is not working right either.'

'Oh?' I ventured innocently at which he looked at me gravely.

'Very serious Mervyn, I can take calls from my wife,' he said.

'Well, that's good then, isn't it?' I offered.

'No, no, no, you do not understand! From my wife, I am always getting these calls, everywhere! But it is impossible for me to ring my girlfriend in Germany!'

It was at this point that I realised that Eric, as well as being a 'character', was a slippery customer as well. In my head, I now have him marked as Eric the Eel. I asked him about the forest fires and he showed me on my map.

Eric had ridden up through central Sweden to join the E6 at Trondheim; it was not the route I intended to be taking back because I had a rendezvous in Ystad, Southern Sweden and wanted to cover the distance by the quickest route possible.

As we sipped our expensive beers Eric said, 'We have a day out together tomorrow, yes?' I told him firmly, 'Sorry Eric, I am going into Hammerfest town and not riding at all tomorrow.' He shrugged his shoulders and mercifully his phone rang with a call from his wife.

I made my excuses and left him to his. I thought a day spent with him might have been troublesome for me; who knows where else he might have his hidden girlfriends?

I availed myself of the excellent laundering facilities at the hotel and did a complete wash in stages. Yes, I know not to mix colours and whites, I am not quite that daft, but my laundering skills needed honing because I set the temperature dial on the drier a bit too high.

My double XL tee shirts were now more like a single XL but my challenge picture on the front was really not so pretty anymore. Maybe it was my imagination; the haziness of it though, made me look a bit younger.

I had an early night, reflecting on riding over 1,100 kilometres during the last 2 days. Ha, this proved to be nothing in the days that lay ahead.

# Chapter 9
# A Brief Sojourn before Leaving

*'I forgive you and I ask God to forgive you. I pray that God may open your eyes to enlighten your minds'* – **Samira, an Egyptian Christian woman whose husband was killed when their church was bombed.**

**Day 15 – Saturday** 21ˢᵗ July 2018. Hammerfest town – a non-riding day.

I was up early…again. I breakfasted at 05:30 along with the oil and gas crews. Early because, and I am not proud to say this, I just did not want to get too involved with Eric today; there was something about him that made me feel uneasy. My fellow diners, like most North Europeans met on this trip, were a taciturn group and clearly not morning people.

One huge Norwegian loaded his plate with what would have been enough food to last me for 2 days. Then, after breakfast, the collection began as they all grabbed the provided plastic bags and filled them with food for their lunches, a ritual becoming routine to me now.

The ages of these men ranged from 20 to 50 and hardly any were wearing wedding rings. I think their lifestyle would not be conducive to long term relationships. They were a courteous, if not kind, bunch of guys; I liked them but I felt they had a certain sadness about them.

As I walked outside, I needn't have worried. Eric's bike had already gone which I found quite strange, for he must have been up even earlier than me for his ride today. Perhaps, he chose to go up to Nordkapp a day early. I silently wished him well.

Once again it was a lovely day, a little fresher after some rain overnight and in the cool of the morning I walked down into Hammerfest. On the hill down from the hotel there was an old lady sitting outside in her tiny garden enjoying a cigarette. I waved and smiled as I passed and was rewarded with the most beautiful smile yet seen on this trip.

It suddenly reminded me of my dear aunt Madge who had recently passed away. For a moment, it felt like a punch in the chest and a wave of grief swept over me. I walked along a path south of the lake and tried to read a notice about the fishing but could not make any sense of it.

Down at the lake, I watched a fisherman expertly casting a spinner across its outflow before a series of man-made waterfalls drops it into the harbour, an impressive performance even if he did not catch a fish.

I love harbours and am always fascinated at the life they hold, both human and natural. I like the colour of these places, in the ships, boats and buoys and the promise of adventure they hold for so many. Here at the shallow end of the harbour, the tide was low and in the stream flow among the brown seaweed I watched a large sea trout holding station.

The trout is one of a few species that can exist in both fresh and salt water; perhaps as a small fish, it had been washed over the waterfalls from the lake. As I walked along the quayside to the deeper part of the harbour, it was full of thousands of small fish.

I could not identify exactly what species, but with 3 dorsal fins, they were definitely a member of the cod family. I had not expected to see what would normally be a deep-water species so close to the surface.

Nearing the shopping area, a young woman approached me waving an unlit cigarette and asked me, in English, if I had a light. How did she know to speak to me in English? The morning was not yet warm but she had no coat and was dressed in a light blouse under a thin black waistcoat and was wearing a shortish black skirt.

I found this approach a little odd; she seemed quite out of place. A hotel waitress on her break perhaps or…? I was unable to help her. She shrugged her shoulders and looked for someone else to assist her.

Walking into the town, I was deeply moved by the simple beauty inside the Catholic Church, modern, tasteful and elegant. The peace within was palpable and, unlike the chapel at the Nordkapp, the music playing was quiet and beautifully suitable.

I said a little prayer and left one of my challenge post cards. What I assumed to be the Methodist Church (circa 1950) was not open but the main Protestant

Church at the end of the town was. It was here, for me, that my challenge was personally concluded.

I left my palm cross, the commemoration of my journey, some post cards and wrote about my challenge in their visitors' book. I had hoped that someone in the congregation, just someone, might have followed up out of curiosity on my journey, someone who might have been touched by the plight of the persecuted church. It would have meant so much to me to have been contacted and perhaps asked to go back, but I never was. I lit a candle, prayed for my safe journey home and for blessings over Hammerfest.

I walked along a rough causeway back towards the town and paused for a long time to watch the Arctic terns diving for fish. They dipped sometimes in false attacks but when they did drop into the water they rarely missed, taking wing again with small fishes in their beaks.

Suddenly, I was 14 again walking along the shingle path at Foulney Island, Barrow in Furness, carefully threading my way through the nesting tern colonies to fish for bass at the point. I never did catch one there but I remembered the beautiful birds that would bravely dive-bomb you if you strayed too close to their nests.

In that quiet moment I reflected on how happy I had been living on the Furness peninsula, close to the Lake District, before my father uprooted us once again to move with his job to the Midlands, before my mother's growing mental health issues became so severe that they invoke such sad memories for me to this day. Today though, as then, I was at peace.

Without asking, the very young man at the Hammerfest Gjenreisningmuset (Museum of Reconstruction) gave me the senior rate. I almost felt offended. Walking slowly around, I learned it was miraculous that the town of Hammerfest existed at all. A hurricane all but removed it from the map in 1856; it was burned to the ground in 1890, then the Germans ravaged it at the end of the Second World War.

The Museum was superb but to a large extent unsurprisingly covered the suffering of the Norwegians in this area during the last war. Retreating from the advancing Soviets, the Nazis razed the town (and local villages) to the ground in a scorched-earth policy.

Hitler ordered that 'compassion for the population is out of place.' The escaping townsfolk were forced to shelter wherever they could, in caves or boats until liberation in 1945, and very many died from cold and malnutrition. The temporary accommodation built to house them after the war had only recently been closed.

Somewhat depressed from the Hammerfest history, I sat on an upstairs window ledge looking out to sea and watched the famous Hurtigruten coastal ship coming into to dock. Within 30 minutes, the town was full of pensioner-aged tourists. Perhaps, when I get old, I will travel like this too.

Typically of me, I entered a town café behind the slowest customers in the world. Clearly off the ship, a man and his wife were painstakingly paying for their coffees in coins counting them out one by one, lots of little coins, dropping half of them on the floor in the process and all the while thinking it is a joke.

The young girl server showed incredible tolerance and good humour, whilst I, on the other hand, felt like saying to them 'oh for goodness' sake, please just pay by credit card!' Then, the family just in front of me took forever deciding what cakes to give their fractious children, and of course, when child 1 sees what child 2 has, it wanted the same, so they were back to the counter and even more delay. They really needed 2 or more servers in this place.

I tried not to show any sign of impatience but I had found the war history of Hammerfest unsettling and was beginning to fret over the ride home. I just wanted to sit down quietly and reflect over my coffee. This was far worse than waiting in line at Costa and I was not proud of the frustrated way I felt.

When they did arrive, the Cappuccino and baguette were hardly worth the wait either. I accidentally knocked my glasses case off the table and as I retrieved it, I looked up and realised that some people in the café were eyeing me quite sympathetically. I wanted to scream, 'I have just ridden a motorcycle here from England – I am not one of *them*!'

Back at the hotel, the BMW rider from Finland was a big amiable guy who told me he'd had a bike just like mine but had recently written it off when someone pulled out in front of him. He looked a bit out of character this evening for he was very smartly dressed. He was relaxed, enjoying his cigarette whilst waiting for a taxi.

I liked this man; he was unpretentious and laughed a lot. At home, he would be my friend. He told me that he and his riding buddies were going to a commemoration; 'We shall drink a lot of beer and eat Lutefish.' Lutefish (or 'lutefisk') I should add is dried fish, usually cod, soaked in cold water with certain additives to create a jelly-like substance that is regarded as a delicacy, although I am told, it is very much an acquired taste.

He told me it was in honour of some young people from the region that had died recently in a road accident. He laughed heartily when I revealed to him that to get drunk in UK would cost less than a quarter of what he will be spending tonight. He winked and told me that Russia was the place to buy booze (Hammerfest is quite close to the Russian border) and also cigarettes and that he had just bought a huge carton of them there.

'They taste like shit' he said, 'but are very cheap.' He asked me when I was leaving, '6:00 am tomorrow, through Finland and Sweden' I told him.

'It is very boring, riding through Sweden,' he said, 'dead straight roads through the forests.' His mates joined him as the taxi arrived and he shook my hand firmly and wished me well, as I did him.

I decided to go fishing in the lake, it may have been evening but it wasn't going to go dark on me was it? After all, I had my travel fly rod and a selection of flies and lures, and it would be wrong to bring it all this way and not to try to catch a fish! From my morning walk, I thought I had chosen a nice quiet spot, but it proved not to be so as the world and his wife passed by.

As I was kneeling down changing my fly, again, I heard a burst of Norwegian behind me. I looked up and it was a young man, a very drunk young man, who stumbled forward then stopped abruptly to over-correct his gait and stood in front of me swaying slightly.

When he had established I was English, he gave me some strange story about him thinking I was a kid in trouble. On hearing this, I thought I'm not the kid in trouble here. His perspective on my age was as blurred as his speech. After a brief and confusing conversation, he shook my hand warmly and tottered off to re-join his drinking buddy.

I was deeply saddened for him. Underneath I sensed he was a nice lad and, clearly from a few things he had said, not stupid, but seemingly on the road to alcoholism. How very sad. I remember that boy often in my prayers and wonder what will become of him. But the event had perturbed me and I had little heart for fishing after that.

In any case, the lake was proving to be a 'hard' water, and I gained no hint of any interest in my lures. But another thing had now grabbed my attention. Black and brooding clouds were building up on the hills at the back of the hotel and I could see a beautiful rainbow.

It looked like a big storm. I hoofed it back to the hotel in super quick time. I made it back without a drop of rain falling on me, and the storm had passed through very quickly and was now out to sea.

Hamlet, the Danish motorcyclist who crossed with me on the ferry from Denmark to Norway all those days ago, seemed to have got it right with his, 'I have never known it not to rain when riding in Northern Norway. And as it had rained the previous night, I discovered the 'Air Hawk' seat cover was not that waterproof and, given the storm which had passed through recently, I would rather not start my ride tomorrow with a cold and wet seat under me.

The new girl on reception disappeared briefly into the stock cupboard and kindly gave me a huge black bin liner which I wrapped around the whole seat. She told me proudly it was from Finland. I am possibly the only English motorcyclist ever that has covered his bike seat in Finnish polythene.

The result was not pretty but no rain was going anywhere near my rump tomorrow. This hotel might not have been very up-market but I really liked it and knew I had been blessed here. I did another wash, a non-coloured one this time. Scarily, I could get the hang of this. But I was fussing and feeling a little guilty, for it was early evening by now and there was no sign of Eric.

After dinner, I walked the now dry hills behind the hotel for an hour or two. There were no trees there and an austere landscape of boulders, shale, lichens, grasses, and stunted shrubs. I loved it. It was a time of reflection as I sat on a rock and looked out at a Norway I had come to love.

My overwhelming emotion was one of thankfulness; I had a sense of God smiling down at me. The Bible tells us that Jesus often withdrew too, to lonely places to pray. I felt peaceful and, although I wanted to go home now, it felt a wrench to be leaving. I could have happily stayed here another few days but knew it was time to leave – the challenge was over, time to start for home.

Re-entering the hotel, there was a middle-aged couple checking in. I said hello and he spoke but she didn't and had no smile. Shortly afterwards, I heard a slight disturbance in the corridor down from my room. It was them and I was asked if I could help as they could not get into their room. They handed me the key and I opened it for them immediately. But there was some problem with the lock, after all, it seemed. Later, they told me they had changed rooms. She smiled at me then.

It was nervous settling down to sleep because I had made a commitment in southern Sweden that I was already starting to regret. Not the commitment exactly to visit an acquaintance there, but the pressure it was going to put me under to fulfil it and I was in no doubt about the riding it was going to entail. Some very big days ahead.

# Chapter 10
# Below the Circle – The Long Road Back

*'We will continue to fight against the evil spirits until the day all the demolished churches and altars are restored in our country.'* – **A North Korean pastor remembering that once his country was full of churches.**

**Day 16 – Sunday** 22$^{nd}$ July 2018. Hammerfest to Tornio (Finland). Leaving time – 05:50; temperature range – 18°C to 26°C; distance ridden – 721 kilometres.

I was awake at stupid o' clock. Outside the rain was hammering down and I could hear the rattle of distant thunder. Hamlet's prophesy had finally been enacted. It was the darkest Norway morning of my trip so far. Not natural darkness, as that did not return up here for weeks, but an uncommon creation from indigo boiling clouds.

I found myself on edge anyway because I feared I may have bitten off more than I could chew with regard to my return leg. I should explain. I had arranged to visit someone in Ystad, south Sweden to arrive there specifically on the 24 July and, poring over my dog-eared map, I suddenly became aware of the magnitude of the ride I was destined to undertake over the next 3 days.

I had met Sue and her son Aaron just once before when they visited a mutual friend of ours, Bernadine, in Highley. I took Aaron fishing down the River Severn one evening, something he has never forgotten and yes, he did catch some fish. Sue is not a lady who enjoys the best of health and I sensed when I called her on the way up to Hammerfest that she was keen for some English company.

She had heard of my trip through Bernadine (Sue and Bernadine had trained together as nurses and were lifelong friends) and on learning I was returning through Sweden wanted me to call in to see her, but, looking at the distances involved now, for me to be there on 24$^{th}$ was suddenly going to be a tall order.

Aaron was the manager of the best hotel in Ystad and had booked me accommodation specifically for that night. Perhaps I was going to regret that day off in Hammerfest yesterday and not having a full night's sleep raised questions of tiredness for me today as I rode. Eric's bike had not reappeared overnight, so where he ended up yesterday could only be speculated on, but no doubt he had something set up.

I left Hammerfest just before 06:00, quietly and with some sadness, the rain had passed and the roads were drying, and for a change it was quite cool. I liked this little town very much, as technically the end point for my challenge it too had gained a special place in my heart.

There was no traffic as I slipped away from the town boundaries but I smiled as there were reindeer on the fjord bridge, seemingly a fitting and poignant memory for me to take away.

Essentially I needed to ride over 700 kilometres (400 plus miles) today right across the Scandinavian Peninsula from the Norwegian west coast down through Finland to the Swedish border. And, to set the scene, soon I would turn south west onto the E6 back towards Alta. I was coming home.

My riding seat was dry but I kept (and still have) the Finnish bin liner. The panorama was vast across the tundra, with some mist at the bases of the distant grey mountains, but there was no sign of any storms now. I was comfortable on the bike this morning.

It was not hot but pleasant and I was relaxed and, in contrast to the night before, tried not to think about the distances to cover. Riding down a hill towards the ruler-straight section of road across the tundra, I spotted a large animal loping across the scrubland and quite close to the road. My immediate thought was, 'Who on earth could have lost a big dog like this out here in the middle of nowhere?'

Then the penny dropped; it was a large, lone, black wolf. I stopped immediately to try to take a picture, but the wolf was spooked by my sudden deceleration and took off and, by the time I had fumbled my camera out of the tankbag, he had become a speck in the distance. But what a privilege even to have seen him.

I say 'him' because he was so big. I had seen a lone wolf just once before in Ontario and this beast was very much like him, black and big. The Ontario wolf appeared out of the undergrowth ahead of us as we were driving slowly along on a gravel road up to a remote fishing lake.

I'd sensed something and said to my fishing buddies, 'Watch, he is going to turn and look at us' and no sooner had I voiced this he did, looking back at us defiantly. We'd stopped too and for a few seconds there was an awkward stand off before he decided he didn't like the look of us and loped back invisibly into the greenery. I'd recalled at that moment I was glad I had not been on foot.

Back on the bike and enjoying the isolation of the tundra and empty roads a few kilometres on I saw an Arctic hare. The wolf, the hare and the lemming were the only animal wildlife I was to see on the whole trip, not counting reindeer and birds of course.

At Alta, I said goodbye to my old friend the A6 as I turned due south onto road 93. This road ran alongside a fast-swirling river for many kilometres and the waterfalls were spectacular as was the road that skirted it. The sinuous corners following the ever-twisting river were fantastic to ride.

I tried to be sensible by keeping loosely to the 80 kph limit for a while, but the road proved to be too much of a temptation. It was so unbelievably quiet, with little traffic and no villages to speak of and after not many minutes of enforced 'goodness' this once again went out of the window.

I rode the 93 in the fast and flowing manner all motorcyclists would understand, happy to be gaining on my time. I can only recall overtaking 2 small commercial vehicles; it was a blissfully uninterrupted ride on a fabulous road.

Late morning, I stopped at a café at a place called Suolovuobme. I only knew the name because I'd bought a sticker there, for it was not on my Scandinavian map. Why should it be? The place was just a café and a few out-buildings, and were it not for the roadside sign I would have missed it.

It was a small Sami community, the café and shop being built in a traditional pine style. I found it cosy, scrupulously clean and tidy as I leant back in my seat and stretched my now tired legs.

Would they speak English way out here I wondered? Of course they did! The young waitress apologised that it was cash only as their credit card machine was not working; fortunately I still had enough Kroner to pay for my sandwich, coffee and some quality souvenirs.

It was an excellent stop. Suolovuobme sounded Finnish. Finland is called Suomi in their language so the link seemed reasonable to me. It did not quite seem a Norwegian name and I had noted too some of the place names on this road seemed to have become 'different.'

Naively, I asked the girl if I had actually crossed into Finland. She laughed. 'No, no, you are still in Norway.'

When I did reach the Finnish border there was actually little doubt about it. It was a proper border crossing, or perhaps it would have been, had it been staffed. There were no security guards in evidence.

I stopped and looked up at the border control office window just in case, but it was empty and, as the barrier was open, I rode into another country without having been seen or noticed by anyone. I was disappointed to note that the speed limit was unchanged at 80 kph. I was now on the E8 still heading due south.

I knew it couldn't all be like this; Finland is a very beautiful country. I mean I was primed because I'd seen the 'Hairy Bikers' on TV cooking some hapless fish or other at stunning rural locations there. I have friends who visit family in Finland and have seen their holiday pictures, but my impressions of Finland, at least this part of it? Sorry Finland, on the route I was riding this day, it was flat and lacking in much interest. Its sandy soils and pine forests reminded me very much of Northern Michigan (sorry Michigan too), interlaced with long mainly straight and unchallenging roads, and these were to mark the rest of the day's ride.

The Swedish border was not many kilometres away to my right, and I was skirting it all the way down to the coast. It was to be another 'grind-it-out' riding afternoon on an unexciting road just purposefully heading south. The only thing of real note was catching the edge of a thunderstorm, not really heavy enough for me to cover my tank bag but certainly dark, menacing and brooding over in Sweden.

I was glad it was going away from me. It was, thankfully, a cooler afternoon in the saddle today, a rare thing since leaving home. I rode alongside another river, wide and powerful looking (the Torne) with many signs indicating the possibility of fishing for salmon. Even in Finnish I got that, but I did not stop to investigate.

I arrived at a town called Tornio, named after the river presumably. I had no forward hotel booking so once more I was winging it. I rode over the river bridge into the town. I could see one hotel immediately, the Park Hotel, but decided to do a little ride around to see what else is on offer and stopped outside the 'Boutique' hotel, Mustraparta, and went in.

It was busy and extremely twee with a lot of purple hangings. I felt out of place here and as I could see no obvious car park, I decided against it. I rode back

173

to the Park Hotel where there was ample and fairly private parking and thankfully secured a good room from which I could see my bike below.

I was amazed when I checked my trip log that this has been my biggest day in the saddle to date, some 721 kilometres, but I felt fresher than I expected to. Even though it got a little warm towards the end of the day the riding was easy and untroubled, the distances just rolling away. Tomorrow however…

I walked into the town and found a Vietnamese restaurant. They had no English whatsoever, I had no Finnish, but the menu had pictures (always helpful in my case) and by a system of pointing, grunts and squeaks we found an acceptable compromise on the menu.

I had never eaten Vietnamese food before and it turned out to be a kind of flavoursome combination of Thai and Chinese. The meal was very good; a satisfying end to a long day's riding. Returning to the hotel I paid for my accommodation before retiring, as is my custom, and slept deeply.


**Day 17 – Monday** 23rd July 2018. Tornio, Finland to Hudiksvall, Sweden. Leaving time – 06:25; temperature range – 18°C to 32°C; distance ridden – 795 kilometres.

I awoke early, refreshed by an undisturbed sleep and was on the bike and away swiftly, intending to ride today until it seemed reasonable to stop and secure accommodation. I crossed from Finland into Sweden within a few kilometres, with no designated border crossing, only a sign informing me of the change. Just another country, just another day.

I was now riding the infamous E4; I say infamous because what I had read about it was not very complimentary. I asked Finland's forgiveness for saying their roads were boring, but very quickly I realised that riding through Sweden was going to be a challenge too, the traffic being immediately heavier and, after such quiet roads recently, menacing.

I would stay on the E4 for virtually the whole length of Sweden. The speed limit was slightly more generous at 90 kph, but there were speed cameras everywhere. The Sat Nav began pinging monotonously almost immediately warning me where they were, but after a while I got a feel of where they were likely to be anyway and anticipated them.

In the north, the E4 was mainly single lane with the occasional third lane for overtaking. The most important thing for me to note as a motorcyclist was the appalling wire safety barriers erected in places on long stretches between the carriageways. It paid not to think too much about the consequences of ending up tangled in one of these, although I understood the need for them for more 'normal' vehicles.

This route through Sweden was, as my Finnish friend at Hammerfest had predicted, tedious too. It consisted mainly of long straight road sections through pine forests which masked any perspective beyond them, so I had no real idea of the topography of the country beyond the confines of the tarmac strip I was riding along. The landscape was at times gently undulating and although I knew I was following the coast of Sweden somewhere to my left, I could see no sign of it.

On and on I rode, trying to take my mind off the monotonous nature of the developing ride. Fuel stops became a relief instead of an inconvenience and the weather began heating up uncomfortably again.

I stopped for a comfort break early afternoon somewhere off this endless E4 and as I was a bit disengaged with the region and area I did not note where it was, only recalling a dual carriageway section and it being very busy. As I rode up the slip road into the service area, I could not fail to notice a male hitchhiker who was placing himself in a vulnerable situation by standing so close to the incoming vehicles.

My immediate reaction was what a stupid and potentially dangerous place for him to stand as he assertively waved his thumb at approaching vehicles leaning over at a less than sensible angle. They all ignored him of course. I didn't think he was very good at this hitch-hiking game because to me it would have made far more sense for him to be standing at the exit catching vehicles as they were coming out.

He cut an odd-looking figure too, a man in his fifties I guessed, with long, almost shoulder length hair, yet bald on top. He was medium height and wearing severe square framed glasses and he had a slightly gormless but perhaps harmless look.

He was hardly dressed to kill in green shorts and a yellow tee shirt set off by a less than matching purple backpack. It was not a good look. I think his appearance alone would not be in his favour. I noted all this in detail because after hours of seeing very little of any interest he was suddenly it.

As I came out of the service area, he had changed tactics, now going from car to car knocking on the windows and asking directly for a ride, and I could see he was getting curt responses from the drivers.

I felt quite sorry for him at this point as he was clearly desperate to get somewhere. I gave him a little wave as I rode out and he nodded in appreciation and I even said a little prayer for him which, as we shall see, may have been heard.

There were many more road works cropping up now and the contra-flows alongside the biker-unfriendly barriers kept me on my toes. The traffic was beginning to become much heavier as the more populous parts of Sweden were approached and some towns, which were not yet by-passed, were almost gridlocked.

One, Skelleftea, was particularly bad and it was a horrible chore riding in the growing heat at such low speeds though these bottlenecks.

The ongoing ride from this town did not become any more entertaining than before and by early evening and I was getting fatigued and thinking of finding accommodation. I stopped and tapped the 'food and lodging' icon on the Sat Nav and apparently there was a guest house off the very next junction.

I rode to it through 7 kilometres of rural Sweden which proved there was very pretty countryside away from that blessed road. The little guest house looked really nice too. I walked in and rang the desk bell, but no one came. Some guests arrived behind me picking up their rooms keys off a reception table. They gave me a look of mild apprehension, registering perhaps their fear that I might actually get a room. I felt a little like a vagrant (not so far from the truth at that moment). The bell chimed out again, and again, no one answered. I gave up. A 14-kilometre excursion for absolutely nothing.

Back on the E4, a bit put out, I ploughed on to the next town, Hudiksvall, and the Sat Nav tried to guide me to a hotel. Following Emilie's prompts, I rode down the correct street towards it but my way was suddenly blocked by a large woman standing in the road centre waving her arms at me in what I felt was quite a belligerent manner.

I had failed to comprehend in my tired state that the road was in the process of being closed for a fair. There was a road sign, which was in Swedish. It could have been telling me the way to the nearest zoo for all I knew!

Perhaps it was. The field adjacent was peppered with unkempt looking people wearing oily overalls erecting large and garishly coloured rides with luridly painted murals tempting a satisfaction that the ride would never actually deliver. These were matched in their awfulness by the equally tawdry half-built side stalls.

Whatever warmth I might have for fairgrounds (very little actually) was rapidly being dissipated by my fatigue and her overly aggressive attitude. She blared at me in Swedish and I was quietly muttering my annoyance back in Anglo Saxon inside my helmet.

I really felt like taking it off and giving her a verbal blast in my best Derbyshire accent and now wish I had. I was not impressed; she was shooing me away like some errant cow that had strayed into a forbidden pasture. The road was not yet blocked, it was not at all busy and frankly it would have cost her (and the others who had by now joined her to endorse the intimidation) nothing to let my bike slip through.

But no, this was about authority not common sense. I could have ridden around them and thought of doing so but I knew these people have a reputation for not being messed with and I didn't fancy coming down to a kicked over motorcycle next morning.

So, I turned the bike around, very slowly, just to frustrate her a little more as she stood there with her hands on her hips. Her attitude was very bad, and mine towards her and the show people wasn't much better being honest. This is what extreme tiredness can do to you. Looking back on it now, I see the funny side of it.

After circumnavigating the town a couple of times, somehow, we, Emilie and I, found an alternative route to the hotel (Hotel Hudik, another Best Western) and I could see immediately from the number of cars in the car park I might be in trouble with a room. But, God's providence and kindness to me was in evidence once again. The young man on reception, Lars, could not have been more helpful to my situation or indeed sympathy for my cause.

'I only have one superior room left' he says, 'but I give it to you at the normal rate'. He winked and said, 'don't tell anyone though'.

It was a lovely room too, as was the restaurant meal and, at last, an almost normally priced beer; in fact I confess I had two. I retired de-stressed and relatively contented. I think I dreamt of fairground rides.

**Day 18 – Tuesday** 24th July 2018. Hudiksvall to Ystad. Leaving time – 05:00; temperature range – 20°C to 38°C; distance ridden – 975 kilometres. .

Knowing of my need for an early departure the hotel placed a pre-prepared continental breakfast outside my room in the wee small hours. Sipping my orange juice, I was getting nervous about what lay ahead today, common sense telling me I had somewhat over-committed myself after riding 1,516 kilometres (942 miles) in the two preceding days.

I rode out of the hotel car park bang on 5:00 am and my unease was not helped by attracting the attention of two bored police officers in a marked police car who latched onto me like a leech. I had to endure their close attention for a few kilometres before they peeled off for elsewhere at the E4 roundabout.

Not the best of starts for what I knew was going to be a very tough day's riding. Realistically, I knew my ride through Sweden should have been at least another day longer, but I had no choice. No matter what time I arrived at Ystad later today the scene was set for keeping calm and carrying on, and on, and on, ever southerly on.

My Sat Nav was pinging warnings much more regularly now; clearly there were many more speed cameras from this point on the E4. At my first stop for fuel today, I lost valuable time. I pulled up at a 'Preem' filling station and, as I had on countless occasions on this trip, looked to pay for fuel at the pump; actually there was no alternative here as it had no staffed kiosk.

For some stupid reason (yes, stupid when you consider this is the primary route through Sweden and many foreign tourists would be taking it) their pumps did not give an option for instruction in English, and to compound the situation they seemed to be configured to deliver fuel in a very different way to all the other pumps I had come across on this trip to date.

Try as I might I could not work it out and, unlike the kind van driver in Belgium, there was no one around to assist me. I gave up after many fruitless attempts and rode on but was really annoyed to have lost this valuable riding time. Fortunately I did have enough fuel to get me to the next non-Preem facility. But what if I hadn't?

It was back to riding in very high temperatures again and the sun beat down out of a merciless sky and soon it became almost uncomfortably hot on the bike. I had to stop much more frequently now (I lost track of how many times I was forced to do so this day) just to rehydrate myself and replenish my water supply.

After just an hour's riding the water was beyond tepid and almost hot when I took my bottle out of the top case. I realised, after riding into a rest area by a huge lake the wrong way, much to the tutting consternation of the already parked motorists, that I was becoming a little drowsy and fatigued.

(Actually, logically coming in from the junction it was the right way in, their set up being oddly wrong; the entrance and exits ought to have been reversed which would have made much more sense to me). Missing a small 'no entry' sign is understandable but a worry, for clearly I was not as alert as I should be.

All these rest stops were slowing me down too, giving rise for concern on my time, but I could not really raise the riding pace, as the route was well policed, the traffic was too heavy anyway and I was getting too hot for anything other than regular breaks.

Because I could not be bothered to turn the bike around, I rode out of the rest area, past the shocked motorists, the wrong way again. In my head, I was excusing myself; after all, the sign had been in Swedish, hadn't it? No excuse Merv, you're just an awkward so and so sometimes.

Mercifully, the E4 became a motorway-proper as Stockholm and other major cities came within reach, the speed limit increased to 110 kph, occasionally 120 kph, and I made the most of the opportunity for better pace with the extra flow of air around me being most welcome, if hardly cooling.

I pulled off again near Stockholm itself at a very large services and went in to buy more water and my energy-reviving (well it seemed to work for me) chocolate milk drink.

On exiting, my eye was caught a by a large white tiled angular building on the other side of the huge car park. It looked rather like the superstructure of a very modern ship. On a large mural facing me were the words, '*there is no other name.*'

It was a church, and clearly a very prosperous one. Then I noticed the black circular wall sign that said in funky lettering 'Hillsong STHLM' and immediately I knew what I was looking at. Hillsong is a megachurch, started by Brian and Bobby Houston in Sydney, Australia and described by musical scholar Tom Wagner as '*a confluence of sophisticated marketing techniques and popular music.*'

It is a modern church phenomenon, professional and slick in everything it does. I was to learn later that there were no less than 7 Hillsong churches in Sweden. Although I didn't really have the time, I was drawn to it for some reason. I walked across and over the covered bridge entrance to the door but did not venture in – I was just curious.

I discerned a reception area that would rival many a hotel and noted the designated parking slots for the pastor and other leaders, one being taken by a new white BMW. I was overwhelmed by the sheer opulence of this worship facility.

What I write next is not meant to be a judgement of Hillsong particularly, for I know they excel in worship and their influence in Christian circles is without question. As a result of attending their churches many people have become Christians and who am I to criticise that in any way? But suddenly, I felt profoundly uncomfortable and did not want to be anywhere near it. What struck me, powerfully and forcibly, was how at odds this facility was with the experience of the persecuted church. It was almost an affront to my tired mindset at that moment in time. I walked back to my bike with genuine sadness as I thought of the Christians in North Korea who could not even admit to owning a Bible without fear of imprisonment or death and where a secret church meeting could be within the confines of a stinking prison toilet.

What I saw here today was the complete opposite and comfortable end of the church scale. Yes, of course, it has its place, but largely it would be touching people who possibly would never consider the cost of following Christ in a dangerous place. That thought did not, does not, rest comfortably with me at all for sometimes that person is me too.

I rode past Stockholm and well south of the city at another rest area I found a quiet picnic table in the shade of some large pine trees away from the noisy families, small yapping dogs and the torrid heat radiating up from the concrete car park and crashed out for about 10 minutes.

There was little respite from the heat even in the shade, but I was so tired now it mattered little. It would have been dangerous for me to continue riding in this state. On waking I grabbed a snack and drink then it was back on the bike for another toilsome leg of this epic riding day.

Soon I was riding past the cities of Norrkoping and Linkoping on and endlessly on in the searing heat of that July day. Now I had eaten and taken on water again, like some human camel, I was resolved not to stop again until I exited the E4 for the roads down to Ystad.

At junction 74 I took the 114 due south where it was disconcerting to see a sign telling me Ystad was still some 130 kilometres away. Once again I sensed the onset of fatigue. I cannot describe exactly how it feels when you are riding, but traffic situations start to become a little surreal in your head. When you feel somewhat disengaged with your riding it's time to pull over and rest.

I stopped at a lay-by and, as I dismounted, I felt like all the vitality had been sucked out of me. I was exhausted. I walked across the road into a shaded area and lay down under some trees. I felt a bit like some saddle tramp at that moment and wondered briefly what passing motorists might make of me, but I didn't care. I was so blooming tired that only an apocalyptic event would have stirred me. I slept again for about 20 minutes and awoke reasonably refreshed and ready to complete my journey.

The 114 is a rural single carriageway much like an English 'B' road, and with it comes the traffic challenges this kind of road presents. Within 10 kilometres of my rest stop I rode up to a snake of about 20 vehicles happily following a tractor and trailer doing about 30 kph.

I asked myself what is wrong with these people? No one is even attempting to overtake it. On a bike I had the advantage and took it, and in a series of staged passes I left them behind to continue to enjoy their traffic conga. I was suddenly very grateful for my rest stop because I felt engaged and mentally sharp again.

At a small town called Vassleholm, I turned onto highway 23. On a stretch of dual carriageway I saw in my mirrors a car approaching me at speed. I indicated I was taking the next junction for highway 13, mercifully the last stretch of road before my destination.

I could discern the car was obviously a sports car of some sort and he was pulling off here with me too. He came quite close, not dangerously, but close enough and I could not resist dropping down a gear and accelerating away from him (sometimes I think I need to just grow up) around a beautiful sweeping left-hand bend leaving him for dead.

On the next stretch of road, he'd caught me up very quickly, a seriously fast car, and, because I was intrigued, I let him come past. It was a bright blue Corvette convertible being driven by a middle-aged man and his blonde female companion. I held my hand up as they go by. They took the next junction off and both gave me a friendly wave back as they pulled off. Respect.

My Sat Nav had been set for Hotel Continental, Ystad since leaving this morning and now, finally, I was relieved to hear Emilie voicing that I was very close. I pulled up outside the main hotel reception door. It was *the* hotel in Ystad, a seriously posh establishment.

I looked at myself in the handlebar mirror and groaned inwardly. Matted hair, my weary and lined face streaked with road dirt and sweat, it was now me that did not have a good look. My clothes were insect spattered and dusty from the ride; in short I was a bit of a sight.

Carrying my crash helmet, which by now looked like it had been used as some sort of battle weapon, I tentatively walked up to the immaculate reception area and desk graced by an equally immaculate and beautiful girl receptionist. She had icy blue eyes and was blonde of course.

I suddenly felt out of place and quite embarrassed. Very well-dressed guests were descending the marble stairs for their evening cocktails; they pretended I was not there. I did not blame them. Bless her; this girl was totally professional and not fazed in the slightest by my dishevelled appearance.

I explain that Aaron Alger had booked me a room. She smiled knowingly, having been expecting me. Aaron, who was in the adjacent office, had also seen me. He had grown into a very handsome young man from that teenage lad I took fishing all those years ago and he was clearly very much in charge here.

He showed me where to park my bike in their small car park among the Porsches, BMWs and other upmarket cars. He insisted on carrying my bags up to the lovely room and handed me two bottles of ice-cold water. I felt cared for, if not loved, and was suddenly quite emotional as he left me to refresh.

It was 18:45; I had been on the road for over 13 hours and in searing heat for most of it. Later, I was alarmed to see I had actually ridden 975 kilometres. This was a day's riding I would never forget or indeed be keen to replicate again. It wasn't so much the distance, for I think under normal temperatures on those roads it wouldn't have been a big problem. But the heat made it more like an endurance test and I was very thankful to have completed the day safely.

I rang Sue who told me she could not see me till 10:30 tomorrow, this being a little later than I had intended was a concern because, as I told her, I needed to be back on the road by early afternoon at the latest.

She did not sound very well, a little confused almost, but I knew she had to take many drugs for her myriad of physical conditions. Sue asked me if I could bring 4 fresh bread rolls with me when I came as she wanted to make us a bit of lunch.

Looking almost human again and reasonably well-dressed, I perkily arrived back at the reception desk. There was another pretty girl on reception, again blonde naturally. I asked her about the possibility of a dinner reservation. Aaron magically appeared by my side and apologised that I was now too late for dinner rightly explaining he could not pre-book for me as he was unsure what time I was arriving. He wasn't the only one.

He recommended the local Italian restaurant which proved an excellent choice. The carbonara was possibly the best I have ever had, but I was stupid for, in my relief at a safe arrival and by way of personal celebration, I had one too many bottled lagers (total of two, that's all, honest).

I then took a leisurely walk around the harbour and watched the sun going down. Ystad was full of beautiful people and never have I visited a place where almost everyone I saw that evening could instantly be included a photo shoot for an M&S life-style advert; perhaps it's the Ystad water.

Alas, I was not one of them and once more I felt out of place and, if I am honest, just a little old.

As he was having a day off tomorrow, I said my grateful farewells to Aaron before retiring. He was a young man with a very bright future, I think, and he had allowed me to stay at this super hotel at a preferential rate. But my expected rest was interrupted by the consequences of my slight over indulgence; I found myself awake with a thumping headache, halfway through the night. I had only myself to blame.

# Chapter 11
## And so, to Home

*'We have really been trained on how to stand strong through the storms of life as children of God and as lights in this dark age.'* – **John a northern Nigeria Christian**

**Day 19 – Wednesday** 25th July 2018. Ystad, Sweden to Derboven, Germany. Time of leaving – 14:15; temperature range – 30°C to 40°C; distance ridden – 647 kilometres.

I was not up very early this morning. It was not the best of nights for me and I needed to allow the painkillers and the extra rest to do their job. I sat in the comfortable chair in the room doing my readings and updating my Facebook page.

Actually, I did not wonder I was feeling a little less than human this morning considering the ridiculous riding commitment I undertook the day before and the temperatures I rode in. I have always struggled at getting my personal hydration levels balanced on days when I have become excessively hot, which under normal circumstances I try to avoid.

I was in no doubt whatsoever that in spite of all the water I drank yesterday I was still in a state of dehydration when I retired. The alcohol from just two bottled beers had triggered a monster headache in the middle of the night; it is something I have suffered before. Okay, if you want to, you can call it a hangover.

When I did go down for breakfast, along with the majority of other guests it seemed, I entered a beautiful and tastefully styled restaurant where everything from curtains to cutlery smacked of quality. In spite of my misgivings about buffets, this one was simply superb and I made the most of it.

No hairy workers with plastic bags snatching their lunch provisions here; the clientele at this establishment were prosperous and not afraid to show it, with many pairs of Gucci and Dolce and Gabbana sunglasses in evidence.

This buffet was conducted in a genteel manner and nothing like the breakfast rugby scrums experienced at some of the other establishments on this trip. But one similarity covered both groups; they weren't speaking much to each other. Perhaps they needed to be wearing posh sunglasses inside at 8:30 in the morning because their cocktail hangovers were bigger than mine.

I had to vacate my room by 10:30 and take my packed inner bags down and secure them in the bike side cases. My riding clothing, helmet and tank bag were left in the hotel security room to retrieve later and I walked into town.

The carillon chiming in Ystad town centre told me it was 9:00 and I had an hour and half to relax and enjoy this beautiful little town full of beautiful people. Sea, harbour, small pretty park areas and colourful buildings. What was there not to like?

I watched as the local market was being set up in the square and bought my soft bread rolls from the friendly bakery opposite the main church. Of course, English was universally spoken here too in Sweden and when I told the baker who I was visiting and that they were for our lunch, he insisted I have four different kinds of rolls. It was the kind of customer service one rarely finds in the UK these days.

Yet as I strolled and sat occasionally on a shaded seat in this seemingly well-ordered town, I occasionally caught the unmistakable smell of stale urine. I noted a filthy coat that some 'down and out' had discarded and realised that Ystad has a dark underbelly of social issues too.

As I sat on a bench outside one of the churches, a very fit looking lady of mature years sat on the other bench a little way down from me. In khaki shorts and strong boots, she was purposefully dressed for a long walk I thought, but in her hands was a large and rather ungainly looking plastic bag.

She did not speak to me then but got up to try the door handle of the church which was locked. She took an iPad out of the bag and proceeded to do what all of us seem to do these days, check her social media. She got up and disappeared but was back a few minutes later.

By now, I was intrigued and said hello and she told me she was about to go on a walking pilgrimage to another Swedish town but because of her accent I was unable to catch exactly where. As we were talking, the lady minister arrived to unlock the church along with another lady who introduced herself as the organist and she, thinking me another pilgrim, came over to shake my hand.

She was middle-aged, tall, blonde and clearly another product of the Ystad water and nothing like my common perception of a crusty church organist. It seemed that there was to be a service to bless these pilgrims on their way.

I explained the very different nature of my own pilgrimage to these three ladies; they were mildly interested but not exactly wowed with what I shared and I am certain they thought me somewhat peculiar. How very perceptive of them. By now, the square was filling with other pilgrims, it was 10:00 and time to begin my search for Sue's apartment.

I was late arriving. Even though her apartment proved eventually to be not so very far away from where I had been sitting, Liz, who had been given the address for me by our/Sue's friend Bernadine, had written it down incorrectly.

As a consequence, in the now growing heat of another baking day, I walked up and down the blessed street for ages before eventually working out the apartments are through an entrance into a quadrangle; even then it took me more time to locate the right floor (the lower one in the end) and the right apartment. I was not best pleased with myself for being 15 minutes late.

The Sue who eventually answered the door was a very different Sue to the one I last met; Aaron had warned me that his mum had become increasingly frail. She walked now very slowly with the aid of a wheeled walker and she was coughing mildly as she invited me in.

As I entered the apartment, I immediately noticed the smell of tobacco smoke and it turned out Sue, in spite of her health issues, had remained a committed smoker and it wasn't long before she was lighting up. I make no judgement about this because people have the choice to make their own minds up about their lifestyles. And indeed who am I to criticise that, I after all ride a motorcycle, and that isn't exactly the safest life style choice either?

As we sat and talked, she told me she had cheated death twice last year; the kidney cancer operation she had to undergo was complex, she almost died and had to be given multiple blood transfusions. Then on her return home, her carers came in to find her unconscious and very close to death.

The cause of this proved to be carbon monoxide poisoning from faulty equipment in her rented apartment. She told me the owners of the apartments had not been as helpful or caring as they should have been given the circumstances and the case was still ongoing.

Sue talked about how she valued the close friendship with our mutual friend Bernadine and how they kept in close contact with each other. The time quickly passed, we had a lot to catch up on, and in spite of her obvious discomfort she did not allow me to make the cheese rolls.

We sat and enjoyed our lunch and coffee on her little veranda overlooking the communal courtyard and she told me of the kindness of her neighbours who waved to her as they walked past. She had perfect Swedish of course, so communication with them was not a problem.

After telling her about my challenge and Norway, she revealed she had a dream to go there on a cruise to the fjords and I strongly encouraged her to follow that dream. She was not a Christian, had a slight belief but underneath was really quite sceptical. However, she did allow me to pray for her and Aaron.

Time marched on there was much more we could have talked about but I just had to go. We had had a lovely time together and we hugged as I left but I was really quite sad to leave her. As I walked back to the hotel, I felt a little emotional. I am glad I made the effort to go and see her but was sorry because Sue had a kind of fatalistic way about her; but I thought that in Aaron she could not have a better son to care for her and it lightened my spirits a little.

It was early afternoon as I rode out of Ystad and with not even the solace of a cloud the heat had built up to an almost expected sauna-like scale. On the outskirts of Malmo, I took autoroute E20 crossing over that fabulous bridge (it really is a spectacular thing) which was the backdrop for the popular Danish crime TV series, 'The Bridge' and then I took the E47 due south to Germany. For the first time in days, I felt as if I was now actually going home.

Liz had been looking at my route and in our regular evening catch up she informed me, 'you've got a tunnel and a ferry crossing too on that route tomorrow.' How did she know that? 'I don't think so' I said, but I had not really checked and indeed she was quite correct on both counts.

As it happened it was a moderately long ferry crossing as it happened on a seriously big ship when compared to those used on the fjord crossings. At a place called Rodbyhavn, as I sat and waited for the ferry to arrive from the German side, the rider of a Honda Goldwing came up to chat with me (this, I might add, is normally how motorcyclists interact with other).

He was tall and German and had perfect teeth and perfect English. He seemed very excited, 'I am going to a bike festival at…' I did not catch the name, but somewhere in Germany. 'Yes,' he said, 'I get accommodation for only €50 and do you know? They serve the beer through an old Kawasaki Z1300 engine!'

I smiled and was tempted to ask him if he liked his beer with an oil flavour, but I knew the Germans often really do not get our sense of humour and thought better of it. The Japanese are even worse though, laughing when you are not joking at all and when you are they often become as inscrutable as only the Orientals can.

My German friend was a really nice guy and clearly looking forward to his biking holiday. We spent the time passing the day; he was very impressed with the ride I had undertaken. The motorcyclists were first to board the ship. Upon paying they told me the crossing was 45 minutes and being tired I went onto the upper deck, found a quiet seat and had a much-needed snooze.

Being a roll-on/roll-off ferry, we were first down the ramp and as we had crossed the German/Denmark border on the water, I was once again riding in Germany. I overtook my friend on his Goldwing, and he waved. He was in no hurry, I on the other hand…

It did not seem very long before the E47 joined what I assumed to be the primary autobahn in Germany since it was designated the A1 and, at my first fuel stop, I could not quite believe my eyes. It was him, the hitchhiker from Sweden!

You really couldn't mistake him or easily forget him. Still wearing the green shorts and yellow tee shirt, he was holding his map prominently whilst wandering up and down approaching people directly to ask for a lift and as before getting short shrift from them. But he had done well to even get this far.

He was over 1,000 kilometres further on than the last time I saw him and he'd got there ahead of me! Okay, I did lose most of a day going to Ystad, but even so it was an impressive achievement and I gained a grudging respect for him. But here was the odd thing; whoever dropped him here would have been going on and as there were no immediate turn offs on this section of autobahn I wondered if perhaps he had over-stayed his welcome.

As I refuelled, I watched him approach a car driver close by who was also filling up. It was a very short conversation. I nodded to him as I rode out, and he nodded back. What was his story, I wondered?

Heading towards Hamburg and being late afternoon, I began thinking of accommodation and I turned off the A1 north of Lubeck stop and inquired of the Sat Nav where local accommodation might be. In the now heavy rush hour traffic and on congested roads, I pulled up outside the first indicated hotel.

Something didn't look quite right as the car park was empty and yet it looked every bit a hotel. A man sitting outside what I assumed to be the reception had his head down into his iPhone. Bob McMillan, my friend and former Honda boss, has a doppelganger in Germany and I did a double-take for a second as he really did look like him.

However, unlike Bob, this man was scruffy and bare chested, his shorts were filthy and he was irritable. 'Hotel?' I enquired cheerfully, feeling more uneasy by the second. 'Nein, kaput,' he said sweeping his arm sharply in a gesture of finality as if I didn't understand him.

I pointed down the road; 'More hotel?' I asked. He knew very well what I meant but pretended he didn't, shrugged his shoulders and looked back down at his phone. Nice chap I thought, the second example of rudeness in this trip and just when I didn't need it. My day was not quite over though in this regard. I was starting to fret a little and he had not helped.

I tapped on the icon and Emilie was soon guiding me to hotel number 2. I was not quite sure where I was exactly, somewhere just north and east of Lubeck. I had no map for this area, so I was relying solely on technology now.

On the way I saw a motel and it looked outwardly acccptable, so I stopped to see if they might have a room. The rather ample German Frau owner wasn't rude, but not exactly friendly either. The answer was 'nein' and, when I noticed the appalling reception décor and the rather dodgy looking clientele, I was hardly disappointed.

Emilie next had me coming down a hill into a resort town of some sorts and here it is confession time. I was not concentrating on exactly where I was. I do rcmember that on the outskirts there was a massive car park full of tour buses and people dressed for all manner of water sports and carrying all the paraphernalia associated with a day at the coast.

Further on, there were many posh hotels around a square, but I never glimpsed any coastline or quayside though it must have been very close by. I was tired and a bit dumb I guess. I did note that every other parked car was either a Porsche, BMW, Mercedes or Audi. I stopped and didn't care, 'take your pick' I thought and walked into the first hotel I came across. I did not get its name but it was one of those boutique hotels, all glitz and trendy.

I was fully aware, not for the first time on this trip, that I looked a bit of a road tramp. Because it had been another long, hot and sweaty day, my bike was filthy with over two weeks of road dust and I was probably not looking very much better. I was tired and not really in the frame of mind to be messed with.

The young man on reception made it fairly obvious even as I walked up to his desk that he did not like what he was seeing. He gave me the sort of imperious look that would have done Kenneth Williams proud.

I asked him the obvious question and he almost sneered at me and was very patronising when he explained, in excellent English, that they were fully booked and he went on to tell me, condescendingly, as if I was possibly the stupidest person on the planet. 'What do you expect? (He did not add sir, but he should have done). 'It is actually the holiday season here you know. Most of the hotels around here were fully booked months ago.'

Not exactly the sort of customer friendly attitude one would expect in such a nice hotel. I knew I was being judged on my appearance and that he was being quite, well actually very, rude. But he had made a mistake; I am not one for being intimidated. I stood my ground and looked back at him defiantly for quite a while before I spoke again. 'Well,' I said sarcastically and quite angrily, 'even in these hotels people are known to cancel sometimes aren't they?'

I was not impressed at all. He was being exceedingly disrespectful and now my return attitude was clearly indicating he had overstepped the mark. I was all the while looking around his reception with a put-on air of disdain as if to indicate the hotel was not up to scratch anyway.

He stared back at me his eyes narrowing thoughtfully and I could tell I'd unsettled him; he was not quite so sure now what manner of potential customer he was talking to, and I was possibly not, after all, the motorcycle vagrant he had first taken me for. He got the message; he knew full well he had offended me, that I was not best pleased and I think he was concerned now where I might take this. I almost gave him a lecture on the value of good customer-facing service attitudes, and thought of calling for his boss, but just hadn't the will or indeed the time.

'Thank you *so* much for your time, it's been illuminating' I told him in my best Basil Fawlty voice, but felt like saying something a considerably more cutting. It was not the fact they were full, but his contemptuous, haughty and judgemental attitude that really annoyed me. He probably hated motorcyclists too; this would be one he would not forget for a while.

I walked across the square and tried to gain reception at another hotel opposite. I press the button for entry but suspected that entrance here was monitored and assessed by a camera. They didn't open the door to me. I stepped back and watched as an immaculately dressed woman and her teenage daughter, their arms dripping with bags displaying designer labels, gained entry as the doors magically swished open for them.

I chose not to follow them in. They too give me a belittling look as they passed, and yes, now I was feeling awkwardly out of place. I decided I was not demeaning myself any longer in this pretentious, pompous, proud place, full of nose-in-the-air attitudes from rich holiday makers.

I found my way back to the autobahn and in the general direction of Hamburg. On reflection, I was over-tired and maybe I was over-reacting a little, but at the time this is how I was feeling.

As I reflected upon this failure to secure accommodation and the places I called into that afternoon I noted something quite interesting. I could remember the roads I rode along from the A1. I had some recollection of the faces of the people I interacted with, distinctly remembering the conversations and their reactions (and mine), but that key piece of information that had frustratingly escaped me, was where I actually was!

This was not me at all, and as I analysed it, I was becoming a little bit too focussed on the accommodation itself rather than where I was seeking it. I really was not thinking straight and relying solely on technology rather than a good map and Godly intuition which frankly should have had me staying on the A1 till well south of Hamburg before I even started looking.

I wasted well over an hour looking for the right thing but in the wrong places. Later, at home using Google maps and a road atlas, I tried to piece together exactly where I had ended up and I was annoyed that I did not record it more accurately in my written notes, relying instead on the entries made in 'notes' on my phone which for this particular day I had inadvertently deleted.

Emilie did not keep a record either. However, on investigation, I am fairly certain I was in a place called Travemunde. I will not be going back there.

Back on the A1, I mused that my Garmin was not doing well for me today and I could have really fallen out with Emilie, yet undaunted I followed her next instructions and the route for a Best Western 'Tulip' hotel on the outskirts of Lubeck itself.

As I stopped right outside the hotel I noted the car park was roped off which was not exactly a good sign. The receptionist was also a young man so I approached the desk with a little caution after my earlier experience. His attitude, however, could not have been more different to the guy down the road. He was sympathetic and apologetic.

'I have lost count of the number of people we have had to turn away this afternoon. Normally sir, (yes sir) we could find you a room, but we really are completely booked at the moment. It is not just the season, there is also a major concert taking place in Hamburg tonight too.'

He kindly offered to ring the next hotel in the group but was not that hopeful. I told him not to trouble himself and thanked him for his help; in fact, I shook his hand because he had been so caring and kind. 'You will surely find a room south of Hamburg' he said helpfully. Outside the hotel, I rang Liz and told her I may be sleeping rough next to my bike tonight.

The autobahn ground to a halt within a few kilometres of me re-joining it. More road works, more contraflows and, as before in Germany, filtering between lanes was a nightmare. The day was not ending well. In a kind of growing desperation, I tapped Hotel Kuhl back into the Sat Nav and was surprised to see it show that I was at least 35 kilometres away. Then suddenly, I realised (it should have been obviously had I actually thought about it) I was going around Hamburg to the south and not north west as before. Doh!

When I eventually emerged from the chaos and the traffic flows again, I saw a sign for a rest area with a bed on it which raised my expectation levels.

I took the exit but my hopes were short lived as the whole service area was a morass of vehicles and people. The accommodation hostel looked iffy to say the least and I noted 3 rough looking types outside leaning against the front of a red van. I don't know why exactly but I sensed they were Eastern Europeans, swarthy and unkempt (I should make it clear I am not generalising about people from Eastern Europe here, it was just what I was sensing), and they made me feel uneasy for some reason.

I also knew that there were many criminal gangs, especially from that area, uplifting and stealing motorcycles throughout Europe and in the UK. I made an immediate decision that even if there had been rooms available there was no way I was leaving my unsecured motorcycle outside overnight in that place. I could see it being uplifted into a van, possibly a red one.

In a previous life, I would have been panicking a little by now but there was an air of acceptance and peace about me, although I confess I was not trusting God in this matter as I should have been. It was almost as if all the other times I had been blessed weren't Him at all but actually me, my resources and my technology.

I wonder at times if I will ever learn to be less self-reliant and trust in a God who knows all the parameters of any given situation. There was a resignation about me in this matter; what was the worst that could happen? A night sleeping beside the bike at a rest area? I was now fully prepared for that eventuality or maybe I could just keep riding south and see the dawn break in another country. God, as ever, had a plan. I said a little prayer and rode on.

By now the light was slowly failing and back on the autobahn a little south of Hamburg I took one last stab at a hotel knowing that if this did not pay off I would stop at the next rest area and sleep alongside my bike. With it being so warm it would not be so much of a hardship anyway I thought.

I tapped the food and lodgings icon again and thought my tired eyes were playing tricks with me the first hotel listed looked like 'Derbyhaven'. This made me smile as I knew Derbyhaven was in the Isle of Man, a favourite place in fact. I felt it to be a good sign and, as it was not too far off the autobahn, I went for it.

Actually it was a place called Derboven and as I arrived at the Derboven Hotel its car park also looked full. Undaunted I parked up and walked in. The man behind the reception counter looked up at me quizzically; I don't think he was expecting a passing traveller enquiring about a room so late in the day.

'Do you have a single room?' I asked.

He smiled, 'I have just the one room only and it has 3 beds in it.'

'I only need the one' I told him,

'Would you let me have it at single rate?' He laughed at my boldness.

'Okay' he said. He was small, wiry and kind. He told me his name was Andreas, 'but call me Andy' he said.

'Follow me' and he walked me back into the car park and opened a huge garage door which also served as his wine cellar. 'You can park your motorcycle here overnight for security.'

Back in reception he told me that he and his wife owned this hotel and that if I went into the restaurant now I could still get a meal, but added that service finished promptly at 9:00; it was 8:45.

'I really need to freshen up Andy' I told him.

'Okay, we fix you a sandwich then' he said. I could not believe the kindness being shown to me here.

As he booked me in, the reception desk phone rang and there was a short conversation in German. As he put the receiver down he said, 'You are very lucky, that was someone looking for a room, had you been five minutes later it would have been gone.'

I enjoyed my typical German sandwich, fresh dense brown bread with a salami type meat filling, pickled gherkin slices and a salad. I treated myself to a glass of draught beer. At that moment, I could not have been happier.

Call it coincidence if you want, but Liz had triggered a prayer request for me (I had been praying myself) and there were a number of friends praying for me back at home to find accommodation; this hotel was God's provision and I was in absolutely no doubt about it. I told Andy as much and that he had been a real blessing to me, at which he smiled thoughtfully.

I reflected back on the 6 places I had tried to stay at today. I was treated with rudeness, scorn and then kindness. I think you do not need me to tell you, I slept very well that night.

**Day 20 – Thursday** 26th July 2018. Derboven, Germany to Eurotunnel, Calais, France. Leaving time – 08:40; temperature range – 32°C to 41°C; distance ridden – 929 kilometres. Then Eurotunnel Folkstone to Great Chart, Kent; distance – 17 miles.

For 2 days on the trot, I was not up particularly early. Buffet breakfast was much as expected and once again the 'workers' were much in evidence and stocking up their 'gander' bags for their lunches.

Catching a glimpse of the front page of the local paper I saw a familiar face and think I now knew why there was not a hotel room to be had in the general Hamburg area last night. I asked the waitress.

'Was Ed Sheeran playing a concert in Hamburg yesterday?'

'Yes, it was a complete sell out' she said. Ah, that explained much; thanks very much Ed. But I realised, this close to Hamburg, how fortunate I had been to even secure a room here. I enjoyed my breakfast but was fretting that I had another big riding decision to make.

Some days earlier I had changed the ticket for my return leg on 'Le Shuttle' to a Flexiplus ticket. This was simply because I could not determine exactly what date I would be returning and it gave me complete freedom on what day and indeed what train I could take.

In the event, it proved a fortuitous decision. I'd checked the weather and today I knew it was going to be possibly the hottest day of riding so far. I was no longer in northern climes and if it was hot up there, well coming south was obviously proving even hotter.

I was sort of acclimatised to it on the bike now but, even so, it was a long way to Calais in one hit in that torrid cauldron of weather. I decided to go for it. I just wanted to get home now and avoid any extra time riding in the heat than I had to. I e-mailed my dear friends Tim and Catherine in Great Chart telling them to expect me that evening.

Andy gave me a friendly wave as he drove out on business somewhere and the girl on reception gave me a few anxious minutes because she could not find the key for the garage. After consulting the waitress and the cleaner the key magically appeared and I carefully walked my bike down the garage access ramp. It was warm already, really warm.

I could give some flowery description of what the weather was like that morning and what I knew I was riding into…again. You know, the glowering and radiant sun blazed out of an azure sky which was devoid of clouds, sort of thing. But there was something rather odd about the sky that morning.

I cannot adequately describe it but there was every indication it was going to be a scorcher of even increased magnitude. It was not just the already building heat but the unrelenting brightness through an odd kind of haze that had a cruel sheen that glared at you both from above, and was in turn, reflected back from below.

Other days had certainly been extreme but this one I sensed was set to surpass anything to date and as incredible as it seems to me as I write this, so it proved.

I rode out of the car park at 8:40 and back to the autobahn A1 and it was not many kilometres before the oppressive regime of this summer hit me once again, perhaps more than ever before, like riding into a blast furnace. To make matters worse the road works south of Hamburg were almost as bad as the north side.

Within a few kilometres, I was into more contra-flows through very heavy traffic. Even normally it would have been hard work, but in that heat! The lanes were extremely narrow and filtering was made almost impossible, so I rode in the outside lane which made for lots of commercial vehicles on my right and particularly nasty temporary barriers on my left. Not for the first time on this trip, if you thought about how vulnerable this made you, then you just wouldn't do it. The temperature gauge was now hitting 41°C and the cooling fan on the bike was working overtime. I could hear it constantly whirring away because my pace was so dreadfully slow.

Eventually, as we left the Hamburg region the traffic thinned out and progress could be made again. There were more road warriors around on this return leg through Germany, up-market cars (the brands would surprise no one) being driven extremely fast. I needed my wits about me on some sections of the derestricted autobahn, especially when changing lanes to overtake, as some of them were coming up on me very fast indeed.

I crossed into Holland, but didn't really know it. At a rest stop I went across to talk to a big 'fella' who was riding a Honda Transalp, a similar style of bike to my own, but at 700cc a smaller engine size. He was Spanish and told me he was heading south to home. He shook his head and pointed to his bike's engine; 'running too hot, too hot,' he said.

He was worrying about it. I had a quick check over his bike; 'You have no coolant leaks', I told him reassuringly. 'Your bike is liquid-cooled, so if your cooling fan is working okay then don't worry about it; mine is running very hot too.' We talked motorcycling and the heat of course. 'We're not like them' he said pointing to the driver of a nearby car.

'They all have air conditioning. Riding a motorcycle is different; in a car, it is like you are watching a movie; ah…but on a motorcycle you are *in* the movie.' I liked that and laughed. 'What a great description,' I told him. He was amazed when I told him of my journey and naturally he was given one of my promotional postcards. We parted friends; I liked him a lot, another fellow adventurer.

Once more around Antwerp the traffic was dreadful and I lost time because of it. Listening later to some experienced fellow travellers who ride and drive this route regularly I am moved to ask the question, 'When is the traffic anything other than bad around Antwerp?'

I lost perspective on exactly what road number I was travelling along, Emilie taking care of all that, and I was just responding to her prompts and the purple ribbon of the set route on the screen (when I could actually see it that is, as the Sat Nav screen was often lost in the reflected glare). All I knew and cared about was that I was on the fastest route to Calais.

I stopped many times to rehydrate and cool down in some air-conditioned service area. Just to sit in cooled luxury for 10 minutes with a cold drink was heaven. Actually, perhaps because I had the additional motivation of coming home, I was not yet that tired.

At one rest area, I needed a top of fresh water for the next leg and I was annoyed by the inconsiderate action of an RV driver who was using the only small public water fount to fill up 2 huge containers. Fortunately, I could see he was almost done so I waited.

As the water was only dispensed in short bursts it was clear he had been there a very long time, much to the inconvenience of all his fellow travellers on that very hot day. As he finished, I walked up to fill my bottle and tutted at him for his selfishness in a way he could not fail to misinterpret.

He waddled off in a stoop, hardly able to walk as his containers were so big and heavy. I was in no mood to assist. I put the filled water bottle in the top case. An hour or so later at another rest area the water was hot!

In one of these service stops in Belgium I began to sense the growing closeness of home and it was exciting. As I walked back to my bike another motorcyclist, a young man, was carefully looking over it. He was Belgian and like my earlier Spanish friend, he too was riding a Honda Transalp, off to visit some local relatives.

I gave him my postcard, (I still had a lot left). He was amazed at what I had done and could not quite believe it. He asked me, 'How have you been coping in this heat? I see you are wearing Gore-Tex clothing which is breathable, but does it help?' I explained my clothing choice dilemma for north Norway and added, 'Excellent though this riding suit is, I am finding it much too heavy for this kind of weather', going on to tell him what a struggle it had been on some days, like today.

He shook my hand warmly, firmly and friendly and I think to him I may just have been elevated from saddle tramp to road hero. To be honest, just at that moment I felt good about it.

As I entered France there were a few spots of rain, but I could see from the sky that there was no threat from a serious downpour. Now the day and the ride were really starting to affect me, and I began to feel very fatigued.

This relatively short hop of 50 kilometres to Calais felt like an eternity and the heat was now almost unbearable. My primary motivation was to finish the day back in England and it became a sheer head down grind to Le Shuttle. I had taken a lot on by going for it in one hit but my resolve was to just push on through it all and get it done.

At the Eurotunnel terminal, the UK border guard was thorough, for which read painfully slow. Sitting and waiting in the heat was torture – I looked down at the temperature gauge on my bike and it was showing 44°C! I felt as if I was melting. He called me forward and asked me to take my helmet off as I handed him my passport. He was a nice chap though.

He saw how hot I was and expressed sympathy; I told him as we spoke that my bike was now showing an outside temperature of 47°C. He shook his head in disbelief and with a friendly wave I was through. Having a Flexiplus ticket proved a God-send; you were on a special train, no waiting.

I did not sense it at the time but later read that both sides of the tunnel had been chaos that day, and indeed all that weekend, with so many people just arriving on-spec expecting to be able to cross. I just could not imagine how I would have coped with that sun beating down on me waiting in some stand-by queue. Not very well I think.

I know I said it before and I say it again – the staff at Eurotunnel are superb, pleasant, courteous and friendly which, as I was now one tired and overheated motorcycle rider with my uptake a bit on the slow side, I appreciated.

I waited in a select queue to board behind the rider of an old red BMW R80RT, similar to Eric the Eel's but much more 'used.' We chatted in the carriage as we trundled under the English Channel. He told me his name was Russell, a Tai Chi instructor who was returning from a seminar in France and now on his way home to Godalming in Surrey.

We talked about our respective journeys and I gave out my final card of this trip. His bike was not pretty, having a large fairing which was well cracked and repaired, the once clear windshield by now so opaque it would be impossible to safely look through it, the engine leaking oil, and I noticed he strapped up his side stand with a wire which was hanging down.

As we readied ourselves to decamp our train, in a Tai Chi move worthy of his calling and no doubt practiced over years, he just swept his side stand up with his boot and deftly caught it in one movement in the wire. His BMW looked so bad it would shame any chapter in the book 'Zen and the Art of Motorcycle Maintenance' but it had taken him successfully on a journey too, so who am I to make judgement? He was a super chap; we shook hands, exited and went our separate ways.

Back in Blighty, I was just too knackered to feel exultant about being home. It is only 17 miles (yes, we were back into miles now, it was like finding an old friend) to Great Chart. I was wondering how I would cope with keeping to the left as keeping right had become almost second nature over the past 2 weeks. It did not prove to be a problem.

I had called ahead from the terminal in France so was expected. When Catherine opened the door to me, I could see she was a bit shocked at the apparition standing before her but tried not to show it too much. I looked a state I know. I had just ridden over 500 miles on the hottest day of my trip, my face was filthy and etched with weariness, my eyes red and puffy, my hair matted to my scalp. It was not a good look.

After showering and making myself look almost normal again, I met their lovely daughter Naomi, who was just a little girl the last time I saw her. She gave me a huge hug; our son Gareth is her Godfather. I showed Catherine my routes on the crumbling map of Scandinavia and recounted some of the adventures along the way; she was amazed at the scale of the challenge. As Tim joined us, I shared supper with this lovely family, and a beer, and sought an early night.

**Day 21 – Friday** 27 July 2018. Great Chart, Kent to Highley, Shropshire (home); leaving time – 08:30; distance ridden – 218 miles; temperature range – 30°C to 40°C. My closing mileage was recorded at 12,222.

When I awoke it was bright outside and I lay in my bed listening to the occasional distant bang of a farmer's bird scarer. I found myself feeling quite low and contemplated why. Was it because the adventure was almost over?

Was it because I still had some way to go on my target towards the £10,000 goal? Had I under-achieved? What was going to follow this challenge I wondered? Then, as I thought about why I had even undertaken this trip and who I had been doing it for, my perspective returned.

I was last to surface in the Wilson household that morning and breakfast was a "help yourself" leisurely affair. Outside, Tim was tinkering again with the Hayter lawnmower and Catherine busying herself with her tasks for the day. Tim was preparing for the church 'open house' event there the next day with a maze to cut in the long grass and I never did hear that mower start up.

It would be one of their last organised events at Great Chart before they moved to Bedford so for them it was possibly a bittersweet time. I had no doubt it would be hard for them to move on from the wonderful people I met there and whom they have shepherded for many years. These are dear and special people.

I became pensive as I loaded my bike which now included the extra bag and items I had left there. The last leg, just the ride to Shropshire and home, it really was coming to an end. I thanked them both and made my farewells. I want to record how grateful I was for their friendship, encouragement and their hospitality. It was very precious to me.

As I rode through Great Chart, I became very annoyed with myself. In my efforts to be on my way this morning I forgot to also thank Tim and Catherine for the generous donations made by them and their church fellowships to Open Doors.

It was something rectified immediately in an e-mail on my return. Had I become so focussed on getting home that common courtesies had gone out of the window? As I rode, I was now thinking keep left, keep left instead of my previous keep right mantra.

But I was not very sharp that morning, missing the turning for the Sainsbury's petrol outlet (the same Sainsbury's that had started the continental leg of my trip 21 days ago) and had to turn around; the day wasn't starting too well. As I rode in, I was reminded immediately that it was a bank holiday weekend. Oh, did I tell you it was a hot morning? Well, I think by now you might have guessed.

A modern phenomenon that has overtaken the UK is queuing at the pumps to fill up at these busy outlets. This morning it was absolute mayhem with cars even queuing on the service road. I drifted passed them and found the situation not being helped by the driver of a large people carrier towing a huge caravan who was blocking off pretty much a whole row of pumps.

The driver was nowhere to be seen, probably inside doing his weekly shop and buying his lottery tickets. On the bike I could just about squeeze in on the end pump behind him. It was very tight; a car would have struggled. I wasn't queue jumping exactly; okay I was a little bit, but no one beeped and no one complained.

I used the pay at the pump facility which alleviates the other modern phenomenon of buying fuel at outlets like this which is standing in the payment queue behind drivers, who, like him, have just left their cars parked on the pump whilst putting said weekly shop through the till. Just an observation; this is modern British life on the road and at times it is not very nice.

The traffic was also queuing heavily to even exit Sainsbury's that morning, I had to be careful how I by-passed the queue because I could sense some drivers already getting stressed and I was not in the business of cutting in on anyone or deliberately winding someone up. I planned the overtaking of the string of stationary cars to minimise any inconvenience to them and to expedite my own exit; this is why I ride a motorcycle. But…welcome home to the UK.

The M20 had a 50mph limit through road works which frustratingly, as there was nobody actually doing any road works, went on for miles. But given it was a Friday and the start of a bank holiday, the traffic was flowing relatively freely even as I joined the now busier M26. But as I rode towards the M25 I had a sense, a portent, of it being anything but a sensible ride home today.

The M25, that much maligned motorway that encircles London, has rarely been as bad in my experience as it was on this particular morning. I had hoped, perhaps prayed, that it might be benign today, that the traffic would flow. But, immediately on joining it the warning signs were flashing telling me of a queue ahead and a couple of miles later it totally stopped, all 3 lanes of it.

The traffic signs were telling me of an issue between junctions 5 to 8 and a delay of 2 hours. I began filtering between lanes of stationary vehicles and, as is my preference, in the space between lanes 2 and 3. It was not quite as difficult as around Antwerp or Hamburg, because the lane widths were slightly wider, but let no one be in any doubt it was still not pleasant. It was risky and hard work.

Because there was little airflow the heat was appalling and, now added to by the rows of hot stationary vehicles, the outside temperature was recording 38°C. Let me pay credit to the vast majority of my fellow road travellers that day, many of whom, on seeing my lights approaching in their mirrors, moved over where they could to help my progress. There were however always exceptions to this kindness.

In my own mirrors, I saw the headlights of some motorcyclists slowly gaining on me on that narrow aisle of road between the vehicles. I squeezed in between two cars to let them come past. As they had caught me up there was no point in me holding up their progress. There were two of them and they waved their thanks as they went through.

They were clearly old hands at this and riding sports motorcycles so their width profile was much narrow than mine and therefore they could be a bit more confident in making slightly faster progress between the lanes. I latched onto them for a while and matched their pace briefly, but it was not so easy or indeed comfortable for me so I did not sustain it.

Soon I in turn caught up the rider of a very noisy Harley Davidson, who was two up, but he did not show me the same courtesy by pulling over to allow me to pass. As he was carrying a passenger, I perhaps understood his caution, but for him to impede my progress for so long was annoying because it was selfish riding.

He did, however, have one advantage I didn't. If a wayward motorist was blocking his progress, he had the best way ever of ensuring that they moved. He would sit on their corner and blip his throttle hard and I could hear the noise back where I was sitting!

They moved back pretty rapidly, I can tell you. I laughed when he did it because it was amusing to see the car driver's reaction; some possibly didn't even know he was there until that moment. After a mile or so we caught up another group of four or five motorcyclists who were making an absolute fist of it and progress now became painfully slow.

I was fed up because it was costing me valuable time. In a rare moment the traffic began to move a little and I seized the opportunity. I moved across lanes and temporarily switched to filtering between lanes 1 and 2. This is particularly unpleasant at times and really does need even more careful thought, timing and planning because it is where the trucks live and filtering between two slowly moving trucks is not a good idea.

If two trucks were side by side I tried to wait until one of them was alongside smaller vehicles before passing, but it doesn't always work out and then it becomes quite nerve wracking. If you filter between 2 and 3 it's less of an issue to worry about because trucks, being barred from lane 3, are only on your inside to worry about.

But on this day my strategy worked. I had enough experience and momentum to leave all the other wobbling riders behind and then carefully switched back to 2 and 3 where I had been before.

But you are never immune to the vagaries of other drivers and like a replay of the incident around Hamburg going up, white van man in front of me changed lanes without indicating. But I had sensed it and being far enough back just eased off to let him in.

The young driver of a new purple Bentley convertible with its roof down (how could he even afford that car!) did the same thing but I was closer. He too began to pull across without indicating, a situation where accelerating is perhaps better than braking, for he had left me enough room to get past before he could get across.

All along he knew I was there and he was gauging my reaction. How did I know that? You just sense it I suppose, just like sensing his nervousness that I was getting close to his precious car door, and he pulled back. 'I bet you don't do that to another motorcyclist today' I thought.

I do not know exactly how many miles I filtered that morning along that section of motorway but looking at the maps later it must have been at least 18. And when the traffic did start to flow the traffic issue wasn't even on the M25 itself but on an exit lane somewhere off the motorway at junction 8.

I was moving along at sensible speeds now and no longer filtering and later the Harley rider came noisily past waving cheerfully as he did. I responded in kind, 'no harm done' I suppose. But, around Heathrow, it all ground to a halt again, similar scenarios were repeated and I was filtering again. One old lady driving a blue Peugeot changed lanes very late causing me a little wobble around her as she did so. She was completely oblivious to my presence and I did not make an issue of it or respond as I knew it was not done deliberately.

However, a little later the lone driver of a red Toyota, who by his actions I knew for certain had seen me coming, pulled across left from the outside lane as I was actually starting to go past him and squeezed me right up to the white line. I hit the horn and had no choice but to brake hard to avoid hitting him or risk clipping the truck on my inside. It was absolutely deliberate and it was close. He wasn't changing lanes to gain progress because the middle lane had been stopped for some time; he just did not want me to go past him and blocked me and what he did was unbelievably dangerous, putting me at real risk of a collision. But just at that moment the traffic in the outside lane stopped too and now, like the red Hyundai in Germany all those days ago, he was wedged with nowhere to go. Had the outside lane continued to move my guess is he was going to try to keep me from coming past him for as long as possible.

He'd stopped me, or so he thought, as I certainly could not get between him and the vehicles in the middle lane, for he had made it too narrow for that, but, and this is the beauty of riding a motorcycle, now there was quite enough room on the other side of him for me to get between his car and central reservation barrier.

I had to physically pull my bike back a few feet to do this and mercifully the car behind him was not too close which allowed me to reposition the bike to ride past him on his outside. Because he was stationary, I rode up to his door, stopped dead, and angrily let rip at him.

He was a balding middle-aged man and was visibly shocked; he certainly hadn't anticipated this. Perhaps it was the culmination of the frustrations of the challenge journey, the heat and all the traffic situations I had had to overcome that day in particular, but I confess I was seriously annoyed and let it show.

I do not remember exactly what I shouted at him but recall that his reaction indicated he'd got the message loud and clear. Only skill and experience (and no doubt God's protection) prevented an accident. It was without doubt the worst traffic incident of my whole ride and on the final day too.

I would like to think he will have learnt a lesson and never do that again to another motorcyclist, but if not, he was going to be on borrowed time for I know of some who would have hauled him out of the car. If he had done this to a Hell's Angel type, he might have been enjoying hospital food for a while.

Back to filtering again, my ongoing mood was now very tense; it had been a close call. As we reached the M4 junction the overhead signs indicated that ahead two lanes were closed by an accident and as we came to it the damaged cars were already on the hard shoulder.

Such is life on our over-congested UK roads where an incident may have been dealt with, but the aftermath lasts for hours. But then suddenly it was all flowing again; the traffic may have been slow and heavy but I was not having to filter now which was a blessing and lifted my mood. Soon on, very familiar territory, the M40, I felt home was at last within my grasp.

The traffic, still heavy, was now moving along at more acceptable speeds. I pulled off at Beaconsfield services for a drink and rest. I found it a complete confusion of vehicles, many resigned looking drivers doing a vehicle conga around the full car park seeking that rarest of things, a free parking space. I did not tarry.

This scenario is repeated further on at Cherwell services where the vehicles were actually queuing on the link road down to it. As I alluded to in the opening chapters, I dislike single motorway services that cater for both sides of the carriageway such as Beaconsfield, Oxford and Cherwell as they are simply not big enough.

On days like this, they rapidly become full to overflowing and unpleasant places to be. Even though I was lower on fuel than ideal, (I used much more than normal in those traffic hold ups) I did not stop here either. I didn't join the queuing traffic and carried on around the traffic island, regained the M40 and took the risk of pushing on to Warwick, which has service outlets on both sides of the motorway.

When I arrived there unsurprisingly it too was very busy but not quite as bad. I rode directly through to the fuel station and filled up, albeit at their vastly inflated pump prices. Good move as it turned out. Not only did they sell sandwiches but beyond there was a quiet parking area for those in the know. I rang Liz and told her of my delays, as I was originally hoping to be home for lunchtime.

The ride to home from there via the M42 and Kidderminster was slower than I would have liked but I was not seriously held up again. However, from Bewdley towards Highley however it was unusually quiet and I could not resist giving the Yamaha its head by way of a final riding celebration.

As I pulled into the communal courtyard of our barns complex that very hot mid-afternoon in July my neighbours came out to greet me. There were banners, balloons and yellow ribbons on most of the garage doors.

I was home; I couldn't quite believe it and felt a bit emotional. Liz came out to give me a huge hug and everybody was excited. I was not sure how I felt. Today had been possibly the worst day's riding of the entire trip and I was still tense from the road battles of it. I needed a shower and cold beer and time to process it all but my overwhelming thought at that moment was one of thankfulness. God is good.

I checked my outgoing and returning mileages. I had ridden 5,907 miles since leaving. The challenge had been successfully completed but the story is not quite over.

# Chapter 12
# Conclusions and Why This Mattered

*'They asked me why I don't just deny my belief and go back to my wife and children. I then ask myself what cost did the Lord pay to save me? The death of Jesus Christ on the cross; the blood of the Lamb of God! Yes, this is a huge price. Therefore, I am also able to prefer prison over being set free.'* – **Pastor Behnam Irani imprisoned for 6 years simply because he ran a house church in Iran.**

Some four months later in December 2018, against the predictions of some, the £10,000 target set for the challenge was reached and indeed exceeded. Once again, I acknowledge the generosity of so many people and secular businesses that helped me make that 'unreachable target' and can only thank you all.

I know the amount raised will have made a difference in the lives of many. I did not specify a fund or country that Open Doors should allocate it to. I reasoned that they would know best where the need might be greatest at any given time. I admit as I rode that summer that the plight of Christians in North Korea was often on my mind.

It is the most dangerous country in the world to follow Christ and they, in particular, became a mental rallying point for me when it became tough. I was sometimes uncomfortable and pressurised on the ride, ending some days exhausted if not a little unwell.

But I knew my discomfort was nothing compared to what my fellow brothers and sisters in Christ suffer on a daily basis. Open Doors produce the World Watch List which is an annual ranking of the 50 countries where Christians face the most extreme persecution. Here are some statistics for the reporting year of 2018 that might bring home the reality of what they face.

1. Approximately 245 million Christians were at risk of high, very high or extreme levels of persecution.
2. 4,305 Christians were killed for their faith.
3. 692 churches and Christian buildings were attacked.
4. 1,922 Christians were detained without trial, arrested, sentenced and imprisoned.
5. On average, every month over 100 Christian women are forcibly married.

These facts are why it mattered. It is why I have headed each chapter with a quotation from a Christian living under persecution so that in some small way in this book their voices are heard and not forgotten. They arc why I made a decision to raise awareness of their plight. The ride was something I know God set on my heart.

Of course, I was fulfilling my own dream to ride to the Arctic Circle but God used it to touch the lives of many I hope. But my vision has not ended because this particular challenge is concluded. I have been appointed a volunteer speaker for Open Doors and will take every opportunity to speak about the persecuted church whenever I can.

And there is this book of course; all proceeds made from the sale of it will go to Open Doors. As I write, I am also still mulling over the possibility that I may do another riding challenge for them, so great is the need.

As I began to write my story of this challenge, I was powerfully struck by the other events unfolding in the wider world. Naturally at any time all of us are living in, witnesses of and party to unfolding history. But often we are too distracted by our day to day living to really appreciate it, unless, of course, it is something that cannot fail to stop and make us think.

I rode my motorcycle during a very divisive time for the UK and Europe and consequently there were events surrounding the trip (and subsequently) that have made me think more deeply and make for wider discourse. While I rode through the oppressive heat of that then record-breaking summer of 2018, the political temperature was also rising here.

It has occurred to me since then there was perhaps some prophetic symbolism between the two events. Only history and our response to it will be the judge.

Some major themes were recurrent as I rode through Europe on my challenge.

Firstly, the lack of physical borders between the EU countries, which because of the checks at the Channel Tunnel (and not being a regular traveller in Europe) came as some surprise. I did not expect it to be quite so 'normal' to slip from one country into another.

Only recently have I discovered that throughout the EU member states there is an agreement for open borders and as I passed seamlessly through the countries I felt, well, European, part of it. I felt for the first time that something of unrecognised value was soon going to be taken away from me because this was written at a time when there was a furious political brouhaha over the issue of 'Brexit.' For the record, I am pro-European; however, I recognise and accept that the UK democratically decided to leave the EU.

Reflecting on this, what I sensed from travelling through Europe during that summer of 2018 was whatever shortcomings the EU has, and I would agree there are many, it was balanced by the strength of countries uniting under a common purpose for the overall benefit of the people who live there. Some reading this might have a different viewpoint on us leaving Europe and naturally you are entitled to your opinion.

This, after all, is my personal reflection endorsed by the observations, conversations, and opinions I gained from my ride. The economic situation aside, the peaceful unity we have had through the EU has been a good thing, possibly an undervalued thing, especially given the history of Europe since the early 20th Century. As Oscar Wilde once wrote we are perhaps like the one *who knows the price of everything and the value of nothing.'*

Secondly, and in a way following on from above, I observed the clear evidence, even all these years later, of the effects of the Second World War particularly had on normal life in some of the countries I travelled through, and the persecution, suppression and slavery to everyday people it brought.

Ironically perhaps, as I wrote this in 2019, before the radical disruptions of life created by COVID-19, it was the 30th anniversary of the Berlin Wall being torn down and it made me consider more thoughtfully the consequences of closed borders, nationalism and resultant extremism. We live in freedom in the West and often we do not appreciate just how fortunate we are.

If we were to consider more deeply what life is really like in a country like North Korea', Afghanistan or Somalia for example, I am certain we would be more mindful and appreciative of it. Countries where freedom and rights are not respected and where the very persecution, suppression and slavery I spoke of are still an everyday reality. I rode for Open Doors; the clue is in the title.

Thirdly, the environment. My ride and what I experienced certainly woke me up to the reality of another controversial topic, global warming. When riding I could physically feel the often-extreme heat each day and because I did not have the luxury of some air-conditioned car, I was never protected from it.

Sub-Saharan temperatures 500 kilometres north of the Arctic Circle lasting for weeks on end are not normal, I would suggest, even in midsummer! Experiencing that unrelenting heat and those cloudless skies each day, witnessing forest fires and listening to the genuine concerns of many ordinary people I met about what was happening, has personally left me in no doubt that global warming is real and a threat to us all.

Extreme weather events are becoming much more frequent even in the UK. Some would argue it is all just some natural cycle the world is going through, but the science disputing that argument is now pretty robust and sadly the temperature statistics of the last few decades alone seem to bear it out. I am being made aware this year (2019) is, in fact, proving to be even warmer than last with forest fires raging throughout the whole Arctic region this summer in Alaska, Greenland, Scandinavia and Russia and as I write this (November) bush fires are devastating many parts of Australia and wild fires are ravishing vast swathes of California.

In 2019, the UK experienced the highest temperatures ever recorded. President Trump argued global warming was unproven, a myth created by the Chinese in order to make US manufacturing non-competitive. When the leader of the so-called free world makes such a glib and unproven comment you know that any resolution to solve the issue is going to be very difficult indeed. Something is very seriously wrong with our world. I think it is us.

I was to discover the reason why Tesla vehicles are so popular in Norway. It is because Norway is one of the first countries to propose a ban on the sale of petrol and diesel vehicles as early as 2025.

The country already has a 'polluter pays' tax system effectively fining those who use fossil fuel powered vehicles in certain areas and it seems to be working. Nevertheless, I took the Norwegian environmental department to task. I e-mailed them expressing concern about the dreadful pollution I witnessed spewing out from those cruise ships in Geiranger Fjord and included my very clear pictures of the issue. This was part of their response.

'A more climate and environmentally friendly shipping are an important priority for the Norwegian Government. We are aware of the unwanted air pollution from cruise ships in our tourist fjords. Geirangerfjorden is also listed as World Heritage and shall be given particular protection in accordance with the requirements of the World Heritage Convention.

Therefore, in 2016, our Ministry requested the Norwegian Maritime Directorate to evaluate possible measures to reduce emissions to air and discharges to sea from ships in our world heritage fjords. As a result, a set of new and stricter requirements from ships, also cruise ships, in the Norwegian world heritage fjords will be implemented from 1.1. 2019.

We think these requirements will give a better environment and better experiences for tourists that visit these areas in the future.

This is also a first step to reduce emissions from ships and measures to reduce emissions also in other Norwegian fjords will now be considered.'

Paradoxically all of this is somewhat at odds with Norway's record of environmental damage from their oil and gas exploration and drilling. Norway wants to be at the forefront of international efforts to address climate change, yet it continues to rely on heavily polluting fossil fuel extraction for continued economic prosperity.

And regarding the extreme weather experienced a few weeks after my return on 8 August this was the last entry in my notes.

'The weather is changing, we are losing the heat and it is now raining, heavily. On the forecast this morning the weatherman commented on the heavy storms moving up through Scandinavia. I thought of how different the trip might have been riding through those. Better the heat? At the time of the hottest days I thought not, but on reflection, how much of Norway would I have seen in heavy storms and associated mists? On balance I had the best of it I think.'

But leaving aside the EU, wars and the environment, critically there was also a spiritual dimension to the ride which I have to record. When I worked in sales there was the oft used mantra of the 7 P's. It goes something like this – proper planning and practice prevent painfully poor performance.

The actual phrase is a bit pithier than this, but I think you get the gist. In a business sense it was true, and preparing for something like this challenge the rule applied no less. My trip, however, was to reveal the lesson of the 3 P's which were prayer, protection and provision, and they were all linked together.

## Prayer

Frankly, without prayer this trip would never have happened. It was the quick prayer, 'What can I do Lord to make a difference?' that received an immediate answer with the inception of the challenge. From the beginning and throughout there was prayer, my own prayers (and at the low times they were frequent) and the prayers of so many people supporting me and from my friends at Open Doors.

There were times when my faith was stretched and big doubts crept in about my ability to fulfil the task (as in my physical and mental capability or even reaching the challenge targets) but God never failed me in any of it, not once. Did He answer every prayer I said? No, He did not.

For example, I prayed I might somehow get a boat directly to Norway from the UK. When we don't get answers to prayer it is sometimes because we don't see things from God's perspective. I am glad it was a prayer unanswered because I would have missed so much of what He wanted to show me on the way.

Were there situations that needed faith to overcome? Of course there were and prayer kept me going, literally, on some of the big days, when I was exhausted and almost melting in the heat of the ride. People have written whole books on prayer; I am no theologian and I have no complete answer to why God sometimes answers a prayer and sometimes why He appears not to.

Perhaps it is a question of timing, perhaps it is for our own good (as in the boat situation) or perhaps He is God and there is a mystery about things unanswered that we simply do not understand. All I know is this I was buoyed up by the prayers of so many, God proved to me time and time again that He is faithful, and I am so incredibly thankful.

## Protection

When I state that I had no more riding 'incidents' in the 6,000-mile round trip through Europe than sometimes during the odd few hundred-mile ride into Wales and back, I know that it was God's protection. Some might call it luck, coincidence or naivety on my part for thinking otherwise.

I cannot convince anyone who might hold to those cynical points of view. I just had this sense of being looked after during the whole trip. Of course, being aware of God's covering did not absolve me from being excessively reckless or stupid, because thoughtless actions always have consequences.

Does that make me a hypocrite for recording those incidents where it might seem what I did was somewhat risky? Let me state quite clearly each riding decision was calculated and even if one of my decisions proved to go awry, as in the case of the off-road episode, I am very thankful it did not end with unfortunate consequences. It was not luck or me 'getting away with it'.

If I had any doubts that my actions were going to result in a negative outcome then they would not have been taken. Others might say it was my experience as a rider then. I believe that 'knowing' is also God-given and part of the protection programme.

But as I said in the opening chapter, motorcycling is not the safest mode of transport. I did pray for my protection and safety at the start of each day (and sometimes during the ride itself especially when filtering) and I ended each one with a prayer of thanks. He is faithful and I am so incredibly thankful.

## Provision

When I set out to put this challenge together I hadn't a clue about fundraising and initially it did not go too well. But as I recorded earlier God came through at exactly the right time when I was thinking the naysayers were right and was about to reduce the target.

For me to reach the challenge target of £10,000 was frankly astonishing and without doubt it was God's provision coming through so many organisations and people. But the provision was also in the legacy my dear aunt had left me to fund the trip in the first place.

It was in the countless people who supported my challenge financially or practically, like the hotel receptionists who, when I arrived in their lobbies unannounced looking like a road tramp with no prior notice, not only found me a room, often the last one available, but even gave me a reduced room rate to help support the challenge. Hotel Derboven (I was going to sleep on a bench in a service area that night remember) was perhaps the prime example of that provision.

It was in the kindness of so many people like them and in encouragement I received from others. It was in the simple things like seeing the wolf and certainly in the beauty of the country I rode through. I could go on and on but I think you understand that I believe that God provided in a myriad of ways, and in fact still does as I tell of my adventure to new audiences. He is faithful and I am so incredibly thankful.

After returning from Norway, I was told by our former Highley Rector Clive Williams that I really ought to add a fourth 'P'-Persistence. In one sense, he is right for I never gave up. But frankly whatever tenacity I may have had to see the challenge through is of nothing when compared to hanging onto your Christian faith in a country where your life and that of your family may be compromised.

And it all comes back to that really; the challenge was never about me – it was about them. I was just a conduit God used and whatever persistence I might have will continue to be given to their cause.

And since my return I have been asked many times, what would you have done differently? I have given much thought to this question. The first thing I would do is be much more flexible on my daily riding plans. I have always been a person who likes the i's dotted and the t's crossed and when they weren't it was actually far more exciting and added richly to the experience, even if it got a little 'hairy' on some days.

I would not over-plan therefore and the itineraries would be far looser. Yes, naturally, there has to be an overall plan, a beginning and an end point, but being *there* on *that* day at *that* set time all the while riding on unknown roads became unnecessarily obsessive.

I would have set far higher daily distance targets on some days and on others I would have been a little kinder to myself by allowing more time to chill out instead of seeing the whole trip as a means to an end. I should have gone to Bergen that one day for example, junked the E6 for a day and ridden highway 17, or hiked to Knivskjellodden and now very much regret I did not.

In a perfect world, I would have taken much greater time to talk more meaningfully to people I met on the way and taken pictures of them for, as is obvious from the book, they were part of the story and I think I undervalued their contribution. I would have been bolder in my witnessing to them. I would have taken time to learn how to use IT and social media more effectively in the form of a blog and by use of video filming.

I would have pared down the clothing I packed and would have worn much lighter riding apparel. I would have spent far less time fussing over the minutiae of the route and started my fundraising much sooner. But the perfect trip does not exist and you have to work with and through problems.

But if I am honest as it turned out I would not have changed any of it because, difficult or easy, good choices and bad choices, it was all part of the adventure. Sometimes too you have to fail in order to learn how to win. Without the issues and the victories, it would not have been the challenge it became and I would not have this story to pass on.

And from the trip what other things did I learn? Primarily that fear will always rise to rob you of your dream. The most difficult thing in any enterprise, challenge, adventure, call it what you will, is taking that first step and actually making that first decision to pursue it.

But also you cannot live forever on the back of a past event, for if you do you are in danger of becoming a bore. There is always something new. Will my experience form the basis for another challenge? Very possibly, but at present I am not getting a clear indication of what it might be.

Of course, I have ideas but when you push doors and all seem closed, as they do currently, it is prudent not to ignore that. The opportunity to pursue any new dream will present itself at exactly the right time. I am certain if and when the time is right those doors will open, just as they did with the Norway challenge. I serve a God of opportunity and His timing is always perfect.

For any of us, no matter what our age, there are dreams. You might counter by saying; 'I am too young or too old, too infirm, too restricted by life's pressures to pursue them'. All I can say to you, and indeed myself as I approach another milestone birthday, is 'have courage and go for it!'

It may not be something as dramatic as my challenge but God does give you dreams and will answer the desires of your heart, He really will. Don't look back on your life and wish.

However, I think the biggest challenge I have faced has been post-trip. Being buoyed up and excited by chasing a dream, doing something for other Christians with God's clear blessing, was always going to be hard to come down from.

Yes, I have shared the story many times since and it has been well-received and I have also written this book which, being no writer, presented an altogether different set of challenges for me, in some ways bigger than riding the trip.

Throughout it all, my mission has always been to widen awareness of the plight of persecuted Christians and in doing so perhaps make people think about the value of a faith that is worth giving your life for.

Finally, although I am a Christian, I did not want to make this an overly religious book. If my actions and comments on my journey have surprised you it was because I did not want to write a sanitised account of the trip. I am no saint and I wanted it to be a real account.

Yes, I did get frustrated, angry, stressed, depressed, occasionally swore, broke a few rules and made mistakes. But if we wait for God to clean us all up before he uses us then frankly, nothing would ever get done. Jesus used flawed people, his disciples, and he still does. But my final word on this does not come from me but from the voice of the persecuted church.

One Christian in North Korea was found in possession of a Bible and taken to prison. A friend of this brave Christian described the spirit which gave him the courage to face the punishment.

*'Every Christian in my country has the spirit of martyrdom in him. If you lose that spirit for one second, you cannot carry the burden of being a follower of Jesus.'*

Many give up everything to follow Jesus. I gave up a few weeks in 2018 to promote their cause and allow their voices to be heard. There is no comparison.

**Some Ride Statistics**

1. **Problems with the bike – none**
2. **Problems with the rider – plenty**
3. **Distance ridden – 5,907 miles/9,506 kilometres**
4. **Petrol stops – 51**
5. **Days riding – 18**
6. **Biggest mistake – forgetting to disengage the Traction Control Switch when attempting to ride off-road**
7. **Mileage average per day – 328 miles/528 kilometres**
8. **Hottest temperature – France 47°C**
9. **Lowest temperature – Nordkapp (in sea mist) 12°C**
10. **Longest riding day – 605 miles/975 kilometres (Sweden)**
11. **Biggest riding issue – the extreme heat**
12. **Highest speed – 125mph/200kph (German autobahn)**
13. **Funniest moment – many, but Eric's faulty phone was a classic**
14. **Most poignant moment – my sadness over the drunken young Norwegian**
15. **Best riding day – every day in Norway**
16. **Worst riding day – M25, the final day riding home at the start of a bank holiday weekend**
17. **Amount raised for Open Doors – Target exceeded, over £10,000**

**Postscript**

*'There are far, far better things ahead than any we leave behind'.* C.S. Lewis

For a variety of reasons, as of the autumn of 2022, this book had still not been published. Who is to blame? Well, me obviously, through procrastination, conflicting advice and, if I am honest, a loss of confidence because the many anxieties caused by Covid-19 contrived to overtake me at times, as in fact they were to overtake us all. Somehow, having done the challenge and with what came upon us during 2020 and 2021, my thought process became increasingly 'does it really matter if I record this or not?' At times I felt as if we were all living with some kind of collective trauma. Psychologically I became too unsettled to pursue it or even give it further consideration. In short I felt I had shot my bolt, it was done, retrench, move on and let the whole thing fall to the ground.

The planning of the challenge, the ride itself, and the writing of this book crossed the pre-Brexit era, its 2020 implementation, and what has come since. Brexit alone, I thought, would primarily define the times I rode in and the times we were living through. I had little idea that shortly afterwards our lives were to change dramatically and in ways completely unknown to us in modern times.

Our history now seems to be defined by the pre-Covid-19 and ultimately the post-Covid-19 era. One life we know well, the other is like stepping tentatively into a completely unknown country. The virus, although diminished, is like a spectre that haunts us and we are still not completely free of it. How could we possibly have known that a virus spawned in China in ways yet to be fully explained, or understood, would create a worldwide pandemic that would come to decimate modern life as it did, kill so many people and destabilise whole countries and economies. We all suffered and the uncertainty of the season we faced due to the pandemic became an emotional roller coaster, the like of which none of us has ever known before.

From March to June 2020 as we sat in our first lock-down bubble of unreality, relatively safe in the confines of our modest house and garden in Shropshire, the death rates locally and throughout the world were rising exponentially and alarmingly. Life suddenly looked precarious for us all. The world had changed. On 15<sup>th</sup> April while working in the garden my phone jangled and vibrated, with a message from Eddy Tromp in the Netherlands (see Chapter 4) informing me that our mutual friend Franklin Coppen had died from Covid. I confess the news hit me hard. I sat down on a log pile in the garden and openly wept. Franklin, my oft outspoken and quirky Dutch friend had gone. Being a type-1 diabetic he had little chance of surviving a bad infection of Covid-19 and it brought home, forcibly and personally, what manner of evil disease this was.

Due to restrictions, it was impossible for me or Eddy to go to the funeral which also hit home hard. Covid-19 was now robbing me of friends and it was in danger of robbing me in other ways mentally. I had to dig deep after this episode to see things from another perspective and it came from the persecuted church.

I was to learn that for Christians in countries where persecution had been at its worst Covid-19 added another dimension of danger not just from the virus itself. For these Christians isolation, confinement, lock-down and restrictions are nothing new, it is the context in which they live out their faith anyway, but Covid-19 made their perilous situation infinitely worse.

In many countries Christians were to lose their jobs and all means of providing for their families and, if that were not bad enough, then they were deliberately overlooked for government food aid and often became the focus of blame for the virus itself. Attacks against Christians, already at an all time high, also increased during the pandemic. Learning of these things helped me to understand that no matter how bad Covid-19 has been for us, we had no real idea of the depth of adversity or the pressure our brothers and sisters in Christ were under. It was a wake-up call to me that my support for Open Doors was never more needed. Without such support by so many, thousands of Christians would simply have starved to death during the pandemic. During lockdown I was privileged on a number of occasions to speak out on their behalf to some churches by video link, once again to raise awareness for those who have no voice. It was why I did the challenge in the first place and Covid-19 almost took away my focus.

When I took that ride to Norway and back, my motivation was the challenge and who I was doing it for and I was not really giving that much thought to the freedom I had in actually being able to do it. Unlike now, borders in Europe were simple and free to cross, travel was unrestricted and uncomplicated and the UK was not yet viewed as the pariah of Europe. The unwelcome hiatus of Covid-19 ravaging 2020/21 made me appreciate how incredibly privileged I was to be able to do it at that time.

But world events recently have shifted focus away even from Covid-19 and it almost feels as if we are going into a period of great global uncertainty and the old order of things is changing. By ordering Russian troops to invade Ukraine, Vladimir Putin created a war that could yet threaten the peace of the whole world. This one act of aggression has created huge increases in fuel prices which in turn has helped to cause a worrying cost of living crisis here and elsewhere. It also scotched any idea I had to do another challenge by riding across Russia to the border of North Korea.

However, my riding experience in 2018 reinforced my belief that climate change remains by far the biggest threat to us all. Freak weather events since then have been truly frightening at times, even in the UK. On thinking how we in the UK are responding to it makes me smile as I note we are catching Norway up in one regard. Tesla is suddenly no longer such a rare vehicle on our roads. In fact the Society of Motor Manufacturers and Traders (SMMT) has recently confirmed there are now over 700,000 plug-in (400,000 hybrids) electric vehicles registered in the UK. Whatever your opinion on the advent of electric vehicles and our climate (personally I think the solution lies elsewhere, perhaps in fuel cell technology) we are at least responding to the challenge and that change seems to have happened very quickly.

Since my ride astonishingly we have changed our prime minister three times. Third time lucky is supremely bad politics and hardly good for the stability of our country during these challenging times. There were changes at the top elsewhere too as Hillsong's founding pastor, Brian Houston, resigned from the so-called megachurch he founded in Sydney two decades ago, after internal investigations found he had engaged in inappropriate conduct of 'serious concern' with two women. My uncomfortable feelings outside one of their churches in Stockholm were perhaps not without foundation.

Recently we said goodbye to our beloved Queen Elizabeth, who during her 71 year reign was our bedrock as a nation, her life-long example of duty, honour and integrity, particularly during Covid-19, was a model of leadership not matched by many of our senior politicians. Our longest serving monarch gave testimony time and time again to her strong Christian faith and the value of prayer in her life of service to us. We will never see the like of her again and we pray that her legacy of faith will live on in her son Charles, our new King Charles III.

With regard to this book and the motivation behind it, perhaps the most poignant event occurred on 27th September 2022. Brother Andrew, 'God's Smuggler,' the man who founded Open Doors passed away aged 94. Since then there have been so many accolades and tributes to him I hesitate to add my own but I hope in a sense the challenge ride for Open Doors and this book would count amongst them. Brother Andrew's story and life was truly extraordinary. But he himself was always at pains to stress that is was simply because he followed God.

*'The real calling,'* he said, *'is not to a certain place or career but to everyday obedience. And that call is extended to every Christian, not just a select few.'*

He would tell us and he has told many others, *'the bible is full of ordinary people who went to impossible places and did wondrous things simple because they decided to follow Jesus.'*

Perhaps in my own small way I am one of them.

As I wrote my story, and subsequently, I have become increasingly conscious that our lives really are shaped by the times we live in. I stumbled across this quote from James Baldwin which now seems particularly pertinent.

*'I am what time, circumstance, history, have made of me, certainly, but I am also much more than that. So are we all.'*

So are we all, indeed. Within each of us, from our experiences, are the seeds of the best or of the worst. But a life given to God, as Brother Andrew's was, makes us that much more again and I can testify to that too.

For me, therefore, this is not finished and my postscript is my way of saying the book will not be the end. What follows is unknown, but as Brother Andrew once said, *'through prayer we can reach into the future and with loving hands touch those beyond our reach.'* My primary focus must remain to touch those currently beyond my reach in whatever and whichever way I can.

Mervyn Smith, Highley, October 2022